FINDING MY RIGHT MIND

FINDING MY RIGHT MIND

One Woman's Experiment to Put Meditation to the Test

Vanessa Potter

TRIGGER™
The mental health & wellbeing publisher

First published in Great Britain 2021 by Trigger

Trigger is a trading style of Shaw Callaghan Ltd & Shaw Callaghan 23 USA, INC.

The Foundation Centre

Navigation House, 48 Millgate, Newark

Nottinghamshire NG24 4TS UK

www.triggerpublishing.com

Text Copyright © Vanessa Potter 2021

Thanks to Barbara Jachs, University of Cambridge for supplying the data and graphs

British Library Cataloguing in Publication Data

A CIP catalogue record for this book is available upon request

from the British Library

ISBN: 9781789562163

This book is also available in the following e-Book formats:

ePUB: 9781789562286

Vanessa Potter has asserted her right under the Copyright,

Design and Patents Act 1988 to be identified as the author of this work

Cover design by Emily Courdelle

Typeset by Lapiz Digital Services

Printed and bound in Great Britain by CPI Group (UK) Ltd, Croydon CR0 4YY

Paper from responsible sources

ENDORSEMENTS

"From page one of *Finding My Right Mind*, you will feel like you have taken the hand of your best friend as you go on a truly meaningful adventure. From hypnosis to mindfulness and yoga, Vanessa leads us on an inspiring journey to understand how different modalities impact the ways that body, mind, and spirit Know, and why they react the way they do."
— Dyan Haspel-Johnson, Ph.D, psychologist, Consultant for the American Society of Clinical Hypnosis and creator of The Deep & Easy Sleep Self-Hypnosis Package.

"Meditation is everywhere! We are told that it could be the answer to coping with a busy life, feeling more relaxed and even sleeping better. In this fascinating book, Potter embarks on the most incredible journey, providing personal reflection on different meditative techniques… and her ability to communicate them clearly is exceptional. As to whether she finds the answers she is looking for, I highly recommend that you read this book…"
— Professor Alice Gregory, author of *Nodding Off: The Science of Sleep from Cradle to Grave* and *The Sleepy Pebble and Other Stories: Calming Tales to Read at Bedtime.*

"In *Finding My Right Mind*, Vanessa Potter, aka Patient H69, writes lucidly about the farther reaches of human experience. Her insatiable curiosity and hyper-awareness of the world around her makes for a compelling account. Personally, I found this book funny, comforting, honest, moving, and at times just so damn weird that I had to keep reading. It raises a glass to spiritual adventurers everywhere."
— Dr Roger Bretherton, clinical psychologist and associate lecturer, School of Psychology, University of Lincoln

"By exploring the depth of our own mind, this book will teach you that we have much more in common with everyone than we ever thought."
— Dr Andrés Canales-Johnson, neuroscientist and host of Talking Brains

"Vanessa takes us on an awe-inspiring journey through the tremendous variety of meditative practices. The recollections of her experiences are sharp-witted, illuminating and hilariously funny. I deeply enjoyed reading her book."
— Karin Matko, meditation researcher

"I've followed Vanessa Potter's journey with great interest and really appreciate the quality of her writing. Her book is most interesting in that it shows her firsthand experiences with different techniques. I was impressed by her courage and skill in turning around a life-shattering trauma. Her subsequent experiments with different techniques offer an unusual contribution to research."
— Charles Hastings, meditation teacher

For Dad

CONTENTS

INTRODUCTION

THE START OF IT ALL

Epiphanies happen at any time and often without warning. Suddenly, during a work meeting, you realize you need a new job. Or, wedged on a train, your nose against the glass, you know it's time to leave the city. My epiphany happened at the age of forty, when one morning I woke up blind and paralyzed.

Many remember 2012 as the year Britain hosted the Olympics. My family remember it as the year I got ill. We received no warning of what was to come – no health rumbles that something was afoot. Married to Ed, we lived in a leafy London suburb with our two small children. Ed worked in pharmaceuticals, often commuting for four hours a day, slumping home each evening too tired to complain. Sixteen years as a television producer in the advertising industry had left me strung out, with a military approach to family life. Too often, late to collect the children from the childminder, I bundled sleeping tots into the car. I loved my job, the excitement of foreign shoots and the creative thinking involved, but I wore rally-driver gloves to get through the day. Projects were fast-paced and my terrier-like instinct for detail brought awards and recognition, yet the hours took their toll. When an opportunity to go freelance came up in the spring of 2012, I took it. Freed from the constraints of full-time work, I scheduled a few months off.

For all the chaos and the fight for quality time, Ed and I made a good team. I was the planner and "doer" of the family, he was the one building dens behind the sofa. With his boyish smile and affable charm he took the role of good cop in our house. That summer, I finally relaxed and spent lazy days playing boo with our toddler son and chasing our daughter around the park. As September brought warm jumpers out of the closet and the last of the tomatoes, I planned our daughter's fifth birthday party. This was to be pony-riding at a petting zoo and a hideously pink cake. Having spent two weeks bedridden with a flu-like virus, I welcomed the distraction. I hated being ill, hated the inconvenience and disruption. I'd even missed our daughter's first day at school, relying upon new friends to step in and help. Finally recovered, party invites were delivered and presents were wrapped.

Yet for all my planning, I never made the party.

Losing Sight

It started with a fizzing – an unending dizziness and a sense of doom. Blinking rapidly on the morning of 1 October, I tried to wake up – yet I was already awake. Wandering dumbly around our kitchen, a film of static – like a visual snowstorm – blocked my view. After the childminder had collected the children, I called the doctor's surgery. When the dizziness turned into nausea at my appointment, they called a taxi to take me to the hospital.

After a fruitless day in A&E I was sent home. Tests had revealed nothing. Playing down my disquiet, I went to sleep, waking the next morning to the excited shrieks of our daughter shredding birthday wrapping paper downstairs. As I opened my eyes, the room felt unnaturally dark. Thick brown fog enveloped my head as if I'd gone to bed wearing sunglasses. My producer's mind kicked in, assessing the damage: a 70 percent loss of vision. And my fingers were numb. Within minutes I was packing a bag, using my teeth to zip it shut.

In hospital waiting rooms I held my breath, straining to see as the outer world shrunk into an ever-decreasing halo. Fear clamped my chest and my body shook as an invisible disease attacked my nervous system. Ed frantically pushed my wheelchair from department to department, as numbness crept up my legs and desperation raised our voices. Assessed by a consultant neurologist forty-eight hours after my first symptom, my feet were lifeless blocks of ice and my sight had all but gone. When I was finally admitted onto a ward the next morning, I was blind and paralyzed. In just seventy-two hours two of my major senses had been obliterated.

Over the following weeks, I was tested for everything from a brain tumour to multiple sclerosis. Unable to diagnose me, I was dubbed "the mystery patient". My mother arrived, in her unassailable manner, bringing a care rota and gentle interference. An easy chair was dragged into my room so my family could stay with me, day and night. Infused with a sense of detached reality, dark humour kept us sane. After two days of complete blackness, a monochromatic world began to emerge. Consisting only of clouds and wispy lines, I couldn't see the bed I was lying in. Unable to move my hands or feet, a determination grew and I looked inwards for respite. My mind plundered resources from my past: slow yogic breathing and visualization, learned when I was pregnant, soothed my nerves and kept me calm. Imagining a sun-soaked beach became my mental sanctuary, escaping the gut-wrenching anxiety my illness brought on. I didn't tell anyone what I was doing, or where I was going – I let my unconscious mind lead me. Intuition took over as I counted down from ten, reigniting hypnotic triggers and using my mind's eye to see. With two physical senses wiped out, I dug imaginary toes into invisible sand and directed cerulean waves. As I flicked through my memory bank, I plucked out patterns and textures and rebuilt a pictorial world. Firing up the vision centres within my brain meant I was keeping them active – leaving a trail of visual crumbs so that one day I might find my way back.

Who would've guessed that strolling along an imaginary beach could have any effect – but it did. Visualizing had been one of the more enjoyable elements of my antenatal classes, seemingly fanciful until it proved a powerful force during the birth of my son. Visualization often blurs into self-hypnosis and can also be a type of meditation. Not that I appreciated those subtleties at the time. Combined with yogic breathing, my made-up beach was a survival tactic that helped me endure a horrific episode. It was the one tool I had unfettered access to, that I could do for myself. It didn't matter that I was a novice or naïve – visualizing saved my mind.

Three weeks after my first symptom I was discharged from hospital needing a stick and legally blind. A "catastrophic episode" was what they said – a rare neurological illness had stripped my senses. For months I inhabited a flickering X-ray with wobbling grey lines and only hints of colour. With no three-dimensional vision, faces were translucent and bodies ghoulish outlines. Unable to hold a spoon, my children stroked my hair and fed me apple crumble. Then the ice in my limbs began to thaw, and I would wiggle fingers and toes. Using my stick I limped up our driveway learning to laugh at what I heard – not what I saw.

Throughout it all, nights of insomnia blurred my mind, compounding my anxiety, a fear in itself. I had suffered poor sleep in the past, but now I dreaded the night – the heart-pounding panic that bedtime brought on. The insomnia lessened as my vision recovered and my family propped me up. Contrast deepened – blacks became darker and whites more pronounced and colour became a sensory experience – something I felt rather than saw. Visual messages became jumbled when our lawn flashed up as red instead of the green it should have been. As my brain slowly healed, I lived through a visual odyssey where the colour blue fizzed like a lit sparkler, only settling when I spoke the word "blue" out loud. Synaesthesia – a sensory phenomenon – meant that touch and sound blended with my visual senses.

Fragment by fragment my vision repaired, and I logged the improvements on a dictaphone. It was a solitary experiment, prompted by a drive to understand the mechanics of my brain. Unable to explain a shifting world, I counted cars and practised reading road signs. I would stand in the street, whispering to trees, reminding my brain what seeing was – forcing my visual system back online. Documenting every day became a project in itself. I'd spent my life telling other people's stories, now I was telling my own.

Opening up my Mind

During my year-long recovery I learned to live a new normal, a life where the world didn't look like it did before. I learned to adapt my mind too – to cope with the enormous trauma my body had suffered. My legs still shook when anxiety surged, but breathing deeply on my beach built resilience. The more I visualized, the quicker I calmed. Championing every improvement and using repetition and gentle suggestion, I crawled along the road to recovery picking up those optical crumbs I'd left behind.

Perhaps strangely, I never acknowledged what I was doing at the time – galvanized by innate forces, not medical knowledge. It would be two years before neuroscientists would explain how I'd healed my mind – and my sight. My documented experiences would provide invaluable data that corroborated 40 years of vision science. The temporary blindness had closed off my senses, yet it had opened my mind to other levels of consciousness and my own, rather untapped, potential. I'd discovered I had more control over my state of mind than I'd ever thought possible.

In the end I was left partially sighted – like a vintage photograph, the world was bleached out. Although I could function normally, my career was over. Seeking answers, I embarked upon an investigative journey travelling the country interviewing brain and vision specialists. This uncovered the uniqueness and rarity of my sensory experiences and how little we know about the brain. Creating the pseudonym "Patient H69" from my NHS number, I blogged about how a hotchpotch of self-hypnosis, breathing and meditation techniques had provided a surprisingly effective coping strategy.

In 2014 – two years after my illness – I had my first conversation with Professor Tristan Bekinschtein, a neuroscientist at Cambridge University. My investigations had developed into a science-art installation anchored around my own experience that I hoped might inform the public (people like me) about their brains. My concept used electroencephalogram (EEG) technology – electrodes placed on the head – which was Tristan's area of expertise. When I shared my exhibition idea that explained the healing effects of meditation, I was surprised that he wanted to help. In his late thirties and easy going, Tristan had a quirky sense of humour and talked constantly in a thick Argentinian accent. Before I knew it, he'd invited me to Cambridge to meet his team.

I'm not the sciencey one in our family – that's Ed – science was my least favourite subject at school. Yet I had found something to be interested in – *my brain*. By combining my producer background with my own sight loss story I'd inadvertently become a science communicator.

Tristan wasn't the only scientist interested in me. Barbara Jachs, a young Austrian masters graduate studying the effects of meditation on cognition, was keen to collaborate too. Tristan introduced us when we started discussing ways to develop my installation. Barbara was interested in how meditation affects the brain "in the moment". She was looking for ways to define and characterize meditation practices and how they impacted "state changes" in the brain every time we meditate: how meditation influences how we're feeling *during* the practice. This has been mostly ignored by traditional meditation research which focuses on "trait changes" – how meditating changes us as people. Any project that considered the inner experiences of meditators got Barbara's attention so we hit it off immediately.

EEG technology had first intrigued me when I'd had sticky electrodes glued to my scalp in hospital. Back then, this had provided reassurance that my brain areas responsible for vision were still alive. EEG electrodes record and measure the tiny electrical impulses the brain emits – our brainwaves. Like a musical score, these neural communications are converted into oscillating, wiggly lines of data. This allows technicians to identify repetitive and rhythmic patterns that can help diagnose brain conditions such as epilepsy – or in my case – measure visual activity. Our brainwave activity can also be used to identify different states of mind – from alertness to sleepiness to meditation. In this way, I could bring my beach to life not with pictures or words, but by letting my brainwaves do the talking instead.

My meditation exhibition-cum-research project was, perhaps not surprisingly, called The Beach. This launched at the Cambridge Science Festival in 2015. For one week Barbara and I invited members of the public to wear portable EEG headsets while watching a film about how an anonymous woman (Patient H69) used meditation to overcome a terrifying trauma. After the film, and still hooked up to the EEG monitors, participants closed their eyes and allowed their minds to wander for one minute. By allowing their minds to think and make shopping lists, Barbara could record a baseline. Straight afterwards, the participants followed a five-minute guided mindfulness meditation – with the headsets still recording. Exiting the room (invariably feeling more relaxed), Barbara revealed each participant's brain activity converted into animated visuals and music. Screens showing red, green, yellow and blue graphics represented the four main types of brainwaves EEG captures (Beta, Alpha, Theta and Delta). These identified how alert, focused, meditative or sleepy they'd been. A dominance of red Beta brainwaves suggested an active mind, clusters of blue Delta and yellow Theta animations indicated a relaxed, meditative mind. These dancing animations, driven entirely by each participant's data, illustrated how they had gone in and out of a meditative state. By comparing this to their individual baseline, each of our 120 participants could observe clear differences between thinking and meditating. For many this forged a new, more respectful relationship with their brains (a part of their bodies some said they ignored). Many had never sat still for five minutes to focus on their minds, and for those who had believed they "couldn't meditate" or that meditating "didn't work", the experience provided a crash course in self-awareness.

In 2016, when the exhibition (along with my own vision research) culminated in a TEDx talk and a book entitled *Patient H69: The Story of My Second Sight*, I was surprised again. I hadn't thought I was a writer – or a speaker for that matter. That story now merges into the one that follows. The next journey would never have started if it hadn't been for the first.

CHAPTER 1

THE IDEA

It was during The Beach exhibition that I had the idea. As a woman was leaving, she paused at the door. "I didn't know what meditation was before I tried it – but it's just mindfulness, isn't it?" Even though the project had been based upon my own use of meditation, I still lacked knowledge in this area but I'd learned enough to respond to this simple question.

"Not quite. Mindfulness is *one* form of meditation, but there are lots of other types." When the woman asked how many kinds there were, and how they all varied, I let her leave. My ignorance plagued me. Like many visitors I hadn't tried mindfulness before. Aside from the visualization and self-hypnosis tools I'd gained during my pregnancies, I'd only experienced meditation fleetingly at a Buddhist retreat several years earlier. After that, horrified at the monks' expectation of sitting twice a day to meditate, I'd forgotten it all.

While I'd found answers to many of the questions I'd had about my brain – new ones had taken their place. I'd come to realize that meditation was not one-size-fits-all; there were many ways to train the mind. And, meditation really was training – be it mindfulness, visualizing, compassion work or, indeed, any of the other variations. The EEG had allowed us to peek beneath the hood – but there was so much more to explore. The curiosity that had driven me to Cambridge in the first place was fired up again. Suddenly, meditating regularly didn't seem like a crazy idea. Tristan had recorded my brain at the exhibition, so I'd seen for myself how meditating changed it. Yet if I knew it worked, why wasn't I doing it? At the first flicker of recovery I'd plugged straight back in, desperate to start living life at breakneck speed again.

I started to wonder if meditation could be more than a sticking plaster in a crisis. Could it be a long-term investment – a way of life? Even though I'd recovered much of my sight, I still had a sense of "dis-ease". It wasn't the anxiety of my illness, but a faint discontent. I constantly rehashed past events, criticizing the things I'd got wrong, and forecasting how "next time", I'd get them right. My family was healthy and we could pay our food bills, yet time ran dry, haemorrhaged by the domestic scrum of everyday life. Could the right technique help me tackle my constant worrying and stop me yelling when my kids acted up? Too often I got cross, only to be wracked with guilt later on – my anger turning inwards. I rarely switched off and my phone chirruped constantly in my back pocket. I never seemed to find time for the people in my life. Even though we were close, I didn't talk to my brother Dan enough, and weeks would pass before I Skyped my dad. We didn't lack affection for each other, yet a deeper connection was missing.

Frazzled and tired at the end of the day, my mind would fret over tomorrow's to-do list. I'd nurse a glass of wine, feeling disengaged and numb, realizing I was teaching my children how to worry, along with good table manners.

Questions flew around my mind. Could a meditation practice help ease these ills? Should I start visualizing again, or might a new technique be better? Would Transcendental Meditation or Zen soothe my jumpy mind? Or how about a compassion practice like loving-kindness? There were so many styles to choose from – maybe one would even cure the insomnia I still suffered at night?

A plan began to crystallize. I saw how my desire for peace of mind could become the basis for an extraordinary science experiment. What if I was to record my *own* meditative brainwaves and embark on a "meditation discovery tour". A shiver of excitement ran down my spine at the thought of lifting the lid of my own consciousness and taking a look inside. Life wasn't bad, but things needed to change. I grabbed my notebook and wrote down three questions:

Could I meditate every day for eighteen months?

Could I try out new mind-training techniques?

What might science learn if I did that?

I scratched out the word science in the last question and replaced it with "I", trying to imagine what Tristan and Barbara would make of my scribbles. Could I pitch a one-woman study where I was both researcher and participant, or was that a ridiculous notion? Would they be interested in data captured from a stressed-out woman juggling work and family life?

Something told me they would be.

Emboldened, I decided to pick up the meditation gauntlet and put it to the test. Science would be my objective observer as I test-drove popular ways to train my mind. After all, there *was* more to meditation than mindfulness. I would help science *and* reconnect to myself and my family at the same time. An experiment like this might reveal similarities and differences between styles which could prove constructive for others. I knew I wasn't the only person looking for a better life – hell, for an easier life. Many of my friends were meditation sceptics, eye rolling and giggling "Om" at the mention of the word. I didn't blame them. Even though I had curated a meditation project, I still found it confusing and a bit embarrassing. Like something I might admit to. It was time to come out of the meditation closet and start practising every day.

Casually mentioning my plan to Ed, a day or two later, he was less convinced.

"Can you keep that up?" he sighed, his voice betraying his misgivings. "I mean, it's an awful lot of navel gazing." He was right of course, but this time, unlike my descent into blindness, I'd be documenting a journey I have chosen to take. Science was coming with me on this adventure and would reveal if meditating really did change my life.

The Experiment: Summer 2016

Barbara didn't take much convincing to get on board. We'd become firm friends, even keeping in contact when she'd moved abroad for work. Although considerably younger than me, Barbara's patience and openness had made her my go-to for all things neuroscience. It turned out my idea complemented her PhD proposal to study meditators' experiences across a range of techniques. She explained why she was excited on a phone call.

"It's too easy to associate meditating with feeling calm and relaxed, or perhaps agitated and fidgety. But lots of shifts in cognition, emotion and mental activity occur and I want to capture all of those experiences."

"Like a meditation brain-spill?" I countered.

"Yes! If we can just get inside a meditator's mind and observe their stream of consciousness, it might help us understand *exactly* what they're experiencing – not just some vague 'I felt calm' or 'I was distracted' statement. I want to create a system that unscrambles *all* of their experiences across lots of different meditation styles. No-one has done that before."

With one in four of us likely to suffer a mental health problem at some time in our lives, meditation and its health benefits is a popular area of study. Barbara hoped her holistic approach would provide insights into how meditators' experiences change over time and how that impacts their nervous systems, their behaviours and beliefs, as well as how their brainwaves change during meditation.

My offer to try out ten different practices was just what she needed. Nicknaming our plan the Top Ten study, we discussed when I might pitch the idea to Tristan. As Barbara's supervisor, there could be no study without his agreement.

Excited that our Top Ten study might change the direction meditation research was going in by revealing the experiences and neural changes during meditation, we investigated which techniques to include. Within a few clicks I discovered countless ways to "train my mind" and "transform my life". Gurus offered stress relief, increased concentration, healthy sleep habits – oh, and the love of your life. No wonder my friends were confused. Meditation had become a commodity, a paid-for product to be consumed at an alarming rate.

Seemingly endless posts from media-savvy personalities described how meditating had helped them find their inner celebrity and Google spewed fluffy mysticism with images of sunsets and skinny women in impossible yoga poses. Yet those sunset images didn't resemble my life, and I was suspicious of anyone who claimed to turn their life around overnight. Surely the celebrities had an army of nannies who took on the grind so they had time to find themselves.

Considering its recent popularity, it would have been easy to write off the mindfulness boom as a modern invention – *a fad* – but meditation has been around for thousands of years and has featured within most world religions. Aside from a raft of scientific papers reporting the benefits, it was hard not to notice that global giants had adopted mindfulness programmes. Or, that it was offered in schools, prisons and the military. We knew to maintain our physical health with good sleep, exercise and healthy eating, yet we were slow when it came to our minds.

Staring grumpily at the images, I was reminded that the only reason I'd meditated when I was ill was *because I was ill.* Time was the one thing I'd had in abundance. It was going to be a challenge to shoehorn a meditation practice into my life when it was already bulging at the seams.

Eventually, Barbara and I decided mindfulness was the best place to start. I'd not been taught it, and it was the foundation for many other practices. We wanted to include a technique that would require me to repeat a mantra word over and over, so Transcendental Meditation could follow. I also wanted to try a Buddhist practice, perhaps Tibetan Tantra or Zen, and I was curious about compassion practices. Barbara persuaded me to include a form of prayer (although I had reservations about that) and I wanted to revisit self-hypnosis (even though it's not a form of meditation) and we agreed a movement-based practice like Kundalini Yoga would be good. I would finish with the ultimate concentration practice − Vipassana.

On my next visit to Cambridge I had coffee with Tristan. After The Beach project ended, we had remained friends, regularly meeting up with our families. With his goatee beard and rock band T-shirts he'd never fitted the university professor stereotype I'd had but I needed Tristan's go-ahead. I pitched our Top Ten experiment as he sipped an espresso listening with raised eyebrows.

"Yes!" he cried. "You'll be a human guinea pig on a consciousness road-trip. Barbara will record your brain using EEG." Sneaking a sidelong look, he added, "What about psychedelics, Potter? If this is to be a proper mind experiment, we should include this too…" With only nine practices lined up, I agreed to consider it.

A month later Tristan called me.

"Potter, can you come to Paris next week? We can have some interesting discussions with a new tech start-up."

"Sure…" I hesitated, uncertain as to why I was being asked along.

"They make portable EEG headsets," he added. I didn't need asking twice.

Six weeks later, a Rythm Dreem EEG headset arrived in a smart-looking box. Embedded into this nifty padded headset were five sensors that would silently monitor my brainwaves. Other sensors tracked my movement, heart rate and respiration.

Tracing Time

With the green light from Tristan, I still needed to understand exactly *how* Barbara would collect my data. As every meditation encounter is undeniably subjective, she wanted to capture my "phenomenological experiences". In other words, how I felt during every single meditation experience. This would provide a vital companion to the EEG data from the headset, allowing Barbara to compare the two data streams together.

Barbara had built an app to load on my cellphone. By using my finger to draw on my screen immediately after the end of each meditation session, I'd create a record of how I felt. She identified eleven experience "dimensions" or categories to keep track of. They included: aperture (how broad my attention was), how bored I felt, clarity (how clear or vivid an experience was), conflict (how irritated or content I felt), focus (how my attention shifted), lens (was I focused on one or many thoughts?), meta (how aware I was of my own awareness), source (whether the contents of my thoughts were generated or I was passively thinking), effort (how hard or easy the meditation felt), stability (how distracted or stable my thoughts were) and, finally, how awake I felt.

On my next visit Barbara explained what these dimensions were and how they'd help her track my moment-by-moment experiences.

"Consider them 'experience categories'," she says. "Like what you're thinking about and how you're regulating your emotions. If you're really focused at the beginning of your meditation, the line you draw will start at the top. But if you lose focus midway, the line will drop creating 'waves of data'. You just draw a 'wiggly line' on your phone screen after each session. It's easy."

"I can do that, but where does the EEG fit in?"

"Your 'traces' – that's what we call your wiggly lines – become data in themselves, and will be compared alongside the EEG data we'll collect. The two work together; that's what's different about this study."

My traces will help Barbara identify my state of mind during every single meditation, combining all of the experience categories she is recording. These states will differ with each meditation technique and change over time. This is how Barbara will categorize my experiences systematically and mathematically.

To support her study, Barbara has asked that I fill in an online diary which gives more detail about my life generally. In this I can "name" my emotions – like "contented", "sad" or "worried". I should explain what events are occurring in my life, my relationship with Ed and any interactions with our children (now aged six and eight). Anything that affects my emotional state is relevant. Of course, this diary will also be useful for me to keep track of the impact each meditation has upon me and any changes I notice.

An Example of Traces Data – Awareness

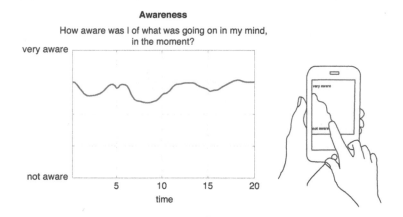

Barbara explains there will be a cumulative effect as I gain more experience. She expects me to get *better* at meditating the more I do it. It seems that my meditation road-trip wasn't such a crazy notion after all.

Laying Out the Plan

Experiments can be run in different ways and the word *research* has various meanings. My project contains two main strands. The first is the ambitious long-term study – the meditation Top Ten that Barbara and I will undertake. The traces I draw on my phone will be digitized and compared with the EEG data recorded by the headset.

Barbara's study is unique in that it will examine my meditation experiences both subjectively *and* objectively. The EEG data will give an objective snapshot of the electrical activity the brain emits. My traces will offer a numerical representation of what I believe my thoughts to be. It's the first time this has been done.

My own research forms the second strand. I will document any changes I feel over the next eighteen months, and then compare those experiences alongside existing meditation literature. Rather than being guided by what others have observed, I'll undertake this book research at the *end* of my meditations. I want to discover how meditating affects my thoughts, feelings and behaviour *before* I match it to what others have written.

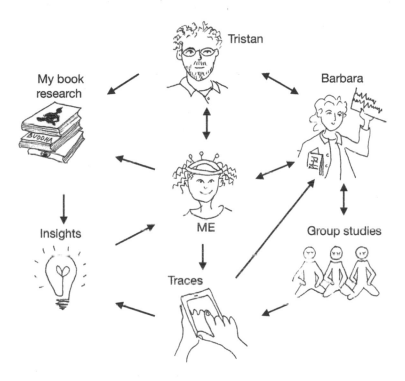

Ready to start, I was determined to learn to meditate and "find my right mind". I wasn't out of my mind, but a calmer, more equanimous attitude would bring about a shift in my life. With my project coming together, I could feel my old producer genes lighting up. What better mission was there than my own wellbeing?

CHAPTER 2

GROWING PAINS: MBCT

January 2017

It's cold out, but as I leave my local café I'm grinning. Barbara and I agreed to start my adventure with a course in Mindfulness-Based Cognitive Therapy (MBCT) and there's one starting soon. I've never been taught mindfulness meditation before and this eight-week programme will provide a good foundation for the later practices. A sense of mindfulness, settling into the body and following the breath are part of many forms of meditation. Mindfulness is a hot topic today; its emergence in the 1960s prompted extensive research and hundreds of published papers. Studies began when psychologists saw the potential in this unchartered area, establishing the international Society for Neuroscience in 1969.

A chat explaining my project to Dave, the MBCT course leader, confirms I can join the class as long as I don't wear the EEG headset there as it might distract the others. This isn't a problem as Barbara and I have agreed that I'll record most of my data in my practice at home.

Getting to Dave's first class is a challenge. A few days earlier, I had been sat on the sofa late at night working with my laptop. I was tired and my brain was foggy, yet somehow I knew my right foot had gone to sleep. When I tried to stand I collapsed in filmic slow motion, my ligaments tearing like a sheet as I went down.

As I shuffle in to the first session on crutches, it's dark and freezing cold; anaemic lights flashing outside remind me that Christmas is over. The community hall where the course is held is often inhabited by pregnant women practising antenatal yoga and, even wearing woolly socks, the chill creeps through the floorboards. As I sit on a plastic chair, one of several set out in a circle, I notice rolls of purple squishy yoga mats piled in the corner. Dave, a sandy-haired man in his forties, sits casually at the front, nodding genially at his recruits. Next to him is a row of red folders, alongside a prayer bowl and gong (a surprise as I'd always associated prayer bowls with Buddhism). There are ten people in our group, aged between about 30 and 50. Out of the corner of my eye I spot a couple, their feet casually touching. Alongside them is a bald-headed man wearing sweatpants who lounges in a nonchalant manner. Scanning the rest of the room, most appear to be middle-class professionals – and look remarkably like me.

MBCT courses are group-based, and were adapted from an original programme called Mindfulness-Based Stress Reduction (MBSR), developed in the USA by meditator and scientist Jon Kabat-Zinn in the 1970s to treat depression, anxiety and other disorders. In the early 1990s, therapists Zindel Segal, Mark Williams and John Teasdale created MBCT, and both programmes are taught in the UK.

As MBCT is secular, this is a gentle start to my experiment and will, I hope, introduce me to the mechanics of my mind. It combines meditation (taken from Buddhist traditions) and Cognitive Behavioural Therapy, also known as CBT. The idea is for me to learn to observe how my thoughts – particularly those insidious, pervasive ones – often manifest into uncomfortable feelings, causing me to behave in ways I'd rather not. Dave's job is to translate this concept into some kind of tangible experience that I can make sense of and use.

Dave starts by asking us why we are investing this time in ourselves and what we hope to get out of the course. This catches me unawares as we've agreed I won't discuss my project. The woman next to me explains she's looking for ways to manage stress. A man, with a surprisingly soft voice, whispers that he has depression, and the woman next to him, wearing a pink fluffy jumper, explains she has insomnia. When it's my turn, I mumble that I'm curious about meditation and instantly feel deceitful. At least the curiosity bit is real. Listening to the others, some of us have prior experience of meditation, but others have none.

For our first practical exercise, Dave gives each of us a single raisin with instructions to hold it in the palm of our hand. I smile faintly as I recall the glee of my six-year-old son after a mindfulness teacher visited his school and did the same exercise. I feel silly knowing I am repeating a task given to a roomful of young children.

As I slowly chew the raisin, I remember eating fruitcake as a child and how much I disliked it. As the sharp, syrupy flavour triggers memories, time seems to fast-forward and the taste gets better. Of course, part of this torchlight awareness is because I'm focusing my attention on eating, which I rarely do. I'm often doing something else at the same time – talking, watching television or, worse, working. It makes me realize that I also eat too fast. I guess this "noticing" is the point.

Next on the agenda is a body scan, which is a form of Focused Attention (FA) meditation. This just means that the meditation directs our awareness to one thing – such as our breath or a candle – any real or imagined object or concept. A body scan requires us to focus on one part of our body at a time. This is traditionally done by moving the attention sequentially up the body to help develop concentration.

Concentration, Tristan has explained, is a skill the brain can learn through practice and is necessary to reap the benefits of meditation. The regions in the brain that create and manage attention can tune in more efficiently the more I practice meditation. Training makes them better and allows me to focus on something – my breath, my body or completing my tax return. In turn, this activity switches off the regions of my brain that activate when my mind is not concentrating (scientists call this "mind wandering"). Activity in the brain reflects the "sharpening" of attention shown by complex patterns of higher activity in some brain networks and lower activity in other regions. This supports the idea that neural mechanisms engage and disengage during meditation. This interplay sharpens the attentional networks the more I practice, "flexing" them. In this way, mindfulness is a bit like a workout for my brain.

The blue mats are dragged out for this first body scan and, floating my blanket over my legs, I settle down and prepare to focus my mind on different areas of my body. Having already dispelled the myth that we need to somehow clear our minds, Dave reminds us that random thoughts will appear and we will be distracted. This is fine – and normal. It's noticing that we are distracted that is important. *Hmm, so I don't have to berate myself for thinking about* House of Cards? *Can I have little indulgent moments considering Robin Wright's perfect hair and uncannily good posture?*

There's something strange and slightly disconcerting about lying down in a room surrounded by strangers, but I'm not put off as a body scan is familiar territory to me. Yet a few minutes in, I'm uncomfortable and my back is twinging. Every muscle spasm irritates my damaged foot, causing frustration to ripple up and down my body. *Ow, that hurts.* I drift in and out of concentration, losing Dave's soft voice as he directs our attention to different parts of our anatomy. I am with him on ankles and calves, but when he reaches knees, I will the session to end. "Relaaaaax your thighs," he says, elongating the word relax. *God, I'm cold.* Frustration bubbles up as the sound of gentle snoring permeates the room. *This is stupid, how can anyone go to sleep?* I bristle as anger prods me in the side. Opening one eye I try to spot the culprit. *Is it the bloke in the baggy sweatpants?* "Focus your attention on your buttocks," I hear Dave say. *No, that's a woman snoring.*

At the end of the meditation I drag myself onto my plastic chair, rubbing my back. Previous body scans had never left me so irritable. When I share what feels like a perfectly normal (albeit negative) reaction, Dave suggests in a level voice that perhaps I could be kind to myself. He suggests, pausing and looking me in the eye, that I don't need to judge the experience. I know he's talking about my reactivity, but damn it, the floor is cold and I do have torn ligaments. It's not my fault I feel this way.

Dave is picking apart my feelings and I want to thump him. However, along with fantasies of violence, his comments stay with me. Swaddled inside that word "kind" is the awful truth that I am not always kind to myself. I realize this is something I need to learn how to do – and recognize when I'm not doing it. Resentment surfaces again and I remind myself to remain open. Zoning out while the others relate their experiences, it dawns on me that I'd only ever done body scans in comfortable settings before. The physical distractions today have removed my ability to focus and have rattled me. It is my choice to embark on this experiment and I need to embrace new tools and a fresh approach to life. Yet this first class is already more than I bargained for.

At the end of the night, Dave gives us all a handout, neatly filed inside one of the red folders. Homework is part of an MBCT course and we are expected to perform a 40-minute body scan each day. This, I notice, causes several members of the class to glance at each other. Of course, I have my own home study as I intend to follow each new technique for eight weeks, starting tonight. As I limp out of the studio, my mind is playing ping-pong with my thoughts. It's not just my injured foot that's causing discomfort.

Capturing my Attention

At home I pull on the EEG headset and, lying on my bed, I follow the recorded body scan Dave has sent by email. In the warmth of my bedroom, I become soporific. Once again my attention wanes and I lose concentration.

Afterwards, using the app that Barbara gave me I score how I felt during the meditation. Placing my finger on my phone screen, I begin tracing a line. Starting at "drowsy" (halfway between "alert" and "sleepy"), my line dips dramatically toward "sleepy".

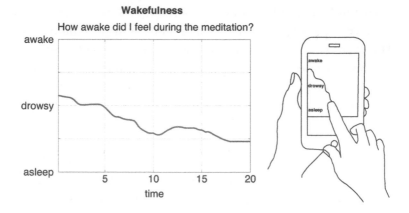

Scoring "effort", which is how arduous I found the practice, I surprise myself when my trace remains close to "high" for the whole time. Moving onto "distraction", I realize I'd spent much of the body scan fretting that my son hasn't practised the piano in weeks – so this scores consistently high too. I pause a moment before I mark "boredom". Testing the app over the last few weeks, I've had to train myself to notice the subtleties between boredom and distraction. They are not the same thing. Boredom is a disconnect from the technique I am practising – feeling that "I'm not into this". Distraction is when thoughts bombard my mind so much that I lose track of the practice (which I might quite like). It's important that my traces reflect these nuanced emotions.

In my online diary I add several notes to Barbara telling her how uncomfortable I'd felt during the meditation. Although Dave had started the MBCT course off with a relaxing body scan, I've found meditating hard work.

Barbara's novel research approach has the potential to break new ground. A few weeks earlier, I'd been on a Skype call with Tristan and Barbara. We'd just finished chatting to a technician at Rythm in Paris about how he'll transfer the raw EEG data from my headset back to Barbara in Cambridge. When he left the call, I asked Barbara to explain how her PhD (and our experiment) differs from other meditation research.

"Historically, meditation studies report how long participants meditate for and over what period of time," she says, perched next to Tristan. "But this misses detail – like whether they followed the instructions, or if they're knackered after a late night…"

"Researchers can't know if participants meditated correctly – or nodded off," Tristan adds.

"Exactly," Barbara continues. "This data gets lost and disrupts the results. Your wiggly lines will capture how your state of mind changes during a meditation."

"Your traces," Tristan explains, "become data in themselves as Barbara continuously measures your experience. This tells us much more. Barbara's method is not so much a means to quantify your experiences, as *describe* them. This continuous monitoring of your experiences is the important difference."

"The key thing to understand is that we aren't describing your experiences over time," Barbara cuts in again. "If you were to describe an experience you might say: 'One afternoon I went shopping and had a manicure. Afterwards I went dancing.' If we scientifically *measured* those experiences it would be more like: 'I experienced concentration and relaxation, then heightened physical activity.'" Of course, Ed's experience of any shopping trip would be indifference and frustration, but I got the point.

"The diary you'll keep will capture the back story to each meditation," Barbara continues. "By digitizing your wiggly lines, we can overlay your EEG data and get objective measurements of your dynamic experience."

I get it. This study paints the full meditation picture. Barbara will be able to attribute my feelings of intense concentration or sleepiness to specific neural responses within my brain. Eventually, she can create neural signatures for each technique being studied. What we learn from me will help direct future studies. We are going to collect my moment-by-moment experiences and fill in some important gaps for science.

"Cool, but what might this data tell *me*?" I ask excited.

"It gives us sexy data – not superimposed meaning," Tristan says, suddenly serious. "This is how science should work. We are mathematically representing your experiences. No one has done this before, let alone for as many as ten practices. If you spend eight weeks practising each one daily, Barbara will get hundreds of hours of data. That's a lot to compare! You're testing this model, but we need to see if it works before we get into the analysis. Your data is going to work much harder and could impact how therapists work in the future and how we understand the relationship between the experience reported by people and its brain dynamics. What you personally learn about yourself during this experiment – is for you to find out."

Growing Pains

It turns out that Jon Kabat-Zinn, the originator of MBSR, found inspiration for his programme in an unusual setting – on a Vipassana retreat. Vipassana meditation (which follows the teachings of the Buddha) is a physically and mentally challenging practice requiring meditators to examine their bodily sensations in microscopic detail for hours on end. It's on my list to try later in the experiment when I can face the thought of meditating all day long.

The story goes that as Kabat-Zinn sat immobile, he experienced intense pain in his legs. He'd been taught to acknowledge uncomfortable sensations, but to avoid labelling them as pain. When the agony became unbearable, it suddenly dissolved into pure sensation. By objectively examining the flow of throbbing, hot sensations, Kabat-Zinn had discovered that he could uncouple the emotional attachment of pain from the physical sensation. Taking his findings back to the University of Massachusetts Medical Center in America, he extracted the mechanics of Buddhist meditation and re-packaged them into a secular programme. He went on to launch the first MBSR programme in 1979, treating patients with chronic pain.

Over my lifetime pain has been many things: a nuisance, a distraction and, occasionally, a debilitating experience. Of course, pain is the body's natural warning klaxon, but it can be liberating. The birth of my son in 2010 was triumphant and pain was part of that process. Is it possible that pain can be a conduit to some kind of perceptual shift? Kabat-Zinn dedicates a number of chapters to this in his book, *Full Catastrophe Living: How to Cope With Stress, Pain and Illness Using Mindfulness Meditation.* And yet I'm not convinced I can observe my injured foot objectively. I can't ignore the pain, but weirdly that is not what is being asked of me. As if my nerves were listening in, a spasm causes my foot to jerk. *Ow!* Intellectually I might understand what Dave is suggesting, but I'm not sure I am experiencing this yet.

Autopilot

It's week two and, after practising body scans every day at home wearing the headset and noting my responses in the app and diary, I'm back in the studio again. Staring out into the inky blackness, Dave's voice echoes around the room as he talks about how often we're unaware of our thoughts. I'm weary, so my attention is waning and I drift back in time to the previous summer: I'd dropped my daughter at her friend's house and was walking home, sweating in the heat. I was wrapped up in my thoughts, replaying an earlier, somewhat difficult, conversation. Turning a corner I flashed an involuntary smile at a bespectacled man who appeared out of nowhere. Neatly sidestepping him, the keys clutched in my hand jangled. The sound made me stop, but I wasn't sure why. Suddenly, I remembered I'd forgotten my car – I had driven my daughter over. Furious at myself, I marched back down the hot street, toward a mother with a weaving toddler. As I passed the mother, I didn't smile. In truth, I have no idea what my face did. It was only when she shot me a hurt look that I knew I'd scowled.

Snapping back to the chill of the studio, I'd been so immersed in the memory that I'd blocked out Dave's voice. I catch him saying that if we get snarled up in past events, we often miss out on what is happening now. *Oh God.* It's a double whammy: I distracted myself *now* by reliving a time when I was distracted *in the past.* The irony is awful. On that hot summer's day, my anger, aimed only at myself, spilt out into the real world and dictated how I reacted to a complete stranger. How many times has that happened? Other moments pop up: like the friend who didn't return a smile when I saw her on the school run, and a stranger today who huffed when I didn't hobble out of his way quickly enough. Were they caught up in their own heads too? Was their coldness nothing to do with me?

Dave is making some good points. Learning to notice and rein in my runaway thoughts is probably a good thing. What he's talking about here is "autopilot". This is what was responsible for me forgetting to collect my car that day. It's funny to think I have a biological mechanism that I'm not in charge of. Sometimes, my unconscious mind kicks in to help me function. Autopilot is how my son jumps onto his bike and pedals off before I can scream – stop! It's a very useful skill, this ability to mindlessly go about essential tasks. But what happens if my autopilot switch gets stuck? Even meditating for a few minutes makes me aware I'm *actively* doing something, bringing home how much of the time I'm *not* aware of what I'm doing.

It's not unusual for my emotional state to get stuck too, often veering into a heightened state triggered by who knows what. For example, with my reduced vision, just thinking about busy crowds makes me panic these days and my "fight or flight mode" kicks in. A hardwired defence mechanism, this response is triggered by fear. It's another example of when the unconscious mind has grabbed the steering wheel. This primal system allows us to react quickly and efficiently to scary situations. It was this response that helped me run like the clappers the time I feared I was about to be mugged: my adrenal glands pumped out hormones, my heart rate escalated, blood rushed to my muscles and, hey presto, I was Usain Bolt.

It's at these times that our bodies are amazing and respond to the world in the way we need them to. However, we do not live in caves and there aren't often bears (or muggers) chasing us. Hyper-arousal puts a strain on our bodies and can be hard to switch off. This is even worse when we can't identify what has made our heart race in the first place. Sadly, it's often an unconscious trigger that acts like rocket fuel for our nervous system.

SAGE Advice

It's week three and I've continued to meditate at home daily, scoring each meditation straight afterwards and filling in my diary. Sessions vary between 30 and 40 minutes long, but I sometimes find myself mentally writing notes for Barbara before the meditation has finished. It would appear that the experiment itself is becoming a distraction.

Tonight, Dave is teaching us a meditation acronym, cleverly entitled SAGE. This stands for Stepping out (of automatic pilot), Acknowledge (what's going on), Gather (your thoughts) and Expand (your awareness to the whole body). Dave uses well-trodden terms to decode the concept of mindfulness: "be here right now" and "the present moment". I flinch because popular culture has made these words cliched through overuse. It's a shame, as they *are* the right words.

We sit on our chairs with our backs straight, preparing to learn a breathing meditation. As I learned during The Beach exhibition, mindfulness is not the same as meditation. Mindfulness is just one style of meditation. Annoyingly, the word "mindfulness" and "meditation" are often used interchangeably, but they aren't the same thing. Dave is teaching us how to be mindful. This is intentionally being aware of what's happening around us at any given time. It's only when, like now that we're sitting down and being more formal about this mindful awareness, that it becomes *mindfulness meditation*.

Dave tells us to close our eyes and, regardless of whether our thoughts come fast or slow, to let them come. He doesn't expect us to focus on breathing in and out for more than nanoseconds at a time. Every time we remember our breath is a success. That is mindful meditation at work. Getting tangled up in memories is not failure but he warns us not get snagged onto a spiky thought, or board a "thought-train", speeding off toward self-criticizing doom.

"We *let* our minds think, we don't try to stop that process. We become aware of the fact we are having thoughts," he says.

Dave hopes that we'll learn not to fight the to-do lists, great ideas or rambling monologues that come up, but to (somehow) stand back and watch them. Without getting involved. And I know a hackneyed phrase is coming: "just be in the present moment". *Ugh.* But as quickly as Dave loses me with his "be here now" adage, he throws a curveball.

"You don't have to believe your thoughts."

What? My eyes fly open at this sledgehammer statement. *Not all of my thoughts are true? Why has no one told me that before?* Blinking in shock it dawns on me that this is the cognitive therapy aspect of the course at work. It's such a simple, obvious statement and yet, however fundamental it is, I had never acknowledged this fact before. All the times I have blamed others for events playing out in the way they did, I never stopped to consider that it might be my *own* mind deceiving me.

Sneaking a look at pink jumper woman, I wonder if she's experiencing the same slap-in-the-face self-awareness I am. As she catches my eye I look away. This self-reflection malarkey is too much like a truth serum.

Mindfulness, as I am coming to see, is not as simple as I thought it was. In the West, the practice is often a health intervention, a means to manage our troubled lives with aspects of mindfulness – such as acceptance and openness – becoming the basis for a number of mental health therapies. The Buddhist interpretation of mindfulness is somewhat different. For serious meditators, mindfulness of the breath, or "sati" (the Pali translation), provides the bedrock to a meditation practice. Meditation is as interwoven into their lives as brushing their teeth. They walk the path to "nirvana", rather than navigate the south circular to work.

Dave doesn't mention nirvana, of course, as the Buddhist roots have been omitted from the MBCT programme. That's why this course is a great start. While it might require me to take responsibility for my thoughts, it does not require me to fully understand Buddhism, enlightenment or think that Nirvana is anything other than a band I once saw at Glastonbury.

Frankenstein's Monster

Thankfully, a month into my course my foot is healing well and I'm walking without crutches. This is good as I have a daunting task ahead. Our homework this week is a walking meditation and I'm debating whether to wear the EEG headset in public for today's meditation. Over the last few weeks we've learned seated breathing and stretching meditations that use gentle yoga poses to encourage us to connect to our physical bodies. As I have practised these slowly with my eyes closed, Barbara hopes that the muscle movement the EEG headset can pick up won't interfere with my neural data.

Dave has also taught us a static mindful breathing meditation, asking us to observe our breath as it flows in and out of the body and the sensations that creates. We have been filling in diaries for Dave that record unpleasant and pleasant experiences and logging our reactions to these. Along with the diary I keep for Barbara plus the daily scoring of each meditation on the app, it's been a lot to remember.

The walking meditation today is about taking time and using slow, deliberate steps in order to increase our self-awareness. Dave wants us to stop "living inside our heads" and to gather up our scattered minds. He's also asked us to undertake everyday tasks like showering, walking or shopping mindfully, requesting we are aware of this activity in a new expansive way. He says "the mind is like an excited puppy, running around collecting toys". Personally, I think my mind is more like a Rottweiler, barking at anything suspicious.

I decide to be brave and wear the headset out for the walking meditation, but I have a problem. The padding around the top is bulky and sits high upon my head. It might be cutting-edge technology, but it resembles a torture prop from a sci-fi movie. I've already tried four hats to see which covers it best. A baseball cap was a non-starter. Ed's old beanie is a possible, but I look like an egghead. The mock deerstalker covers it completely, but given I laughed out loud at myself, that's out, too. In the end, a woolly bobble hat is the best option as the fluffy ball disguises my elephantine head.

Peering out of my front door, I scan for neighbours. It's all clear so I scamper down the road and in through the park gates. Breathing hard, I look for dog walkers, tots on scooters or people I know. As my hands flutter around my hat, I realize I'm acting strangely. The handful of people here are oblivious to me, so I take a few slow paces – and stop. Standing with the sun toasting my back, I'm now aware of being still. Really still. Closing my eyes, I can feel my feet encased in fleece socks inside my trainers. They're warm, a little clammy, but comfortable enough. I hadn't been aware of them until this moment and it feels strange to connect. But, nice strange.

I roll forwards, savouring the movement, the pressure on the balls of my feet. Taking a slow step forwards my body shifts, tipping me off my axis. Each step is pacifying, drawing my body into neutral gear. I hear noises, a buzzing, a car door slamming in the distance. Opening my eyes, colour floods my senses. I'm momentarily shocked as this kind of vibrancy is a distant memory. I don't just see the trees and the branches, I see the spaces between – the harsh stencils the sunlight has cut. I take another step and a shrill tone splits my ears. Leaping into the air, my fingers frantically press buttons on my phone.

"Hi," I hear my voice say – remarkably level. It's a local parent asking if I can collect his daughter from school. "Sure," I breeze, wondering if I sound mindful. The call over, I return to my contemplative state. I can see now – because of the call – that I have returned to this entirely different place. I am floating down the path in an intensely sharpened way of being. Each step is gratifying and the world looks so close I want to touch it. As my heart slows, I wonder why I don't do this more often.

Iceland

It's week five and I'm in Iceland – the supermarket. The kids love potato waffles so I'm braving the chill and fluorescent lighting. Approaching the checkout gripping my frosty carton, there's a queue. A checkout person opens a second till, but as I shuffle forwards a man pushes in front. *How dare he!* I fume, not quite sure how to respond. Heart pounding, I take a breath and say, "Excuse me," in what I hope is a polite, yet firm voice. I don't get any further, as the woman behind cuts me off.

"*You're* pushing in!" she screeches at me, spittle spraying my neck. Taken aback, I stand my ground. *Surely she saw the man push in? Why is she screaming at me?*

"He can do that, he can do that!" she parrots in a strange Mickey Mouse voice. As she shifts restlessly, something isn't right. *This doesn't make any sense.* The other customers stare, curious to see what will happen. My initial outrage is replaced by apprehension as I silently urge the checkout worker to move faster. The machine is bleep-bleeping its way through the man's Weetabix and frozen peas. His face is infuriatingly impassive as I fire invisible arrows at him. *You caused this!* I scream inside my head, not daring to speak out loud. The woman behind is panting now. I'm only buying waffles; how did this happen?

When I get home I record this event on the sheet called "unpleasant events" which Dave has given us. That evening, relating the incident to the class, I realize my shopping trip was anything but mindful. I exclude how I mulled over the altercation for hours afterwards – hours spent justifying my distress and ruminating over the woman's behaviour. Then came the slow dawning that the woman probably needed help – and none of us gave it. It was the unfairness of the situation that upset me. I sought some kind of meaning, a rationale. Of course, there was none. My reaction was, and still is, over the top. I know Ed would have let it all go – so why can't I? Retelling the incident has made my face go hot. I feel sweaty and angry and somehow, agonizingly, I am back in Iceland again. Dave explains how thoughts are sticky, how they gain traction through repetition unless we stop them in their tracks.

Dave is right. My brain's executive centres, the frontal lobes (located behind my forehead) are causing the problem. As humans, it is our ability to worry about the past and fret about the future that separates us from other animals. According to Dan Goleman and Richard Davidson, in their audiobook *Altered Traits: Science reveals how meditation changes your mind, brain and body*, there are paradoxical advantages and disadvantages to these skills. Epictetus, an ancient Greek philosopher, sums it up nicely: "Men are disturbed not by things, but by the views which they take of things." It is my view of Waffle-gate that is the problem, not the event itself.

This may be true, but changing habitual responses takes practice. I'm relieved when Dave guides us through a seated meditation. Closing my eyes, I wonder if these practices are just a weird form of distraction. By focusing on my breath, my ankles or even my bum, I point my attention toward that thing and away from Waffle-gate. Breathing in and out, I start to gain perspective. Unfortunately, my thoughts are spring-loaded and my anger boomerangs back. *Damn it. Why does my mind have a hotline to my emotions?* While I'm not sucked into the story quite so bodily it's hard work and requires actual effort. I'm not sweating this time, but my body is behaving like it's trapped in Iceland. My mind is conditioned to whirr and obsess. I might have been in charge of buying waffles, but I was not in charge of my emotional or physical reactions. It's a sobering thought.

Running on Empty

It's a dark evening in late February and there's hideous traffic. All I have to do is collect my daughter, now aged nine, from her after-school class, but I'm already late. It's raining hard and managing unpredictable events are emotional triggers since my sight loss. After my daughter darts into the back seat dripping wet, we sit motionless in the traffic.

"This is ridiculous!" I moan, a little louder than I intended. My children are quiet in the back seat – they know I don't like driving in the dark. Sighing, my gaze drops to a red flashing light on the dashboard. The petrol gauge is empty.

"Ed!" I bellow, making the kids jump. My husband didn't fill the car up after he used it last night. Yet as waves of panic and anger flood my body, a funny thing happens. Dave has taught us to recognize these moments, to become aware of our lightning-fast responses. He asks us to intercept our reactions as they happen, but that interception has *already* occurred. As I force my attention onto my body, I'm already breathing slow, calming breaths. What's more, this breathing started *before* I realized I needed to do it. I blink a few times to process this. *Dave has been teaching me something I already knew!* This is body-memory at work. Breathing was one of the techniques I used to get through the panic-inducing trauma I suffered during my illness five years ago. My body has intercepted and put this dormant skill to use once again. Staring through the rain-streaked windscreen, I'm humbled at how clever my brain is.

Silence Please

I'm dreading our penultimate class. Dave explains we are to spend an entire day in silence. Total silence. The nominated day is a Saturday in early March, which clashes with a family commitment. My request to leave early was gently rebutted – there's no getting out of this. With the threat of not getting my MBCT certificate hanging over me, I arrive armed with blankets, snacks and extra-thick socks.

Dave explains the rules: no phones, no speaking, no unnecessary eye contact and no reading. We start with a walking meditation where no speeding is permitted. Only if our pace is naturally faster than the person in front are we able to "overtake". We haven't even started our plod and I hate it. I'm annoyed because I actually like mindful walking; just not in a tiny circle in a tiny room. I'm bored and frustrated and don't want to be here. I feel like an unhappy lion in a zoo.

After several hours of structured activities, we sit down to lunch. I drink mint tea, trying to read the ingredients on a pack of biscuits. It occurs to me that reading the label is breaking the rules and this pleases me. As instructed, we have avoided eye contact all day, so I sigh and stare at the sunlight outside. I feel cooped up and fretful, but I don't mind the quiet. I can smell the sulphurous residue of egg sandwiches and the musk of human bodies. And yet, mulling over the (annoying) comments Dave has made during our imprisonment, something new has come up.

Tara Brach, in her audiobook *Radical Self-Acceptance: A Buddhist Guide To Freeing Yourself From Shame*, asks a penetrating question: "What is asking for attention?" The stillness in the room has allowed me to sink down and really feel what is happening within my body. It's a profound yet subtle feeling – something beyond normal cognition. I realize I want to connect more to those around me – *to feel more*. This day of silence is reminding me of the disconnect I felt at the beginning of this experiment. There is a wall of numbness that often surrounds me, an invisible force-field keeping this mad world at bay. For a second, I feel a stranger in my own life, like I've been yanked out of my own body, leaving only the shell behind. It's a disconcerting feeling and one I recognize. Sometimes, standing in our house surrounded by Ed and the children, I feel empty. Mulling over who left the lid off the toothpaste or unfinished homework, I forget to ruffle my son's hair or touch Ed on the elbow. These acts of tenderness get lost in amongst the jostle of life, leaving me emotionally distanced from those I love.

As the silence in the studio consumes me now, I feel frustrated that I can't voice these feelings. Is this what isolated introspection has revealed? Brooding on the cold floor, I have unplugged myself from the room *yet again*. I have to stop doing this.

A New Lens

It's late March and I have travelled to Cambridge to check in with Barbara. We've decided to do this every couple of months to review aspects of the experiment. We are still fine-tuning the design as recording individual experiences during meditation hasn't been done in this intricate way before. Barbara wants to use the lab's high density EEG equipment to capture my brain activity periodically while I meditate. Explaining how this data will prove valuable during the analysis process, she likens my headset (with five electrodes) to a bicycle, and the lab's 128-electrode headset to a Rolls Royce. It's a good analogy and I understand how much more detailed this data will be. We plan to start doing this once I have four or five disciplines under my belt, and these "meditation marathons" will involve me coming to the lab and practising one meditation technique after the other, along with recording some baselines (two minutes of just "thinking") for comparison. As we hang out in Tristan's lab at the university, Barbara quizzes me.

"So would you still call yourself a beginner meditator?" she asks, munching on a sandwich. Barbara has asked this (rather sly question) as she is trying to define what characterizes and separates beginners from experienced meditators.

"Yes ... No," I reply, unconvinced. "I don't know. Probably."

"Did you learn anything new?"

"Yes. Stuff I didn't want to learn!" I quip. "There were huge gaps in what I thought mindfulness was."

"Like what?"

"Like I thought it was just a tool to calm my mind. To relax. But it's about understanding patterns of behaviour and how the mind actually operates. It's like looking under the hood and seeing the mechanics of your mind."

"Oh, I like that," she grins. "What's next?"

"We said I'd try Transcendental Meditation next, I think?"

"Yes, TM is good as we want to include a mantra-based meditation. Remember to record in your diary how different that is."

Later, on the train home, I replay our conversation. Barbara is aware of the pressure this experiment is putting upon me. Evaluating how I feel during meditating sometimes clashes with the notion of being mindful. Mindfulness is about learning *not* to do, so striving or having expectations is counterintuitive. As Dave said many times during the course, "There is no good or bad meditation." Moving forwards, I'll need to observe my thoughts and feelings without being critical – a tricky task when assessing the experience afterwards. That said, the cognitive behavioural element of the course has enhanced my own "meta awareness" – my ability to stand back from thinking and appraise the thoughts bombarding my mind.

Ironically, the first thing MBCT taught me was that the meditation gauntlet I picked up at the start of this experiment is what I now have to put down. This isn't a competition and I cannot fight this process – if anything I surrender to it. Learning to "let go" is the core of a mindfulness practice and has proven extraordinarily hard. I have to allow myself to be frustrated and to sit with that frustration as it bubbles away.

The MBCT course provided more than just relaxation. The combination of breathing, stretching and movement meditations each brought up subtly different insights. The body scans connected me to the off-the-radar twitches and temperature fluctuations within my body. My damaged ankle provided an opportunity to develop a new, more curious relationship with pain. Following Dave's audio instructions, the seated movement meditation provided "mental brakes", slowing my mind and providing an awareness of my body in space and time. I connected to my senses, hearing birds outside, feeling the tickle of a breeze on my calf. The breathing meditations provided fertile ground for distraction. I had to accept that I couldn't force my mind *not* to be active. Mindfulness is not about forcing – but standing back and accepting whatever is there – even if it's unpleasant.

So it turns out that MBCT wasn't an eight-week secular inroad to meditation – it was an inroad to Why I Do Stuff. Being introduced to my inner chatter was like being invited to a party where I didn't think I'd know anyone, only to find I knew everyone there. This narcissistic, wandering part of my mind obsesses about itself and is often unhappy. It was this brain network that was activated when I replayed the waffle incident over and over. Developing a new, albeit wary, relationship with my inner self has been a pivotal step.

Mindfulness has not been about sitting serenely on a cushion – the biggest *work* was taking responsibility for myself and seeing how my reactions have led to misunderstandings in the past. It turns out, mine isn't the only reality. What's more, I construct my own reality based upon my version of events. Of course, inside my head, I take the starring role (like in Waffle-gate), but Dave has taught me ways to deconstruct that story by employing a different kind of awareness a new lens.

It's been a lot to take in. An MBCT course is like living inside a hall of mirrors with each week revealing something I didn't see before. I'm still processing the sense of disconnection that came up during the day of silence.

As my first, formal introduction to mindfulness I realize my initial scepticism came from what I saw as its over-commercialization, sensing the core intention had been lost. By noticing my thoughts and feelings, I have learned to stand back from difficult situations and to (I hate to say it) pause a fraction before responding. This helps me manage the ups and downs of family life.

When my children fell silent in the back of the car on that rainy February night, I knew what was happening to me. And I talked to them. I said sorry, and that it didn't matter if we ran out of petrol. "We can always walk home!" I said. When I relaxed, they relaxed – and the journey became an adventure, not a war zone.

My reactivity may be ingrained, but I have the choice to change. However, the reality of putting into action all I have learned feels overwhelming. I have a steep hill to climb. We got the first bit of our experiment right – mindfulness is the buzzer on the door to my consciousness.

As I arrive back at King's Cross Station, a message from my friend Louise suggests a walk later in the week. I smile as she also asks if I am still looking for a TM teacher.

CHAPTER 3

KEEPING MY WORD

Transcendental Meditation (TM): June 2017

Following email exchanges with Neville, a recently qualified Transcendental Meditation teacher, he agrees to meet me. Neville was trained by the Meditation Trust, an unofficial offshoot of the original Transcendental Meditation movement after he discovered the technique by chance in his twenties. In his correspondence with me he described TM as "transformational".

TM is one of the more popularized meditation techniques and is normally taught over four-day courses, with follow-up sessions. Employing a mantra, the initial aim is relaxation and stress-reduction, but I'm told it has innumerable health benefits, along with improved self-awareness and spiritual consciousness.

Before Neville can help me with my experiment, he asks that I speak with Colin, the founder of the Meditation Trust so he has permission to teach me the practice. Life has got a little hectic, so I've overlooked this phone appointment and my cellphone rings as I'm jogging to collect my son from a play date. Catching my breath, I pace up and down while Colin tells me his story and asks me questions. Colin is passionate about TM. His 30-year practice came about after TM helped him overcome an addiction to prescription drugs and alcohol. In his words, TM saved his life. The TM movement puts much emphasis on scientific study and Colin directs me to research already undertaken. Due to its powerful nature, he's concerned that any other subsequent technique will be influenced by TM. This is a valid point. All the techniques I try will have an accumulative effect and this, along with overlaps in style and theory, will be something Barbara will consider within the data.

With roots in the Indian Vedic tradition, TM was introduced to the West in the 1950s by Maharishi Mahesh Yogi. Born about 1917, Maharishi devoted his life to spiritual study, even though he was unable to inherit his teacher's religious lineage as his family was not part of the Brahmin caste (the Hindu religious aristocracy). In 1952, his teacher Swami Brahmananda Saraswati allegedly instructed Maharishi to spread the word of meditation internationally. TM became nothing short of a mystic revolution. After Maharishi gained the attention of the Beatles in the late 1960s, they stayed at his ashram in India, bringing along a cohort of celebrities. Much media debate surrounds this famous visit and, indeed, Maharishi himself. He wasn't just a media-savvy guru, but an astute businessman. Streamlining classic Vedic teachings and westernizing the ancient language, he initially taught TM for free, before commanding fees based upon income. Today, the Maharishi Foundation is a large, well-known charity, teaching four thousand new students each year in the UK alone.

Colin, now in his seventies, was part of the original Maharishi movement, but left to found the Meditation Trust, an independent charity, in 1999, offering lower-priced courses in comparison to official UK TM fees (although these have also now come down in price).

Having thoroughly quizzed me about how often the study requires me to meditate, how we're recording the EEG data along with what other techniques we will be exploring, Colin suggests I attend his TM retreat in September, providing I accrue sufficient meditation hours beforehand. While I understand positive effects can be felt straight away, it's normal to need several months or even years of TM to see lasting benefits. The retreat is run over a weekend and encompasses talks, group meditations, yoga "asanas" (postures), "pranayama" (breathing exercises) and a day of silence. Colin tells me this weekend is the equivalent of three months of meditating at home. It sounds like a no-brainer. Colin gives his blessing and suggests Neville teaches me the TM technique beforehand, requesting only a nominal donation.

"Hazim"

Neville, who turns out to be a well-spoken man in his forties, greets me at his front door with a smile and a request to remove my shoes. He directs me into a simply furnished room where diffused sunlight pours in through a large netted window. It's July and unbearably hot, and Neville mops his brow with a small hand towel.

After some formalities Neville explains how the course will work. Secrecy cloaks TM and the teaching is highly structured. The "Puja ceremony" forms part of my induction and involves a yoga ceremony similar to Hindu rituals. Neville explains that the Sanskrit chanting expresses gratitude to the Shankaracharya tradition behind TM.

Perched on Neville's leather sofa, thick incense fills my throat and at one side of the room a lit candle flickers incongruously. On a makeshift altar, a framed photo of Swami Brahmananda balances next to a gold tray upon which are three round bowls. The first contains a red powder resembling paprika, the second is filled with rice, and the third with camphor oil and water. Completing this collection of objects are a bunch of plastic roses and fruit in a basket, covered by a cloth. I'm sure Neville said the bowls represent the four states of consciousness, but I am struggling to remember. It's so hot I'm starting to feel woozy – it's a lot to take in.

After the Puja, Neville gives me a mantra that I must remember. This, he explains, is simply a sound that can connect me to inner peace. I must repeat this one word silently and gently, treating it like any other thought. Questions fly into my mind. *Will you write it down? Can I say it out loud? Do I say it fast or slow? Is this an affirmation?*

My inner perfectionist wrings her hands, desperate to be good at this. Neville smiles and tells me I'm overcomplicating things. Mantras are sacred words or phrases that normally have specific meaning or purpose. However, a TM mantra has no meaning in order to stop the mind from trying to intellectualize it. (It is common to confuse mantras and affirmations, but generally affirmations are positive statements intended to target specific negative beliefs.) Neville explains that my mantra will resonate and even vibrate on a deep cellular level. I feel a bit giddy at this, like I'm being given a toy that no one else has.

"Hazim." Neville whispers my mantra for me and I freeze. *Huh? That's a man's name! Did I mishear?* Turns out that I did. Yet when Neville repeats my mantra, I hate it. It feels metallic and hard bouncing against the walls of my mind. Spiky. I try twisting and stretching out the vowels, trying to anchor it.

"Oh," I say, my eyes flying open. "I've forgotten it already."

"Don't worry," Neville soothes, "that's normal." After a pause he repeats it again.

I close my eyes, trying to keep this alien, ephemeral word mentally tethered. As I chant it, weirdly, the word has a mesmerizing effect, a cyclical reverberation, like I am hypnotizing myself from the inside out.

Neville explains that silence is the mind's natural state and one we can all experience, but we have somehow lost the ability. The idea is to transcend beyond the "thinking mind". The word "transcend" comes up a lot in TM – I'm going to have to look it up. Neville says that the body needs the deep rest experienced when transcending occurs and that sleep alone does not replenish us enough. The process of TM will liberate my mind, allowing it to settle effortlessly into a silence more profound than anything other meditations can offer.

I lose sense of time as my mind detaches into a dreamlike state. I feel odd but my body is surprisingly motionless. The minutes speed along and I have a sense of "being elsewhere", although I couldn't tell Neville where that was. After twenty minutes, Neville tells me to stop. I just need the five minutes of rest that should follow every meditation. Opening my eyes, I feel displaced and sticky from the heat. Strangely, I have no memory of the meditation, only the residue of an old dream slowly fading away – a surreal moment when I found myself driving a steam train. Unlike the mindfulness meditations, my mind had not focused on any one thing, but had flitted freely like a butterfly. I feel calm and relaxed, but not particularly sleepy and pictures rather than thoughts seem to remain. I have forgotten the mantra again and wonder if it will be like my pin number – something I can only recall at the moment I need it. Smiling, Neville explains that losing the mantra is partly the point. The sound is only a conduit for the mind. Neville assures me it will all make sense in time. All I need to do is meditate twice a day for twenty minutes and everything will start to happen. My eyebrows fly up at the twice-daily instruction as this will prove tricky to fit in. I wonder if I can meditate while my son is at karate. *Would the teacher notice?*

Seeing me to his front door, Neville reminds me that my practice must not be discussed or shared with anyone else. This is an important instruction. I smile benignly, knowing I will share everything with Barbara. Before he closes the door, he reassures me that it is often the simplicity of TM that throws people the most. Really, he says, very little is required.

Neville is a good bloke. I genuinely like his gentle manner. He's found his calling in life and, if I'm honest, I'm a little envious. However, there is something unsettling about the rigidity of the Meditation Trust's teachings. When I casually mention that using the mantra might help me sleep at night, Neville is quick to interject. This is not how the mantra should be used as it could stimulate my mind. Better sleep, he explains, will come on the back of the practice. While the MBCT course had a clear structure, with timed meditations and instructions, there were fewer "rules" and more latitude to interpret and adapt the teachings to suit my needs. TM feels considerably more strait-laced.

The Sloth

The next day, after the morning school run, I practise TM at home. Wearing the EEG headset my thoughts race in amongst the mantra, like cars on a Scalextric track. This feels less intense than the body scans or breathing meditations that have come before. Repeating one word over and over is straightforward and the minutes zoom by. I don't feel as though I am doing anything, which illustrates how engrossed I was with the *act* of meditating previously. I'm relieved I don't have to look for the experience – this time it's coming to me. Right now, if mindfulness is a meerkat, alert and curious, TM is a sloth, slowly chewing as the world passes by. I smile, wondering if this metaphor will make sense to Barbara when she reads it in my diary.

Neville is right, *not* having to notice my thoughts is liberating – and simple. By repeating the mantra, I'm gaining a heightened sense of my own thinking. I frown as I write this down too; it sounds ridiculous. Of course I have thoughts, but I've never observed my thinking in this way before. This seeing thoughts thing came up with Dave in the MBCT class. I still recall my shock when he said I didn't have to believe the vitriol my mind spewed. What I'm gaining here is a broader understanding of the functioning of my mind.

The TM Effect

It's my fourth session with Neville and after this my initial training will be complete. The other teaching sessions used diagrams to explain how TM positively impacts the nervous system, including tips for meditating. I tell Neville how much I am enjoying practising twice a day. It's felt easy, sitting wearing the headset on my sofa and I've looked forward to this mental time out. My emotional state has felt recalibrated afterwards, contrasting the initial irritation I'd felt learning mindfulness. A sense of mindfulness is also the preamble to TM, so the skills I acquired (like noticing my inner landscape and settling into the body) are all proving useful.

That said, I'm distracted today as my dad, who normally lives in South Africa, is staying with us. My father moved abroad 25 years ago, after my parents divorced and he retired early. While I see my mother regularly and we have a close relationship, distance has meant I don't see my dad as often as I'd like. He's here to visit me, and my younger brother Dan and his family, who live a few hours away. After staying with us, Dad will head to Yorkshire to see his older sister who's suffering a number of health issues, which is also weighing on all of our minds. Dad's trips back are infrequent so I'm hoping this session won't take long – our time together is precious.

I find Neville standing in front of a flip chart with a purposeful air about him. He points at a diagram showing TM at the top with arrows making up a circle. TM, it appears, has its own mnemonic. Here the T represents *thoughts* and M signifies the *mantra*. Neville draws arrows to illustrate that once meditation commences, mental activity lessens. I interrupt, saying that quite often I experience the opposite. Neville smiles, replying that mental activity will reduce overall, but it may initially increase when stress release occurs. His arrows point toward DEEP REST printed in capital letters at the bottom. I'm told new meditators (like me) don't always experience obvious stress relief straight away. We might be fidgeting or scratching our noses, but despite what our minds are telling us this is stress release at work and we are receiving a profoundly healing rest.

"The body follows the mind," Neville says. Through TM, my body will naturally eliminate deep-rooted stresses, loosening their grip on my nervous system. Neville explains that as my mind releases this tension, I might experience small twitches, or a little loosening of the neck, for example. These are physical manifestations of the processes at work. As my body responds, so does my mind and thoughts arise. Yet even when that happens, I'm still getting rest. I'm told that the mind looks for a reason to exist – so it reaches out for the mantra. However, this in itself isn't meditation. Meditation is coming back to the mantra, treating it like an old friend and welcoming it back.

Much of what Neville says rings true and I'm excited that this technique might exorcise past events. The way he describes the mind latching onto the mantra and the subsequent deep sense of calm – that's real. He has related a huge amount of information, some of which is overwhelming to absorb in one go. I am feeling the impact of the practice though, even using TM for a short time has rejuvenated me in that I often feel lighter and buoyed up afterwards.

Ultimately, the aim is happiness and this was Maharishi's mission statement. Proving its scientific efficacy was always a top priority and as such, there are hundreds of published papers on the subject. In fact, Maharishi's vigorous approach to scientific study helped pave the way for meditation research.

The studies referenced on the TM website suggest regular practise can reduce stress and depression and increase creativity, as well as cognitive and intellectual abilities. There are also claims it can help with drug and alcohol addiction and ADHD in children. A five-year study from the US found that in patients with coronary heart disease who used TM, there was a 48% reduction in heart attacks, strokes and death. Yet (along with other TM studies) the research appears limited in that the control group only had access to a health education programme. I am impressed, even if some of the early TM research lacks rigour, which a review of meditation research notes. However, TM clearly does something. Heavyweight supporters such as Oprah, Hugh Jackman and Jerry Seinfeld promote its health benefits, and David Lynch set up his own foundation advocating the use of TM. A hard-hitting quote from psychiatrist, scientist and author Dr Norman Rosenthal sums up the TM machine: "If this kind of result was observed for a new prescription drug, it would be a billion-dollar industry to make it available to everyone immediately."

There is no doubt that TM means business. Maharishi also made global claims based on the yoga tradition. In the 1960s, he predicted that if just one percent of a population practised the TM technique simultaneously, it would produce measurable benefits for the whole community. (In 1976, a phenomenon called The Maharishi Effect was reported in a published paper claiming that when 1% of a number of US city communities practised TM, crime reduced by 16% on average.) Maharishi's suggestion for world peace received much criticism. However, a later published article in 1988 claimed that when the number of TM meditators and TM-Sidhi practitioners (the advanced programme that Maharishi introduced) in Merseyside grew above 1% of the community, there was a 13.4% decrease in crime (in comparison to the previous year). Whether this curious phenomenon is true or not, I wonder whether if Ed and I were to practise TM just before bedtime, would it reduce childish tantrums by a measurable amount?

A Mental Stress Toy

Before I book the September TM retreat, I decide to attend a group meditation class. Sitting in a sparsely furnished community centre that smells of disinfectant, our teacher Gemma welcomes me and five other meditators. Gemma, a former clinical psychologist, explains that new meditators often feel like they're not doing enough. That had crossed my mind. As a society we expect anything rewarding to require effort and she believes other forms of meditation perpetuate this belief. Many techniques, including mindfulness, require full concentration; in fact, this is often integral. Gemma explains that TM is different. Whereas mindfulness asks me to experience "the present moment" – this moment now, not the one that's just gone – TM's aim is for me to move beyond active thoughts toward a deep silence, a kind of pure awareness. Progressing through seven stages of awareness, TM students learn to experience unity consciousness – an absolute oneness with silence that, over time, can exist in any conscious state. This is where TM loses me. Both Neville and Gemma talk about this deep silence, but what that is is beyond me. I can't imagine there ever being any kind of silence inside my head.

I think what they are getting at is that if I close my eyes and leave my mind alone, it will be able to sink into a kind of nurturing state all by itself. Wrapped up in my overstimulated life, I have forgotten how to *let go*. Sometimes meditating doesn't touch the sides of my busy, stressed-out mind. What it does do though, is tell me that I have a stressed and busy mind. Meditation isn't so much the solution or the cure, but the doctor standing over me saying I have the illness.

I like the idea that my mantra is a stress toy for my mind. Transcending implies diving down into myself, becoming less concerned with my ego and the noise of the outside world. This is why I initially felt relief practising TM. However, something is niggling me. I already know the practice is having a positive effect in that I feel calmer and more balanced, so I don't understand why my teachers continually point out the limitations of other techniques.

Back home after the class, I break a rule. During my training Neville asked me not to Google TM but to contact him with questions. I'm dying to look up my mantra as I've forgotten the damn word *again*. Yet while the internet doesn't contain every mantra TM teachers use, I found mine listed according to sex and age. Now it doesn't feel quite so unique and I feel I have let Neville down.

I like TM. When I relax, the mantra and my thoughts coexist, playing happily like children in a park. While this is pleasing, it only happens when I have my eyes closed. All harmony ceases the moment my eyes open. Back in the corporeal world, I tend to embody my thoughts, losing any useful perspective. Building on the insights I gained during MBCT, I am becoming more and more fascinated by the variety of thoughts I have. Some are irrelevant and easily forgotten (imagining I am a vole in my garden), some are important (signing that school trip letter), some are creative (an idea for a psychological thriller) and some are troubling. These latter thoughts are pushy, elbowing their way to the front. I replay the hurt I'd felt when two friends discussed a barbecue I hadn't been invited to. Revisiting my first "vole" thought, I wonder if it holds a lesson. If I can shrug away that cursory whim, could I shrug away the hurtful thoughts too? After all, neither exist. Realizing that my thoughts are nothing more than transitory electrical impulses is pivotal to a meditation practice (whether mindfulness or TM). Thoughts are neither concrete nor real. They have no substance or permanent place in this world.

TM is helping me practise an intricate thought-analysis. Like a mental administrator, I'm categorizing and filing the flights of fancy inside my mind, but shredding thoughts is easier said than done. And thinking about thinking is headache-inducing. These processes are like a dripping tap – they take time to sink in.

A Hasty Retreat

It's late September and sitting on an overheated train, my body melds into the seat. It doesn't take long for the grubbiness of London's high rises to transform into the orderly green of the Kent countryside. Scrambling into a white minivan with five other women, I'm loath to start a conversation. Instead, I stare out of the window as we drive to the stately home where the Meditation Trust is hosting their TM retreat. Trailing into a grand atrium with peeling paint, a row of grey school tables form an abrupt barrier. Standing silently in line, I feel awkward and alone. I'm starting to have a bad feeling about this retreat.

The man who leads me up to my room (in the old staff quarters) explains that inexperienced meditators, like me, often forgo the first meditation tonight. Of course, this just galvanizes me to go. After a delicious vegetarian dinner I search out the library where the meditations are held. I panic when I enter a large imposing room with oak-panelled walls, oil paintings and rows of dusty books. A selection of ancient Chesterfield sofas and some uncomfortable-looking office chairs fill the room. Blankets drape territorially over the best seats, clearly reserved by those in the know. Refusing to be shown up as a newbie, I squeeze myself onto the end of a sofa next to a large man wearing shorts. I'm conscious that I haven't met

Colin in the flesh, so I keep an eye out for him. Surveying the room, my fellow residents range in age from early thirties up to a couple who I guess are in their eighties. Of the sixteen people I count, there's an even mix of men and women and many seem to be here on their own.

Without warning, a door, hidden within the panelling, swings open revealing a slim man wearing a cream, loose-fitting shirt and trousers. Sporting white cropped hair and an air of authority, I guess this is Colin. With a half-smile he scans the room, nodding greetings. As his gaze reaches mine, his eyes hover for what feels like endless seconds before he moves on.

Colin welcomes us all, reinforcing the strict "no phone" rule that's pinned up on all the walls. Having agreed not to bring my EEG headset to the retreat, perhaps naïvely I'd hoped to use my phone to record notes. Now I need a new solution – I didn't pack a notebook.

Colin explains that the next day is to be spent in silence, interspersed with meditating and yoga. He is a huge proponent of yoga, claiming it could eradicate the world of misery. He also suggests limiting what we eat so we don't become too sleepy. He finishes by saying there will be notelets available in the hallway for any questions that come up and to leave them in the bowl outside. *Aha, paper!*

After the housekeeping, Colin bows his head and launches into a 20-minute meditation. As this retreat is for relatively experienced meditators, he doesn't remind us to use our mantras. Caught daydreaming, I'm a beat behind. Still, I repeat my own mantra as thoughts, like angry wasps, invade my mind. Projected onto my inner movie screen, I replay my arrival, my stomach knotting as I stood in line. I identify how alone I'd felt. I'm an outsider, unknowing of the rules. I can't use my phone. *Stupid.*

Next to me, the man in shorts grunts, a sound remarkably like a water buffalo. Another woman stirs and the collective breathing deepens. The room is strangely somnolent and I catch the mantra as it flies in amongst the wasps.

Seeing Red

The next afternoon I am secreted behind a bush in the woods, hopefully out of earshot of the retreat staff. I'm squatting in the shrubbery, desperate to record notes on my phone. As I peer back at the grande dame of a building, I imagine an asylum.

The morning didn't start well. In fact, the problems started last night at the 9pm bedtime when I realized I had forgotten my toothbrush. Sitting on my oversprung bed, I berated myself for at least an hour. *If you paid more attention, it wouldn't have happened!* I spent the night in a half-dreaming state of anxiety and disbelief. Anxiety about how I was going to commandeer a toothbrush when I wasn't supposed to talk to anyone, and disbelief that I was reacting quite so hysterically. *On a meditation retreat.* The irony does nothing to alleviate my frenzied mind. I was 15 miles from the nearest Tesco Metro and this was a disaster. I imagined what Ed would do, normally so unruffled by unexpected events. Creeping downstairs at 6.30am, my mind whirred with strategies: I could steal a toothbrush from a bathroom, sneak a note to another inmate or break into the staff quarters. Then I bumped into Colin. Mimicking brushing my teeth and shrugging my shoulders successfully signalled I needed a toothbrush. He agreed to have one sent to me. *Done.* It was sorted in less than ten seconds. I had wasted nine hours fretting about something that did not need fretting about.

Whispering into my phone now, I can see my reactions for what they were. Ridiculous. Emotional. Irrational. Knowing that doesn't make it any better. I'm exhausted from lack of sleep, but slowly accepting that this is a learning curve. Relieved that Toothbrush Gate has been averted, I describe the people I met the previous evening at dinner. Several guests have a nervous energy, repeating a need for this retreat "to work". One man, who owns his own business, wants to increase his productivity. He wants TM to make him (in his own words) "superhuman". He's researched the science and views this retreat as an investment. On the other hand, a single woman in her forties is on her second retreat. She's renewing the technique, having let it slip, as she wants to start meditating again.

Then there's the elderly couple permanently camped on the (nicest) cream chaise longue in the library. From her accent I suspect they're Italian, although I haven't heard him speak. He sits statuesquely, a folded handkerchief in his jacket pocket. Together they exude a timeless elegance and I wonder what brought them to TM. She's remarkably open, almost brazen about their meditation practice. I can't help but feel their story is one of positivity and triumph. Clearly TM is part of that.

Combined with what I learned during MBCT, TM is providing a new perspective. I can already see that meditating is useful. I had a misconception that if I meditated regularly, I'd feel calm afterwards, but this is not always the case. Sometimes there's a trapped intuition or message that I need to understand. Occasionally this message follows the meditation, rising up through layers of consciousness, eventually bubbling at the surface. It might pop hours later, revealing what I needed to know. I'm guessing this is the drip effect, often used to describe a contemplative practice. There are a lot of water metaphors in my notes today.

After a better night's sleep (and with freshly brushed teeth), Sunday is already a better day. As the second meditation comes to an end, I stretch like a contented cat. I am now so comfortable in the library that I cannot recapture the initial reticence I felt. As I have done on a number of occasions, I open my eyes a fraction before the 20 minutes is up. Each time I experience a strange moment of fierce colour and objects in the room leap out. Sharp lemons slice my senses – burgundy walls are rich not mottled. By meditating continuously over the weekend, I have evoked a deep relaxation resulting in a heightened seeing. I'm reminded how opulent and vibrant colour can be and I have seconds to soak up this rainbow world before it disappears.

This has been a rich experience. The frustration I experienced at the beginning of the retreat has dissolved, replaced by an unexpected serenity. My overreaction to the missing toothbrush seems a long time ago. Knee-jerk reactions, so habitually ingrained, have been exposed and assuaged. Beguiled by Colin's insistence that TM brings about bliss and happiness, my mind feels ironed out. Intense meditation has channelled my psyche to spit out ideas and concepts. As my body uncoiled, trapped memories have been released – snapshots from my past merge with fantasies and imaginary worlds. My hand ached as I scribbled on the notelets, trying to keep up with the flood of ideas my unconscious purged. Like separate frames from a movie, TM helped me scoop these pictures together. I left the retreat with around 40 notes, written in a torrent (rather than a stream) of consciousness.

A Mystic Legacy

Two weeks on, my meditation has been going well. The twice-daily sessions wearing the headset have been difficult, but I regularly manage a morning slot and another one just before the school pick-up. This often coincides with low energy levels and resets my mood. What's interesting is that sometimes I don't know my mood needs resetting until after the meditation. TM brings me back to a zero baseline. On the whole, one 20-minute session a day has an uplifting effect, but twice is better still. Even five minutes boosts me. TM has become a fix – something I look forward to because, inevitably, I feel better afterwards.

My mind has continued to be stimulated in other, productive ways too. Perhaps due to the lack of focus (it's okay to forget the mantra), I'm still documenting sudden intuitions and an unleashing of creativity in my diary. These imaginative flares often dominate my meditations so much that I find myself writing down a clever turn of phrase or the memory of an old friend I hadn't thought of in years. Even a few snatched minutes seems to free pent-up melancholy and emotion, often translating into deeply personal insights. As this continues I am learning to control the flow and harness this rich material.

Even though I'm still a novice, Maharishi devised a number of optional advanced techniques for students wishing to speed up progress. On the retreat there were repeated thumps and bumps from the Siddhi programme being taught upstairs. "Siddhi" is Sanskrit for paranormal powers attained by enlightened beings. These advanced meditators were learning to levitate which, while sounding a little ridiculous, is taken very seriously. Colin explained they were "learning how to lift their bodies effortlessly from the ground through intention rather than effort". Maharishi developed this practice from the *Yoga Sutras of Patanjali* (dated around 400 AD), from the section entitled *Vibhuti Pada* which describes the development of supernatural powers. Yogic flying competitions, run by the official TM movement, provide extraordinary footage of meditators bouncing in the lotus position, while officials measure the distances they cover. However, Patanjali also suggests that yogis should not strive to attain these abilities (nor show them off) as they can become hindrances on the path to enlightenment. While I didn't experience any adverse effects from intense meditation, several meditators on the retreat reported headaches and feeling dizzy. This was explained as stress releasing from the body and an expected, temporary part of the process. Severe side effects are rare in any meditation practice, but can happen, particularly when techniques are open to anyone. A 1976 article by the clinical psychologist Arnold Lazarus suggested negative psychological effects had been experienced by TM meditators. Also Deane H Shapiro Jr. and Roger N Walsh, in their book, *Meditation: Classic and Contemporary Perspectives*, include a chapter entitled "Adverse Effects of Transcendental Meditation" which analyzes a number of studies that reported participants experiencing anxiety, depression or withdrawal while practising TM. Of course it's difficult to attribute psychological impact solely to a practice without considering the wider context of one's life. Also, few meditation schools were investigated scientifically during the seventies. However, it does suggest a certain responsibility is required to undertake any kind of meditation practice.

TM takes itself very seriously, but I think I understand why. Maharishi's aim was world peace and unity, yet his approach melded spirituality and science in a way that introduced meditation to a wider audience. I was put off by the celebrity endorsements (even though I am a huge fan of Mr Lynch) but I understand why that attracts new students. I am reminded that spirituality in the West is a lucrative industry – self-care is now a necessity. Perhaps the media attention surrounding TM had deflected me from what is a simple and effortless practice. Yet I wonder if TM tells Westerners what they want to hear. In providing access to what the movement calls a "simple, natural technique", this style of meditation is presented as a modern-day cure to improve almost any aspect of our lives. This is possibly true, but a commitment to practise it is crucial, as is a commitment to change. Whatever change that might be. Overall, I find TM to be very accessible. I don't know what the long-term effects might be, but the short-term ones are encouraging. Neville was right, the simplicity of the practice is the most confusing part.

CHAPTER 4

JAMYANG: TIBETAN TANTRIC VISUALIZATION

September 2017

It's a mild September day and I'm meeting the spiritual leader Geshe Tashi Tsering at the Jamyang Buddhist Centre to talk about Tantric Meditation and my previous use of visualization. Jamyang is affiliated to the Foundation for the Preservation of the Mahayana Tradition (FPMT), which is a large international network set up in 1975 by Tibetan Buddhist monk Lama Thubten Yeshe, to preserve and teach Mahayan Buddhism around the globe.

I have arranged to meet the centre's director, Roy Sutherwood, at Kennington tube station. A bald-headed man wearing black trousers and a black shirt strides assuredly toward me. In his fifties, Roy is a Buddhist teacher and we chat as we reach a large nineteenth-century building with an inviting canopied courtyard. Here, Roy invites me to wait for Geshe-la (the affectionate name he gives Geshe Tashi). While I wait, I notice the strawberries my daughter painted on my thumbnails last night. *I look ridiculous!* Suddenly a small man, wearing simple robes, bows in front of me. Geshe-la takes my hands and asks me to sit.

Born in 1958, Geshe-la fled his homeland with his parents when the Chinese Communist Party invaded Tibet. Eventually, his family settled in Karnataka, India where Geshe-la entered the Sera Mey monastery as a young man.

Leaning on the table, Geshe-la's thin brown arms poke out of his robes. I instantly warm to him, although his stillness emphasizes my fidgeting. His face wrinkles in concern when I describe my sight loss in 2012 and how visualizing an imaginary beach became a coping mechanism. He wants to hear more about this mental sanctuary. Clearly interested in neuroscience, he tells me about the Dalai Lama meeting with scientists such as Dr Richard Davidson in the 1970s. He is curious to know if my EEG cap can recognize when I use different techniques, such as compassion or a mantra. I explain that it can't differentiate specific thoughts, or types of focus, but more fluctuating states of mind such as how drowsy or stimulated I feel.

Having recently completed a masters in social anthropology, Geshe-la has studied the Western adoption of mindfulness and how we find it an easy and accessible form of stress relief. Contemporary interpretations of mindfulness differ from Eastern approaches, which are more focused on effort. Effort, Geshe-la says gravely, is necessary to learn spiritual practices. I'm instantly intrigued by this statement as it conflicts with what the TM movement teaches.

Fascinated to know more about Tibetan Tantra, I ask Geshe-la what it is. Smiling, he explains that the word "tantra" has various meanings, depending on which culture or religion you look at. In Buddhism, the word refers to a set of teachings or techniques that offer students a continuous path to enlightenment.

Buddhism didn't originate in Tibet; originally there were two strands that spread out from India. Mahayana is the more widespread form that travelled through China, Japan, Korea and Mongolia, taking on local customs. Theravada Buddhism is associated with Sri Lanka, Thailand, Burma, Laos, Cambodia and parts of Southeast Asia, and is considered to be closer to the original teachings of Gautama Buddha. Both styles share the same core beliefs.

In Tibetan Buddhism, the tantra teachings are known as *Vajrayana*, which translates from Sanskrit (the language of Mahayana) to mean "diamond vehicle", or my preferred "thunderbolt vehicle".

This sounds altogether more exciting and superhero-like. From what I can gather, *Vajrayana* seems to be a kind of Rough Guide to Enlightenment. Here, tantras provide practical advice, rather than a philosophical perspective. Evoking inner experiences, *Vajrayana* texts use highly symbolic language that aim to recapture or instil the same enlightenment that Buddha experienced.

Mahayana Buddhism dates back to the first century and teaches that any practitioner can reach enlightenment. A core doctrine is the concept of non-self. This is a difficult belief for Westerners to understand as it suggests there is no permanent physical soul or ego. I find this idea of losing any sense of self and merging with the cosmos in some kind of energy bubble bath impossibly hard to conceive, but Geshe-la reassures me that practitioners aren't expected to get this straight away.

Tara, a Tibetan Buddhist deity, is the focus of a Tibetan Tantra practice and is here to lead the way. The techniques require repetition of Tibetan prayers accompanied by a guided visualization during which meditators imagine a youthful woman (Tara) seated on a lotus leaf.

Geshe-la warns that this is not a path for novices, nor the faint-hearted. Achieving a full visualization requires much practise and understanding of the technical language used. He worries that pursuing Tantric Meditation might be too frightening for me as it could evoke the trauma of my sight loss. If I am to pursue Tibetan Tantric visualization, I clearly need to brush up my Buddhism – and the last time I studied it was on a retreat with Ed ten years earlier.

A Monk Called Hedgehog: September 2009

We had bickered most of the drive there, blaming each other for our late departure. I'd been battling guilt, having left our baby daughter in the capable care of my friend, Jackie. I knew they'd have a lovely time, but I was regretting booking Ed and I onto a Buddhist retreat.

We arrived at the Tara Kadampa Meditation Centre in heavy rain and were herded into a large airless hall. Shoving our bags under our seats, we sat back as our coats dripped silently onto the carpet.

The centre was set up in 1984 by Geshe Kelsang Gyatso as part of the modern Mahayana Buddhist movement, to bring practical Buddhist teachings to a wider audience. I was hoping their Introduction to Meditation course would provide some skills to combat the heart-pumping anxiety I experienced as a television producer. I was struggling to survive in an environment where stress was a status symbol. Ed was less enthusiastic, seeing meditation as "not his thing", but nonetheless agreeing to be my curious (if sceptical) consort.

For a while all was silent in the stuffy hall. Then, a young monk no more than twenty years old made his way onto a podium. A glass of water and a microphone were set out next to a mat, upon which he settled himself. Looking around, he smiled and proceeded to spend agonizing minutes arranging his robes. When the suspense became almost unbearable, he leant forwards.

"Hello." He paused again. "Bit stressed, are we?"

A collective gasp provided his answer, followed by self-conscious laughter. That was my first lesson in self-awareness and it provided a flash of clarity. Sitting in my sodden coat, the collar clammy against my neck, my hands were fists and my jaw was clenched. Yet I hadn't known that. I'd told Ed I wanted to find some kind of stress release, but, in truth, I wanted more than that. I was at this retreat to, well, retreat inside myself; past the front door at least. I was there to find a safe space in which to discover a few pertinent truths about myself, with no one judging.

When our youthful monk introduced himself, Ed and I missed his name. "Hedgehog?" I whispered, leaning over. "Ketchup?" Ed whispered back. It didn't matter, our young teacher was just that – a teacher and he was the first person to introduce me to Buddhist attachment.

It's important that Buddhist attachment is distinguished from the meaning of the Western term in psychology, which refers to an emotional tie or affection for another person. Attachment in Buddhism is not the same thing, but refers to an inability to "let go" of how we feel about people, objects or events. For Hedgehog, explaining this often-misunderstood concept to a room full of stressed-out teachers, executives and healthcare workers was no easy feat. It didn't help that he started talking about ignorance. Again, this means something quite specific in Buddhist teachings. There, ignorance is simply not knowing why we are miserable, or how to stop being miserable. Counter to Western semantics, ignorance does not relate to stupidity or lack of education, it is simply the inability to recognize how our own habitual responses are the very thing causing us problems.

Ignorance is also referred to as delusion; another rather depressing term. Basically, the man himself, Gautama Buddha, said that most people haven't a clue why they feel the way they do. They literally cannot see the cause of their woes, even though it is staring them in the face. He believed it is never a physical thing or event that causes our misery, but more how we feel about that thing or event. Hedgehog explains we must accept this rather paradoxical concept before we can fully understand Buddhist attachment.

It didn't take long before I felt resentment. Hedgehog seemed to be implying that whenever things had gone wrong, it had been my fault if I'd felt hacked off. Crossing my arms, I glanced at Ed.

Being hacked off or upset has a collective name in Buddhism; it's called suffering. This term also includes being anxious, annoyed, uncomfortable, scared or even just a little bit sad. Suffering (and finding a way to stop it) is the cornerstone of Buddha's teachings. He believed that we live in a cycle of what sometimes feels like unending despair. As I looked around the room I was surrounded by suffering – tension creased many of the faces there. Buddha called this negative cyclic existence "samsara". Today we call it the rat race.

Buddha was a spiritual pioneer. Two thousand years ago, this man spent seven weeks sitting under a Bodhi tree trying to come up with a solution. A solution. And that's why Buddhism has gained traction in the West – because it offers hope. Hope was the reason we were sitting in that hall, pushing aside our misgivings. As Hedgehog talked, though, the solution was not clear cut. It seemed to involve a substantial change of beliefs. Buddha called his solution to misery "The Four Noble Truths". In a nutshell, these are:

One – The truth of suffering: Life sucks. You have to accept that.

Two – The truth of the cause of suffering: Realize what is making your life suck.

Three – The truth of the end of suffering: Make a plan to stop life sucking quite so much; and

Four – The truth of the path that leads to the end of suffering: Follow a prescriptive, tried-and-tested plan that will sort it all out.

Bingo – you're on your way to nirvana.

Nirvana again. Enlightenment is tricky to grasp but I was happy to brush this aside as I was more concerned about navigating onto the nirvana freeway than arriving at the destination.

That evening, Ed and I went out for dinner. We'd opted to stay in a bed and breakfast, as I wasn't going to push my luck and ask Ed to stay in a dormitory at the retreat. We needed space to absorb what Hedgehog had said. After a bottle of wine and some philosophizing we agreed there was some truth in what we'd learned. Even if it made us squirm.

No Strings Attached

The next day, Hedgehog introduced us to craving and aversion. These two gremlins are the foundation blocks of Buddhism and are two sides of the same coin. Craving is just wanting, wearing a different hat (and also called grasping), and aversion is, well, hating something. This was quite easy to grasp. Wanting something in life wasn't a problem but, wanting *more* was. Hedgehog explained that it was our endless wanting of stuff that caused so much grief. At this I perked up, because on a simplistic level I got this. It's rather like the "Keeping up with the Joneses" idiom. The more you compete for what others have, the more unobtainable that is and, in turn, the more aggravated you become. When this is applied to material or social wealth, it's an easy concept. When this is applied to everything in life, including relationships and people, it gets harder to comprehend. The principle is the same: whether you want a new lawnmower, a new job, a new (more sexy) partner, more friends, more party invites, more, well, anything. It is not the lawnmower that makes you dissatisfied – it's the bloody wanting it in the first place.

These analogies were helpful, but everybody wants stuff all of the time. I fancied a glass of wine because I knew our friends were in the pub back at home. The idea of limiting our wanting was hard to swallow.

Glancing around, a charismatic Swedish man I'd spoken to earlier caught my eye. His wife had booked him onto this course as a birthday present because (in her words) his work had taken over his life. It seemed an odd gift to me, given she hadn't come along. Grimacing, he had told me that as CEO of a large advertising agency he travelled almost continuously. I was sympathetic, as I knew all too well the unrealistic pressures he faced. I wondered if, like me, he was wondering how Buddhism might go down back at the office.

If Hedgehog noticed our glances, he ignored them. He explained that all of us wanted things based upon the way they appeared, without thinking about how they existed, or how they might change. Change being the pivotal word here. Change, he explained, wasn't something we paid much heed to – absorbed as we are with what is happening now. Yet nothing in life is static – even unmovable mountains changed over millennia, the chair we're sitting on will eventually rot away. Pausing for a moment, he let that sink in. Hedgehog continued, explaining that we wanted more of what we liked, and avoided what we didn't like. That meant we got annoyed when we didn't get what we wanted and could never get enough of what we did want. Okay, enough. I was starting to see the cycle. This wanting or craving held us hostage. On the whole, Westerners do not get this. We're too busy speeding down the road to disaster, instead of taking that elusive B-road to nirvana.

Attempting to absorb this bombshell, my attention was diverted by a woman in tears. Sobbing, she explained that caring for a convicted (and unrepentant) rapist in the hospital where she worked angered and upset her. The room sighed in sympathy and looked to Hedgehog. Nodding, he suggested it wasn't the rapist himself who caused her pain, but her reaction to him. As the woman's face crumpled, he asked more gently, "Do you feel angry now?" She nodded mutely. "Is he here?" he asked. And, oh God, I got it. Even though this was a horrible situation, I had enough distance to see what Hedgehog was getting at. But the woman was confused.

"How can he be causing your anger now, if he is not in the room?" Hedgehog continued. It was a rhetorical question; the kind of question you could spend hours going crazy thinking about. Yet it made sense. The woman, however kind and caring, created her own anger. That awful man had not crawled inside her head and planted anger in there. She had a choice – she didn't need to feel that way.

This is where I had been going wrong. I had been assigning my emotions to *other* people. And yet, I resisted. Surely there were exceptions to the rule? I couldn't imagine totally letting go of anger. After all, Hedgehog didn't have to work with Candice.

Candice. Now, she really did make my life hell – the bullying, the passive aggression. Cornering Hedgehog on the final morning, I took up the challenge, determined to make him concede that Candice was the exception to the attachment rule. Unruffled and surprisingly reasonable, he suggested that rather than believe what he said, why didn't I try an experiment. He suggested I go to work on Monday, and LOVE Candice. *Bloody love her? He had to be kidding.* On the drive back up the motorway, I ranted about how ridiculous this suggestion was. By the time we got home, Ed had heard enough and told me to just do the damn experiment.

The next morning, I found myself taking a huge breath in as I walked toward Candice's office. Normally I avoided all contact with our account director. A primped and pneumatic woman, she had a tendency to dart out, demanding paperwork and we often came to blows. Pausing at her door, I decided to make the first change. I refused to *love* Candice, but I did concede to attempt civility.

"Hello Candice," I said weakly, peering in. "How was your weekend?"

Not surprisingly Candice stared at me, her jaw hanging open. "Fine," she mumbled, clearly unsettled.

Hedgehog's annoyingly calm face floated in front of me, so I kept going. "What did you get up to?" I asked, not remotely interested.

"I took the kids to Greenwich Park," she replied.

"Oh," I said, inadvertently brightening. "I love it there."

"Oh," Candice mirrored, and we both fell silent. "I've got free tickets to the observatory there," she ventured. "You can have them if you like?" She smiled, and I smiled back.

On the phone to Ed minutes later, I was agog. "It bloody worked!" I whispered fiercely. "I can't believe it. She's giving me free tickets!" Laughing, he replied, "You *Buddhified* her. Good for you."

But I didn't Buddhify Candice, I Buddhified myself. And, that was to be the second lesson I would learn.

Sting in the Tail

It's a warm Autumnal afternoon two weeks after my meeting with Geshe-la and I'm having coffee with a friend.

"So how are you getting on?" she asks, in between mouthfuls of cake. "What meditation are you doing now?"

"Buddhist Tantra," I reply, watching her reaction. I know, even if she tries to hide it, her mouth will twitch. I'm uncomfortable discussing this in public so I add, "The practice is called Green Tara and I have to chant prayers and imagine a green goddess." Even with this description, associations of Sting's sexual revelations will jump into my friend's mind 24 years after his throwaway comment. Or she'll know about the various Tantric workshops available for singles and couples to explore their spirituality and sexuality. In her book *Sensation: Adventures in Sex, Love and Laughter*, Isabel Losada gives an insightful account of what an all-female tantric workshop involves.

Tantric is about connection, love and encompassing unity with others. Like much of spirituality in the West, it hasn't escaped commercialization. In the last 30 years, tantric sex has become a ritual that incorporates sexual activities that many claim don't just produce intense pleasure, but altered states of consciousness. It can also apparently lead to enlightenment, and it is believed that sex tantras can incite magical energy for healing.

Since the 1960s, the West has reinvented many forms of meditation and Tantra is just one of them. It could be seen as a bastardization of those original core beliefs or an evolution of them. Ultimately, in many cases it depends on the historical interpretations óf the Tantric texts. Investigations by a number of academics have suggested that Tantric practices were complex and empowering rituals that embraced both the feminine and masculine within us. The Associate Professor of Religious Studies at Richmond University, Miranda Shaw, suggests women had a larger role within Tantric Buddhism than was originally thought. Her book, *Passionate Enlightenment: Women in Tantric Buddhism*, puts forward evidence to support this.

Secretly curious, I'm not disregarding an all-female Tantric workshop in the future, but for now I'll follow the path of Green Tara and the non-sexual practices taught on a Tuesday night at Jamyang.

Green Feminist

It's already dark and I'm stressed when I head toward Jamyang Buddhist Centre a week later for my first Tibetan Tantra meditation class. A fresh batch of worries compete for my attention – an argument with Ed over tidying shoes away vies with the mouldy walls we've recently discovered in our son's bedroom.

Walking into the old courtroom which doubles up as Jamyang's temple, I nearly miss Roy waving me over to a seat. I'm given a handout and Tibetan prayer book and instructed to join in when prompted. When Roy closes the door, there are seven of us seated on red meditation cushions. This is a regular meet-up, paid for by donations, that focuses on Buddhist Tantra with the group providing a support network for those pursuing this more complex path to enlightenment.

The first part of the evening is a recap of the Buddhist understanding of unhappiness. I'm struck by the concept of samsara tonight, this never-ending grind to which I unwittingly subscribe. It has a sharp relevance given what I was mulling over as I arrived. In the midst of my own anxiety-storm, I can see the shadow that unhappiness casts over my life. Roy says, "Unhappiness is just a signpost to happiness." Our spiritual blindness means we cannot see the good stuff right in front of us. "Happiness is already here," he says, "we just need to peel back the misery curtain to reveal it." This is frustrating and even a bit frightening. I understand Roy's words, but I'm struggling to connect on a visceral level.

We will be studying Green Tara tonight and I'm soon distracted. A Tibetan Buddhist saviour-goddess with numerous forms (and colours), she was widely popular with Tibetan Buddhist practitioners as a means to accelerate enlightenment. In Mahayana Buddhism, Tara is a "bodhisattva", which is a "realized being" committed to helping others. This practice has a huge focus on altruism as practitioners hold off their own enlightenment in order to help others first. Tara is a compassionate goddess who helps people cross to the other shore, overseeing both earthly and spiritual travel.

Tonight's group are regulars and can recite the Tibetan prayers with an understanding I don't have; they are clearly dedicated to this path. Reading these historical texts aloud is strange and unfamiliar, yet I want them to be familiar. Asking us to close our eyes, or keep a loose gaze, Roy leads a guided visualization. With my eyes shut, the scent of stargazer lilies floods my senses. *Strange, I hadn't noticed any in the room.* Roy describes Green Tara and she appears in my mind's eye, sitting on her lotus leaf. She is bright green, gem-like and iridescent. In her left hand she holds a blue utpala lotus flower. Strangely, she is faceless, but I'm not concerned, only curious. I see her in colour, even though there's little detail. I imagine a modern-day funky version of her. We collectively murmur "*Om tare tuttare ture soha*", and the sound is deep and melodic. Feeling calm I am reminded of the purpose of a mantra in the way the sound seems to travel throughout my body.

Afterwards, I am lighter and my body feels soothed – euphoric even. I needed this release from the torment of my thoughts. Walking down Kennington Lane, I head toward the station. Without thinking, I take a shortcut through a little park. Halfway down the path two things become apparent. The first is that the path is unlit and very dark. The second is that I am not alone – footsteps pad softly behind me. While I absorb these facts rapidly, my heart does not beat faster. I am on high alert, but I am not fearful. I know that, if I need to, I can run, but instead I walk steadily, looping my hand through my bag-strap. My footsteps are light but swift and I reach the exit in seconds. As I pass under a yellow streetlight, a shadow swerves and the footsteps are gone.

Sitting on the train home, Tara is here. Behind my eyelids, colours explode as her image lingers. Replaying the park incident, I acknowledge the calm alertness – my lack of panic. This isn't the first time visualizing has had this effect – the same thing happened back in 2012 when I lost my sight. Visualizing a beautiful beach wasn't an amusement, but a primal response. Yogic breathing and meditation soothed my nervous system and kept me calm during a terrifying time. My imaginary beach fascinated Geshe-la for good reason. I hadn't used it as a tool to reach awakening, but as a mechanism to heal myself.

Singing the Praises

Two weeks into my Tara practice and things aren't going well. I've spent most of the time showing my son's bedroom wall to surveyors, with most recommending costly damp treatment. After a lot of sighing, the last guy left muttering that that our roof needed replacing too. Every time I think about the rising damp and the rising costs, I feel sick.

I decide to meditate. I want to dedicate a full hour to this session, as practising in piecemeal has been unsatisfactory and hasn't allowed me to concentrate fully on visualizing Green Tara. One full meditation is better than several short, interrupted attempts. This differs to TM, which could be easily practised in short bursts.

My commitment to this experiment has ebbed and flowed. Sometimes I'm frustrated at the chore of syncing the EEG headset to my phone. Sometimes, I just want to meditate unobserved. However, I remind myself that by recording the activity in my prefrontal cortex (the region of the brain implicated in planning complex cognitive behaviour, personality expression, decision making and moderating social behaviour among the other areas), Barbara is tracking my neural waves along with the subjective experiences of how visualizing Green Tara feels over time. I want to know if this inner experience correlates to the data Barbara collects. Will this experiment reveal if I have a firm grip on reality? Will my brain respond differently during different techniques? And will I have any control over those changes? It's exciting to think we might find out.

Turning to the Green Tara Sadhana Roy gave I settle in. "Sadhana" translates to mean a set of instructions, and this twelve-page handout requiring recitation of prayers and chanting is nothing short of a meditation manual. Sighing, I know I won't be able to memorize everything, so I record myself reading them out loud instead.

Listening back to the refuge prayer, I'm reminded of the reasons behind this practice – we follow this path not just for ourselves, but for those around us:

I go for refuge until I am enlightened
To the Buddha, the Dharma and the Supreme Assembly
By my practice of giving and other perfections
May I become a buddha to benefit all sentient beings.

Becoming a bodhisattva in Tibetan Buddhist circles is basically a crash course in altruism. These guys are spiritual guides on a one-way trajectory to help others. This overwhelming desire to do good is called "Bodhichitta". Bodhisattvas sound a bit earnest to me, a bit goody two shoes. Although, this could be my own resistance. I recognize how busy I have become and how easy it is for thoughtfulness and kindness to take a back seat. Meditation teacher Tara Brach points out, in her audiobook *Radical Self-Acceptance*, how many of us are addicted to busyness. We struggle to not "do", and feel uncomfortable just being with ourselves.

I follow the visualization instructions, imagining a ball of white light inside my abdomen and the letters "AH". Trying to see a white moon disc proves less easy. The "AH" morphs into a single syllable "TAM", which is supposed to represent the omniscience of Tara herself. Wracking my brains, I try to recall what omniscient means. *A kind of super-knowledge for higher beings?* I picture a white saucer-like shape and attempt to keep up with the instructions. Next, the letters of the mantra *Om Tare, Tuttare Ture*, appear on the edge of the saucer, like a kind of reverberating wall. Thankfully, when I recorded the instructions I repeated the mantra several times which gives me a breather. Tara appears in the meditation now but, disconcertingly, I can only conjure up a strangely Shrek-like face.

Lengthening my breath, my voice describes the position Tara is sat in: Left hand on her heart, right hand in a giving position, resting on her outstretched right knee. My own green goddess floats in front of me, gaudy and magnificent. The quality of my recording isn't great, but even with rustles and the distant beeping of the dishwasher, it guides me through this visualization. I may not be religiously inclined, but the prayers mean something today. My scribbled notes reflect how absorbed I have become in Buddhist philosophy. The hour-long session has provided a full immersion.

I sense a shyness developing. My Tara experience is taking me deeper into myself. I'm surprised that these dusty Sanskrit words have touched me. My meditations this week have brought up both positive and negative emotions. Unlike the deep relaxation and spikes of creativity evoked by TM, this practice has left me contemplative and broody. Considering that this experiment was a means to discover useful ways to train my mind and get the most out of life, I'm not finding deep introspection fun. My personal life is playing out in the diaries I keep. It has dawned on me that I am not an anonymous participant. Do I really want my inner thoughts converting to data and dissected by science? Probably not.

Yet, I like Tara and I like this practice. She's a feisty deity, a foot-stamping destroyer of evil and a slayer of foes. There are myths surrounding who she was. Some say she rose up out of a lake riding a lotus leaf (I liked that, it was quite Botticelli-like) or (more historically) that she was a Nepali princess. Some stories suggest her father sponsored Buddhism, but when Tara became interested in the teachings and wanted to become a nun, her male teachers didn't support her. Instead, they suggested she pray to be reborn as a man as they believed women could not attain enlightenment. Tara was having none of this so, in true feminist form, vowed to get enlightened herself. And she did. What's more, she spearheaded a fast-track route to enlightenment along the way.

The *Praises to Tara* (a tantra containing 21 verses designed as a homage to Tara) are full of fighting talk, with Tara throwing off Mara (the Buddhist word for demon) and anyone else who gets in the way. There's a distinctly feminine angle to this meditation, and I'm not surprised Tara is often called the Great Mother. I feel like I have a tribe of Amazonian warriors by my side.

After the meditation, I have an urge to call my aunt. I'm worried about her as she's been hospitalized again. Answering the phone, her breaths come in painful rasps, but her tone warns not to question this. We don't talk for long but I'm grateful that the Tara practice prompted me to reach out.

A Toe in the Water

It's mid-October and the way Barbara and I capture my brain data is evolving. With six weeks of Green Tara practice under my belt, we have identified that bringing "visual content" (in the form of a goddess) into my mind affects some of my experiences. Barbara has added a new dimension – a mental category on the app she calls "object orientation" to record how much my attention was focused solely on Tara. Barbara is interested to see how immersed I become in visualizing my green goddess and how this affects my sense of reality.

I've finally plucked up the courage to try a Tantra for Women Course, held in North London at the Tara Yoga Centre. The blurb says I will awaken my femininity, reach my maximum potential and experience the magic of being a woman. Secretly I love the idea of this, but my inner sceptic is – sceptical.

The theme tonight is "resonance". Our teacher is a stunning young woman, dressed in an orange maxi-dress with matching jacket. Having rushed out of the house, I'm wearing old jeans and a frumpy sweatshirt. Our first exercise, after being asked to hold hands in a circle, is a meditation. Forty minutes later, I sit back up relaxed.

Next, we are to partner up and dance slowly, mirroring each other's moves. I look around for the woman I figure is least likely to caress her boobs in public. I hate this exercise, until my partner flashes me an embarrassed smile and I realize she's as nervous as I am. She has a stain on her jumper that I'm sure is baby sick and I feel a rush of connection. Locking eyes we sway and dance together, and I decide this is almost fun.

After the dancing, our teacher gathers us round to talk about the clothes we're wearing. I groan inwardly, fearing this will descend into frivolous fashion talk. It does a little, but as each woman describes what she's wearing, their stories come alive. There's more to this exercise than I thought. A woman gently fingers a necklace around her neck, explaining it was a gift from her Lebanese grandmother –

the only heirloom she has. When it's my turn, I joke about my old jeans, but ripping off my socks, reveal Dorothy-red sparkly toenails. These, I declare, are my secret weapon. The women clap in delight, but my painted nails are not superficial. They represent time to myself and choices I make. This evening, surrounded entirely by women, I have revisited the feminine, often neglected parts of myself. I don't draw attention to it, but staring at my naked feet I spot the toe-ring I have worn since I was eighteen years old. What other stories are hidden within the clothes we wear?

It's easy to remonstrate, to judge myself and say these trappings are meaningless, these are just labels I put upon myself. My femininity is important. Revealing my ruby-red nails to a room full of strangers allowed me to connect to that. And it felt good.

Every experience I put myself through points a finger at something I can work on. Judgement still sears everything I do.

Christmas Blues

A month later Ed picks up two early Christmas cards that have arrived in the post. I recognize my aunt's neat handwriting and we exchange glances. My son's face drops when he sees that both are addressed to his sister. "They're mine," she snaps, knowing there's probably money inside. It takes a brief tussle before she relinquishes one of the ten pound notes. I'm worried. My aunt is meticulous about details like this; it doesn't bode well.

Buddhist Tantric Visualization has been more than just learning a new technique. It has been the memorization of complex Sanskrit texts (that Roy decoded), recitation of multiple phrases, chanting and the following of detailed visualization instructions. Unlike my previous visualizations (my beach), this was not a technique for relaxation – but for the purpose of spiritual advancement. I had underestimated the relevance of what I had considered to be an ancient, perhaps outdated, practice. Geshe-la was right. Green Tara's path to enlightenment is not a process to be undertaken by a beginner.

The practice required me to apply Buddhist teachings I'd learned in the past – principles that made more sense when applied to this practice. The skill of mindful awareness (learned with Dave during MBCT) has bled into this practice as Barbara expected it to.

Meditation is not a stand-alone exercise, but sits alongside diet, postures, breathing, chanting and mantras, as well as other ethical practices. In Eastern spirituality, the "Sangha" is a critical support network that encapsulates a meditation practice (in this case provided by Roy and the Jamyang weekly meet-ups). In the West we isolate many practices, hoisting them out of their original framework, streamlining them for modern tastes. Transformation comes from embracing *all* of these disciplines as a system – not just nabbing one element of it.

Until now this hadn't occurred to me, but approaching practices as simply *techniques* feels naïve. It puts too much emphasis on methodology, rather than the modality as a system. The MBCT course created its own framework, but this was practical rather than spiritual. TM, on the other hand, felt like something I practised in isolation. Even though the TM retreat included yoga postures, healthy food and group discussions, I never felt part of a community. Because of the Buddhist framework, I took learning Tantric Visualization more reverentially and, in turn, got more out of it in the form of spiritual awareness.

A fortnight after the Christmas cards arrived, Mum calls with the news that my aunt has died – she was eighty years old. My son sobs uncontrollably when I tell him. She is the first person he's lost and his grief is all-consuming. My sadness at her death segues into the sadness I feel at the realization that I have neglected the feminine parts of myself. This practice's focus on a strong female altruistic character has impacted the way I view myself, and my relationship to others. Learning the Green Tara practice has been learning how to reconnect with that. As my son's little body shakes, his sister and I console him.

"It's okay, you can have both tenners," my daughter soothes, appearing much older than her ten years and I see our very own bodhisattva crouched on the floor.

CHAPTER 5

THAT FOUR-LETTER WORD: LOVING-KINDNESS

February 2018

It's a year into my experiment and at 4am on a cold February night, the wind is an irate ghost, rattling our bedroom window. I'm being pulled toward wakefulness when a noise like a gunshot jolts me upright. Shaking Ed, I whisper, "What was that?" But his reply is a sleepy grunt. All is revealed the next morning, when we see half of our roof strewn across the garden. Phoning roofers later that day I wonder if the compassion meditation I'm about to start will help manage the friction this latest drama has brought about.

Compassion-based meditation, and in particular loving-kindness, came up on Google when I first gazed into the gaping jaws of the wellbeing market. When I first came across compassion, I thought it sounded a little benign, wishy-washy even. When I asked Dr Ann Marie Golden, a psychologist friend of mine, what it entailed, she warned that compassion was powerful work. *Work?* What on earth does she mean?

Compassion meditation is exactly what it sounds like: developing a feeling of compassion, kindness and even love toward ourself and others. It's deceptively simple – commonly using imagery and silent phrases, such as "may I be well, may I be safe", that encourage us to feel less judgemental and friendlier to everyone. This is different from batting away irritating thoughts, repeating a one-word mantra or even conjuring up goddesses. This practice is about being *nice*. How hard can that be?

Loving-kindness, otherwise known as "metta bhavana" (from the Pali language), is one of the ways I can explore my new focus. "Metta" means love or friendliness, and "bhavana" means development or cultivation. Compassion is an integral part of loving-kindness, as the practice focuses on those in need, wishing them to be free from hardship.

Now that my Tantra course is over, I decide to sign up to two compassion workshops Jamyang is running. Altruism was a tenet of the Green Tara practice, so I expect there to be some crossover. Alongside this, I download the Matthieu Ricard Imagine Clarity app, as this has a focus on compassion and altruism. Matthieu Ricard, a French scientist turned Buddhist monk, is well-known for promoting a simpler, compassion-based existence. His TED talk entitled Habits of Happiness has over nine million views and he's been author and participant in a number of studies that bridge the gap between Buddhism and modern science.

Moments after booking the workshops I receive an email from Dad to tell me that he's moving back to the UK, as he has been diagnosed with cancer. This is a major shock only two months after my aunt died. Having only seen my father intermittently over the years, his contact with the children has been limited. Video calls mostly end with my daughter drifting away and my son doing headstands on the sofa. While I know my dad feels great affection for his grandchildren, a deeper relationship is lacking. "Grannie" features far more regularly in my children's vernacular.

Dad was absent during much of my youth – often working long hours and then emotionally distanced when my parents split up. During my teens we had a troubled and somewhat separate existence as my brother and I lived with our mother. However, time healed and my dad mellowed, eventually remarrying and living permanently in Cape Town. We reconnected in my mid-twenties when I returned from a year living abroad and forged a new, close relationship which has been strong ever since. And yet, reading the message again, I feel a disconnect. He'll be living permanently in Yorkshire, a five-hour drive away. I'm sad that one of my parents has seen so little of my children and now, when "Grandad" is finally coming home, he's going to be hospitalized and living a long way away.

A Loving-Kindness Workshop

A week later I'm back at Jamyang. A tall man with a crew cut and trendy jeans sits cross-legged behind a table in the courtroom. He's leading a loving-kindness workshop and the Apple logo of his laptop is incongruous amongst the red and gold of this spiritual room. Video equipment is set up to record the evening; for a talk on love, it is surprisingly businesslike.

Most of the meditators here are aged between 25 and 50 and many seem to know each other – there's a friendly hum in the air. I'm glad to be here as I've felt isolated starting my compassion practice at home using a loving-kindness recording from the Buddhist Centre website. Worry about my dad (and the roof) hasn't helped.

In a soft voice, our teacher dispels some loving-kindness myths. Because of the love word, this technique sometimes gets misunderstood. Any love evoked is of the non-romantic variety, and it's the love word that has been making me uncomfortable at home – although I'm not sure why.

In Buddhism, there's an aspiration to love everyone equally. How we express that wish is up to us. Clearly, we'd spend more time with our partner and less time with work friends, but we should wish everyone to be happy in equal measure. The trick is not to view loving-kindness as an *act* of love, but to want everyone in the world to be happy. This sounds reasonable.

When he gets onto happiness and its causes, I hit a stumbling block. *Aren't the causes of happiness the million-dollar question?* This is where traditional Buddhist-speak baffles me. To further confound things, our teacher throws in a quote from an eighth-century Indian monk, Shantideva:

"Those desiring to escape from suffering hasten straight toward their own misery. And, with the very desire for happiness, out of delusion, destroy their own wellbeing as if it were the enemy."

That's depressing. This harps back to what Hedgehog taught us in 2009 and how constantly striving to be happy will always leave me unhappy. While I understand the principle, this feels absolutist. Is there really no other way? What if I never discover these elusive causes of happiness? Thankfully, there is a solution as no one actually wants to be unhappy.

Before we get to the solution, we need to understand what happiness is. Apparently, there is not one kind – but two. The first sort – temporary happiness – comes from nice pleasant things that are stimulus-based. These are transient and unreliable as they are conditional. I know a food analogy is coming, it always does. (Buddhists particularly love ones with chocolate cake.) However, this is quite right. I enjoy the temporary pleasure of a gourmet dinner at our local pub. However, I recognize that if I eat or drink too much, I feel bloated and guilty afterwards. This reminds me that I rely too heavily on wine to make me happy, but I squash that thought for now. This temporary happiness is rarely in my control and does not lead to *more* happiness. I hadn't thought of it that way. It's not the initial high I hanker after, but a way of maintaining it. Actually, I'd forgo full-blown happiness for just feeling at ease most of the time.

Our teacher explains that what we're all seeking is the second type of happiness: genuine happiness. This is that ambiguous state of inner wellbeing that feeds the Western wellbeing machine. This is more stable, but often gets confused with its fleeting counterpart. We hope that stimulus-based pleasures will leave us feeling warm and cuddly, but because we can't get enough, we slide down the happiness ladder to doom and gloom. *I get it, but where do I get this genuine happiness from?*

Fortunately, the key to contentment is contained within a moral code, like a set of ethical guidelines, called the Noble Eightfold Path. I wonder if a modern interpretation might be like the AA's (Alcoholics Anonymous) 12-step plan? If so, it might read like this: First, we need to nail the Four Noble Truths. Remember these?

Life sucks; know that. Realize what makes life suck. Know there is a cure to stop life sucking, and follow Buddha's grand plan to sort out your life.

Then, we get to the Noble Eightfold Path:

Right view: Life has consequences. What you do in this life might revisit you in the next.

Right resolve: Your intentions matter.

Right speech: Don't lie or say nasty things.

Right conduct: Don't do awful things like kill, steal or get up to any weird sexual misconduct. In today's fluid society, I take that to mean no sexual activity that causes harm or distress to another person.

Right livelihood: Avoid a dodgy job that hurts others (slavery is mentioned here, but I get the point).

Right effort: Tame your monkey mind and don't think negative thoughts. Try to be kind.

Right mindfulness: Be mindful of your mind and body.

Right "samadhi" or meditative absorption: Concentrate, really hard. Not much then. I look at my notes and sigh. I wanted a failsafe, easy list to follow, not some cryptic way of life. All of this theory is fine and dandy, but it's not allaying the numbness and unease I feel.

Love Thy Neighbour

The next day at home, wearing the EEG headset, I play the guided loving-kindness meditation again. There are lots of compassion meditations, with excellent offerings from Tara Brach and Sharon Salzberg, but the one I'm using is a traditional five-stage version from the Theravada tradition.

To begin I am asked to generate a sense of warmth and love toward myself – self-compassion. This term was introduced to psychology research by the researcher Kristin Neff, in order to separate the focus of self-esteem from self-care. This is an important point. Self-esteem relies upon evaluation and comparison to others, which can be psychologically damaging. Self-compassion asks for no judgements. There's no need to be special or above average. We can feel good about ourselves and part of humanity even when we fail.

I can't evoke kindness on demand. The best I can muster is something lukewarm. There's a tightness in my chest and my jaw is tense. Mentally scrabbling around, I try to recall what kindness feels like. The voiceover instructs me to repeat phrases to help me connect to these feelings:

May I be open
May I be well
May I be happy
May I have peace
May I be safe

My eyes moisten when I mutter the last one. I don't feel safe. It's a subtle feeling, not easy to identify – more a faint tremor of disquiet. I wonder how much this is a hangover from my sudden blindness. Did my body ever come out of high alert?

These phrases are watering the compassion seed buried deep within me. This isn't positive thinking; these words are suggestions, cleverly designed to grow feelings of loving-kindness. What saddens me is that I have come to see that those feelings are dormant. By propagating a wish for happiness, I am drawing compassion to the surface. This is hard work; Ann Marie was right.

Next under the love-limelight, the voice asks me to choose a close family member or friend. While I instantly imagine my children (behaving perfectly), I'm uneasy. Even though I adore my children, I struggle to evoke feelings of love. This is shocking – and confusing. The numbness I identified during the MBCT course is still here. The voiceover must have read my mind, as he suggests that if I can't feel kindness, to imagine feeling it. He also offers the option of feeling kindness toward a pet as it's not unusual for Westerners to prefer to direct their attention toward an animal.

Next, I am instructed to think kind thoughts about someone I feel neutrally about – a work colleague perhaps, or the postman. This is better as it seems more acceptable to feel numb about someone I don't know. I picture my neighbour, then decide she's a friend, so move onto the nice guy who serves in the pharmacy.

Stage four gets tougher as I have to consider someone I have difficulties with. The trick here is to try and bring this person to mind without the negativity that enfolds my heart like poison ivy. This is almost impossible. Even a fleeting image of one of the more trying people in my life prompts my heart to beat wildly. This is ridiculous. Why can I feel anger but not love for my family? Deciding I need to focus on a less provocative person, I shift my attention to the annoying (if faceless) woman I've been emailing at the council. Breathing into my discomfort, I mentally scroll through our email exchanges regarding bin collections. These missives have been irritating, but I don't feel anger. However, it suddenly dawns on me that I might be evoking compassion for a mailbot, given the mechanical replies.

It seems I have no kindness inside me – only panic, anger and agitation. Then I remember that this practice requires the suspension of judgement. It only occurs to me now, fifteen minutes in, that I have been judging myself. What's more, I have been harsher on myself than I would be on anyone else. This jolts me back to life. When, for the last stage, I'm required to think kindly toward all of the people I've considered and to then emanate that to everyone in the world, I am more successful. I amuse myself by cutting and pasting large crowd scenes, creating an endless sea of humanity. It's really quite powerful. When I finally remove the headset, I feel like I've run an emotional marathon. Writing up my diary afterwards I remember Barbara's instructions again: "Be detailed and don't think too hard. Write what you feel so I can use keyword searches to capture your emotions." Sighing, I realize tonight's keywords are "disconnect", "sadness" and "judgement".

Unspoken Words

Love wasn't a word we used much when I was growing up. I remember having read Nevil Shute's *On The Beach* in my early teens when I had the urge to tell my mother I loved her. I'm sure the post-apocalyptic novel had something to do with it. I practised the words in front of the bathroom mirror, mouthing the shapes –

seeing how they felt. I spluttered "I love you" as she walked down the corridor with a basket of washing.

"Oh," she'd said surprised. "I love you too." I remember my pounding heart, the difficulty I'd had in sharing this emotion. Love in my family was implicitly, rather than explicitly, expressed. Although never discussed, I wonder if it was considered a little sentimental. I didn't come from an unloving family, we just didn't talk about those things. Growing up in the 1970s, I don't recall anyone really talking about love or happiness. Sure, I noticed if our neighbour was grumpy, or if my teacher was having a bad day. It never occurred to me that they probably wanted to be happy.

I didn't have a bad childhood, but bad things happened. In my teens, I felt separate from everyone around me. Apathy became a cloak, a form of protection I wore to stop hurt from drawing blood. The compassion work I am doing now is kneading that sore spot. It's also opening up the possibility of resolution and so much more.

In his book *The Art of Happiness: A Handbook for Living*, the Dalai Lama says, "Happiness is not something ready made. It comes from your own actions." Loving-kindness requires effort. Understanding and seeing myself and the people around me is this practice. The Dalai Lama suggests that if we can't connect with someone else's distress, perhaps considering their very humanness, and how that is the same as ours, is another option. Even people I dislike have a heart, a family, hopes and dreams. Knowing this makes them more real and less villainous. Connecting with another person's life creaks open the door to compassion. It's a two-way mirror – allowing myself to feel charitable toward others allows those same emotions to shine back on me.

Spring is emerging and March has brought with it dampness and daffodils. My experiences synchronize with the transitioning seasons. As the days get lighter, so do I. Compassion, I realize, is an art. It's something I have to learn. It seems counterintuitive to nurture something that must be innately contained within me. Yet compassion toward myself has been grossly missing. In fact, compassion toward others has been a little on the light side too.

I'm starting to see how harsh my inner critic is. This voice is so embedded that I have become deaf to it. It's only now, in the silence of a meditation, that I hear the venom behind the white noise of my thoughts. *You didn't call your brother,* it rebukes. *And you lost it with the kids again. Bad mother!* it shouts. I'd always believed I didn't beat myself up, but the reprimands are there, recited from a long list of poor choices, embarrassing moments and Things I Got Wrong. *Why do you never learn?* it scorns. "Why" is such a cruel, belittling word.

I'm not just tough on myself, I'm tough on my children too, asking them to do their best and to shun mediocrity. I expect Ed to think like me and to prioritize life in the same way. There's an urgency for everyone to be at their best, all of the time. No one is allowed to switch off. I'm not sure who made that rule up, but we live by it. My drive for perfection shocks me. I'd always thought being perfect was a good thing – aspirational even. Have I been using "high standards" as a stick to beat myself with?

There's an abundance of research on this topic. The Greater Good Science Center at the University of California, Berkeley, studies the psychology and neuroscience of wellbeing. Their podcasts, based around practices that encourage positive wellbeing, include one entitled How To Be Less Hard On Yourself. In this Kristin Neff points out how we listen to our friends in a non-judgemental way when they mess up, yet we find it hard to be a friend to ourselves. "People have this resource of compassion in their back pocket, ready to pull at it anytime a friend needs it. And so they just have to really remember that." Neff is right – we need to use this compassion on ourselves too. In one of her studies, 43 percent of participants who practised self-compassion had increased wellbeing, less anxiety, and felt less self-centred and more resilient to stress a year later.

The purpose of loving-kindness is not relaxation. This practice takes me beneath the surface to the squidgy, vulnerable parts below. It lifts the shell and allows words of love to penetrate, even if at first that feels alien. Part of these exercises is accepting that if I go the distance, I may find things I don't wish to find. There's a stripping-back process which is why only meditating sporadically has limited effect. Even without Neff's research to support it, I know the positive, if hard, work I am doing.

The Banyan Tree

Meditating at home, the hypnotic drum of rain is soothing. I remember a majestic, triffid-like banyan tree I saw on an African camping trip years ago. Supported by hundreds of lichen-covered branches, its gnarly arms appeared to be strangling the tree. In my meditative state now, I am that tree. The love I have for my children is a delicate reed – a thin lifeline smothered by the tangled-up modern life I live. It's only when I sit still, alone, here, that I understand how I am moulded by my environment.

I am learning how to be kind and forgiving. It's taking grit to address the emotional debris this practice is kicking up, but I am determined to change. Connecting to (and not avoiding) how I feel is the first step. If I am to leave any kind of emotional legacy for my children, the gift of self-awareness is probably the greatest. That means connecting with Ed too – swapping the anaesthetic glare of the television for human eye contact, for words – for touch. He needs as much time and attention as the children do. I can't believe how much having my eyes closed is helping me to see. By reducing turbulence on the inside there is less blown about on the outside.

Good Intentions

It's a Monday evening in mid-March and I head to Jamyang for another compassion workshop. An earlier conversation on the phone with Dad has unsettled me. His cancer surgery is booked for next week, with radiotherapy to follow. I'm worried and join the class in low spirits.

Roy, the centre director, has agreed that I can wear the headset to this evening's class so I hastily put it on. There are ten others as I take my seat, but nobody seems to notice or care what's on my head. The session is being run by an assistant teacher who sits cross-legged at the front. In a thick but melodic Italian accent he kicks off the session with a discussion about positive intention. This strikes a chord as I know how important this is. The idea, he says, is to set an intention to wake up every morning with positive thoughts, in the hope they will spill out into our day. In our super-busy lives, it's more common to start the day feeling negative and to focus on what's wrong. Yup, the mornings are my most grumpy time.

Buddha, of course, had good intentions, but, while he emanated the most positive of vibes, he did not eradicate negativity. I initially misunderstood this subtlety, believing a compassion practice required me to start liking everyone. A stressful thought. That's not the case; it's okay to feel indifference toward others. I don't have to force feelings that aren't there, or suppress those that are. The work is to notice when my attention has been kidnapped – and to scoop that energy up and redirect it. The point that our teacher is trying to make is that it's possible to feel compassion toward people we don't actually like. I baulk at this statement. That's madness. Then I remember Candice at work. It was compassion that allowed me to alter the course of that relationship. After she gave me free tickets, we eventually became friends.

One of the positive side effects of compassion is that the more I practise it, the less reactive I become. After just six weeks I can see the difference. Even Ed says the sharp edges of my temper have worn away. Yet there's something lurking beneath tonight's lesson. Something I have wrangled with for most of my life: it is impossible to like everyone. And – the killer part – it is impossible for everyone to like me.

There. It's said. Not everyone will like me. And, what's more, it's not my fault. It's the same for everyone. This knowledge is my in-road to compassion.

In his book *The Chimp Paradox: The Acclaimed Mind Management Programme to Help You Achieve Success, Confidence and Happiness,*

Professor Steve Peters discusses the same thing. He provides a simplified model, based upon scientific reasoning, that our emotional reactivity is akin to an untamed chimp, constantly reacting to any kind of danger. This mind struggle, he proffers, is balanced by what he calls the human quieter-and-more-rational (but less powerful) part of one's psyche. Peters explains that it is not possible for all of our chimps to like each other. This is a fact we must accept. Somewhere inside of me, there is a thirteen-year-old child that wishes she'd known this years ago.

After the break, our teacher delves into technique. As I'd been taught in Dave's MBCT class, sati (mindfulness of breathing) is a good way to calm a jumpy mind. I recall the frustration I'd experienced during Dave's classes – the way I'd fought this process of corralling my attention toward one thing. It's ironic and a little humbling that I am being taught the same thing again. It is true – before any compassion can begin, my mind needs to be receptive. Even five minutes of breathing is self-compassion.

As I start the breathing a weight pulls me forwards. An inner coil, wound tightly around my ribs, constricts my chest. My breathing feels shallow, like I am resisting something. My body is taut and my back aches. I consciously lengthen my out-breath, but it's hard work. My daughter dominates my thoughts and recent clashes surface. She has recently turned ten, and I see her arm-folded defiance and recognize she's practising non-compliance. Our power battles are present now as my desire for control surges through me. Uncoil the coil. My out-breath is long and shuddering, but oddly liberating. I am letting go.

Within seconds, judgement is back. I blame my daughter for being strong-willed. *Why? She's a child!* Focusing on the knot inside my chest: What's making me uncomfortable? I probe, touching the hurt to see what it reveals. A quote by Rumi, the thirteen-century Sufi poet, comes to mind, something I'd heard Tara Brach say during a meditation: "The wound is the place where the light enters you."

I probe a little deeper. Control, yes; along with a need to be right, to be The One Who Is in Charge. I sense unfairness here too. I listen again to the stories coming up. That time I was blamed for a project going wrong. An easy scapegoat. The mistake pinned on me when I was away on annual leave. I couldn't defend myself. The pain of injustice roars in my chest as the memory surfaces, ripping the scab off this old wound. Breathing into the discomfort, I realize some of my thoughts need warning flags attached: crimson for those spiralling out of control, amber for others heading that way. I realize I am not meditating on compassion at all, but unravelling the essence of Who I Am. This meditation is an emotional wrecking ball. I am not in control of my thoughts. I'm in the back seat and my emotions have their foot on the pedal.

Tonight's workshop has taught me a number of things. The aim of compassion training is not to remove negativity completely, but to decrease it so that positivity gets a look in. Buddhism teaches that anyone can become a Buddha – that's the modus operandi. Also, I don't need to be held hostage by my emotions, and small improvements should be rewarded. I have devalued these subtle shifts, expecting everything to be "big".

The entry point into loving-kindness is motivation. If I have an intention to be nice, the rest will follow. And, the best bit is that my intention can be really, really small.

Life Issues

A week after the workshop, I'm having a bad day. I'm struggling to see how this practice can be part of my life when I see no evidence of compassion around me. Plastic coke bottles litter the park and vandals have destroyed the playground swing. My friend chased a teen trying to steal his bicycle, the third time in a month. It's hard lowering my guard enough to live a compassionate life without feeling vulnerable.

Putting on the headset to meditate, the pacifying voice of Charles Hastings on the Imagine Clarity app fills my ears. He asks me to think about the people I pass in the street – to notice them and their needs. I suddenly have a powerful vision: the children and I are buying washing powder from Sainsbury's and outside is the young mother I often see. Like a slow-motion movie, I see the man who sells the *Big Issue* and the way he catches my eye while I avoid his by staring at my feet. I see the pensioners standing in the bus queue soaked in loneliness. I rush past so I don't see these things, yet of course my mind has recorded it all. I did see these people, but at the same time I didn't take it in. Perhaps I never processed it fully until this moment. Now all I can see is the pain and despair that surrounds me. And suddenly, that compassion that was so deeply buried is moved like a huge boulder out of the way. I don't want to be numb anymore. I want to put my head up and to see what is out there – what I'm rushing past too fast to absorb.

That evening I cuddle my son. "Mummy, can you do the body scan?" he asks. We started this recently when he was worried about school and struggling to sleep. A legacy from Dave's MBCT class, it's now a ritual we do. I start by asking him to clench his feet then relax. Moving up his body we methodically relax all his muscles. I use hypnotic language and pauses, never directing, only encouraging. He adores this exercise. It's time with me and he falls asleep easily. I'm careful that he learns to sleep independently, whispering that his body already knows this – that he has slept well hundreds of times before. "Your body is clever," I tell him. This meditation is something we do together using the skills I have gained during this experiment – but he is teaching himself to sleep.

Small Steps

I'm meeting my friend Genet outside the station for our weekly walk, but she's late. It's warmer today; fluffy clouds butt playfully up against each other, set off against an endless powder blue. The sun is warming my neck and I know the unhappiness I felt at the beginning of my metta practice is thawing. Recently, I've been making decisions more slowly. I've made small, seemingly insignificant changes that I wouldn't otherwise have made. We buy the *Big Issue* every week now, not just occasionally. I've lent money when I wouldn't have, I've held my tongue more often and I've been kinder to myself and others. There's more I could do, but I have made a start. Sitting in my local café recently, I had a sudden flood of love and gratitude for Ed. It came out of nowhere, but I saw it arrive only because this practice has pointed out the absence of these emotions.

Lost in thought, I jump when I feel a tap on my shoulder. Turning around, an elderly man is leaning heavily on a stick. He has the oaty residue of porridge in his beard and dried mucus under his nose. My instinct is to shrink back, but instead I smile weakly. He doesn't speak but jabs an arthritic finger toward the bus stop over the road. Bobbing his head, I gather he wants me to help him walk there.

"Sure," I say after a beat. I want to make an excuse, to look at my watch and tell him that I don't have time. Breathing in, I push my reservations away and take his arm. His body is frail, bird-like, but I sense a wiry determination.

"Ssssstroke," he mutters, his raisin-like eyes darting around. I ask if he's got any support at home, but he wheezes in reply. Genet arrives and, after a quizzical look, takes his arm on the other side. We deliver the old man to the bus stop and he doesn't thank us, simply waving us away. Walking back toward the park, Genet asks how I came to help.

"It's strange," I start, then stop. "He could hardly walk, yet he weaved past other people to ask me for help. I had my back to him, so it's not like he caught my eye or anything."

"I wonder why he chose you?" she mused. And, for a moment, I wonder the same thing. On the whole, people don't approach me in the street. I don't have one of those faces that attracts strangers.

As we stroll through the park it dawns on me that I'd just experienced a massive hit of empathy. I know it was empathy – rather than its counterpart, sympathy – because it was hard work and felt different. Normally in an uncomfortable situation, I would extract myself, avoid eye contact, mumble that I had to go and reassure myself later that my actions were justified. The research professor and author Brené Brown writes extensively about empathy and sympathy in her book *The Power of Vulnerability*, using a startling example to differentiate them. Empathy, she explains, is the ability to get another person's perspective, regardless of the situation. In other words, if you see someone sitting at the bottom of a large hole, empathy would be climbing down and sitting there alongside them. Sympathy, in contrast, would be staying at the top, calling out, "Oh no, what happened?"

That old man didn't reach out to me to be told how to live his life. He didn't need me to fix anything. He reached out because, for whatever reason, he believed in my ability to see his need for help. By taking his arm, I climbed into that hole with him. The only reason I did that was because of the loving-kindness work I've been doing. Matching Brown's research on shame and vulnerability to my own somewhat confusing array of experiences is empowering. I understand that the split second I take to decide what to do is critical. Do I allow old habits to dictate? Or do I consider what it might feel like to be the person in the hole?

An fMRI study at the Max Planck Institute in Germany investigated just this. The researchers discovered that participants who were taught loving-kindness for only eight hours reacted to disturbing images of burn victims with empathy, lighting up the brain circuitry associated with positive affect and emotional evaluation. Those who had not learned loving-kindness but who had just been trained in "empathy" showed a more negative effect and increased activation in areas previously associated with empathy for pain. In other words, they felt distress themselves.

Approaching my meditation experiment from the "experience up" allows me to relate to Brown's research on a much deeper level. Her findings remind me that compassion meditation is training. I just have to learn this stuff.

Street Compassion

Compassion is just one big loop that starts and ends with me. I wasn't familiar with the term self-compassion before all this, but I can't love anyone else until I love myself. Thankfully, compassion doesn't have to be big or arm-wavy. It can start inside my head.

In her book *Real Love: The Art of Mindful Connection*, Sharon Salzberg suggests a "street practice" that I have customized to practise with my children. Salzberg says that meditation shouldn't be cramming something new into our lives, it's about tweaking what we're already doing.

The street practice is easy and can be done anywhere – on the train, in the park, at the school gates. It requires me to put my phone away, and silently repeat phrases out loud or under my breath: Be well. Be safe. Be happy. I can direct each phrase toward a different person or the whole lot toward one person. If I'm worried about being mistaken for a stalker, I "zap" my compassion, superhero style, in their general direction. It's the intention that counts. Plus, if I zap someone I don't like, I get gold stars. As Salzberg points out, it's harder to love those we dislike, rather than those we like. Flexing my compassion muscles, I zap the mum who once told me that we were not invited to stay for drinks after a children's party. There you go mean lady – zap, zap.

Labour of Love

With my eight weeks of compassion coming to an end, I have a sense of newness, as if a brittle outer layer has melted away. I'm feeling my emotions more, exposing my bare skin to the sun for the first time. I found the practice challenging, which I suspect will be revealed in my traces data at the end of the experiment. At first, this practice left me tender, bruised perhaps, but I have become accustomed to the sensation of feeling alive. I think I'm a little less scared, and a bit more excited, at what lies ahead.

As a "life practice", elements of loving-kindness are relevant to Ed and I as parents. It's vital we don't "unteach" the unconditional kindness I see in our daughter and son. Children, I realize, find giving easy. A 2012 study at the University of British Columbia found that toddlers gave up their favourite toys selflessly, even though they didn't fully understand the cultural value placed upon kindness. The study suggests that altruism is a fundamental part of human behaviour, even when it comes at personal cost.

It's all too easy to skim on the surface of life like fragile ice-skaters, travelling at great speed. By slowing down my inner world, I've had the opportunity to see what is going on outside. "Time out" is something I have misunderstood in the past. Sitting on the sofa or reading a book is not the same thing. Sure, that is slowing down, but it won't reap this level of insight. If I travel too fast, my life will be a blur – it's that simple. Time and space are needed for this practice to work; it takes commitment. Loving-kindness has required me to move beyond the mechanics of meditating to the active participation in uncomfortable feelings. I can no longer stand at the bottom of the mountain describing the view at the top. I have to put on my boots and climb up myself.

I had it all wrong – this practice is not mild or easy. Loving-kindness research undertaken by Julieta Galante at the University of Cambridge investigated loving-kindness as a foundation for a therapeutic intervention. Results suggested the practice might be "too difficult" for some people to process. I certainly found it tough going.

The workshops have balanced what I've learned at home, illustrating how compassion is central to Buddhism. It has to be. It starts with kindness to myself, providing the foundation for it to spread to those around me. I don't need to be a Buddhist to follow a compassionate life, though. Based upon what I have experienced, it's part of everything I do. And, while I'm no expert, I'm surprised at how much I have learned in this short time. In the way the MBCT course was a vital foundation in understanding the mechanics of my mind, loving-kindness was vital in understanding the mechanics of kindness. My compassion journey has only just begun.

The Dalai Lama says: "The cultivation of compassion is no longer a luxury, but a necessity, if our species is to survive." Given our political, environmental and health climate, this has more truth than I would like to believe.

CHAPTER 6

NAUGHTY MONKS: ZEN BUDDHISM

April 2018

It's early April and messages from my family have been pinging all morning. Dad's had his surgery and is recovering at home. I'm behaving like I understand this cancer-talk, typing words to convey my concern. Yet for all the electronic missives, I don't feel part of what's happening. I call my brother, Dan – a sudden need to hear his voice. We haven't spoken in ages, work and busyness getting in the way of what is an easy relationship. Even though we repeat the same words, I feel comforted. Lugging a load of washing outside to hang on the line, broken roof tiles still litter the lawn. My stomach knots. It's another thing not sorted.

Loving-kindness exposed me emotionally, so I'm hoping this next practice will build resilience. The weekly Fundamentals of Zen class I've enrolled onto is held at The Buddhist Society in London and promises something new, something more orderly perhaps.

"Zen" is the Japanese pronunciation of "Ch'an", of the Chinese Ch'an School of Buddhism, and is widely popularized. Many are familiar with Zen Gardens, "feeling Zen" or even *Zen and The Art of Motorcycle Maintenance*. This notion of simplicity and tranquility in the face of calamity has created a kind of mystique around Zen, which is a variant of Mahayana Buddhism. The Middle Way, based on Buddha's teachings, are passed down in a strict lineage from master to student. Zen teachings spread from China and Korea into Japan around the seventh century. According to legend, an Indian monk called Bodhidharma was a key figure, instrumental in spreading the word of Zen.

Unfortunately, I couldn't just rock up to this Zen class as there's a strict entry criteria. New students must first complete a seven-week Introduction to Buddhism course. Joining The Buddhist Society for a small fee gave me access to this free course (also available online) that teaches students the basics tenants of Buddhism along with the terminology used. Membership also provides access to free classes held at The Buddhist Society and details of their retreats, along with their magazine.

After completing the introduction course my notebook now contains topics such as Karma (spiritual cause and effect), the Wheel of Life (a symbolic representation of life, complete with "hungry ghosts") and The Paramitas (six wholesome ways to live). While it was a lot to take in, it was fun to learn and reinforced the knowledge I previously gained with Hedgehog.

A week later, arriving at my first Zen class, I'm nervous I might be tested on my new-found knowledge. The Buddhist Society, a not-for-profit charity, is housed in one of the sumptuous Victorian buildings in Eccleston Square, Pimlico. Inside, I remove my shoes and stuff them into the locker provided. A tall, grey-haired man blocks the entrance to the Zen class, instructing newcomers on "the Form". The Form, it turns out, is the way we enter. We must hold our hands at prayer, bow to the altar, then to the seat we choose – then finally to the others already there. It feels ceremonial and I'm instantly on guard. Given the formality, I'm relieved I haven't asked to wear the headset to the class; I would feel too self-conscious here. I'm worried I am going to Get Something Wrong. The room is as magnificent as I thought it would be, with decorative cornices, plush carpet and floor-to-ceiling bay windows, in front of which is an altar, adorned with Buddhist statues and bowls. I count eleven men and women, aged between about 20 and 50, either seated on chairs or kneeling on cushions. After a few moments, a white-haired man walks in and a hush ensues. The man is wearing casual clothes with a fabric bib around his neck. Staring at this curious garment, I realize it is a "rakusu" – a traditional Japanese hand-stitched item, worn by teachers. He takes the seat in the middle of the room so I guess this is our teacher – Garry.

After welcoming us, Garry explains a little about the practice of Zen. The principle, he says, is seeing into our own Buddha-nature, otherwise known as the true self. This idea of the "true self" came up during the loving-kindness teachings at Jamyang, so while I'm still not entirely sure what it is, this is familiar territory. Garry talks a lot about reactivity, calling it "the fire within" and, sometimes, the "bull". He tells us that fear, anger and frustration are difficult emotions that must not be buried, for they will only return to bite us. Zen is an all-encompassing practice that builds equanimity, enabling us to live with and accept this inner boiling-pot of emotion.

Zen has an emphasis on training and, while there are strong monastic influences, it has been adapted for Western tastes. Garry starts by explaining the deceptively simple daily practice. This is what it sounds like – having a sense of mindfulness in every task I undertake. In particular, this applies to boring things, like cleaning the bath or putting the bins out. I consider mentioning this to Ed next time he's doing the washing up, but baulk when I picture his reaction.

The idea, Garry says, is to maintain this awareness during every waking moment. My resistance to this last statement is immediate and strong. I'm prepared to be mindful some of the time, but sustaining it all of the time seems untenable. When he instructs us to commit to the same bedtime and morning routine, along with meditating at the same times each day, more alarm bells sound. What about my daughter's morning swim squad? Not all days are the same. Garry explains that Zen students get one day off a week, but otherwise they follow these routines as much as possible. Clearly this is the training I had read about. Each class follows a similar pattern, with Garry discussing the history and principles of Zen and the practices involved, often illustrating a point with a story. Zen is well-known for its stories. These often use metaphors as a means to say something, without actually saying it. Today's offering is about an old Confucian scholar who, at the age of 80, travelled many miles to challenge the teachings of a new, younger master from the recently established Zen school. After arriving and spending much time narrating the importance of his own teachings, the old man demanded that the younger scholar explain his – asking whose were the most profound. The young man simply replied that his own teaching was summed up in one sentence: "Do no evil and try to do good." At this, the old man became angry, saying that even a three-year-old child knew that. The young scholar replied, "Every three-year-old child knows it, but as you see, even an old man of 80 cannot practise it."

I nod sagely at the story's punchline. Yup. This morning's shouting match (over my daughter's lost coat) was hardly a great example of me doing good. My children copy me, so how can I chastise them when they mimic my behaviour? As I mull over the messages woven into this story, Garry explains the other important element of Zen – "zazen", otherwise known as a sitting meditation. This word is made up of "za", meaning to sit and "Zen", meaning "dhyana", which is meditation. This sitting practice is to be done twice a day for twenty-five minutes each time, with a short break to stretch the limbs. Garry says if this timing doesn't work, we can split each into two sessions. In order to keep the mind as still as possible, we are to count our out-breaths up to ten. If a thought arrives, we start again at one. Like the bedtime routine, we should practise zazen at regular times. Panicking again, I know I can't do this. I have to be in different places at different times, but I keep quiet.

The class normally ends with a thirty-minute meditation but, first, Garry asks if anyone has a question. Tentatively raising my hand, I attempt to outline my children's schedules and why I can't follow the rules. Garry surveys me for a moment before suggesting, with a half-smile, that perhaps I might consider not having children. A twinkle in his eye tells me he's joking, but it's a clear message.

What's more, it's a message within a message. Zen is about tackling ingrained habits head on and dealing with the knee-jerk reaction that change evokes. This practice isn't about making excuses, it's challenging me to commit to something that feels uncomfortable. And, asking myself why I feel uncomfortable. It's interesting how quickly my mind resisted, how it sought to dilute the instructions and find an easier way. Of course, not having children isn't an option, so when the meditation starts I close my eyes and start planning ways I can get my daughter to her swimming class. My counting doesn't get above a one.

Be Still

A few days later I'm in Yorkshire visiting my father in hospital. He was sombre in spirit, but remarkably upbeat, relieved the cancer was gone. That evening, my stepmother and I eat a subdued supper before I excuse myself, trying to keep to my Zen schedule. I have failed to meditate at the same time every day, managing trains and hospital visits has thrown things. I push this aside as I don't want the rigidity of the practice to compound my stress load.

There's no chair in the spare bedroom so, pulling the EEG headset out of my overnight bag, I perch on the edge of the bed. Sighing, I realize I shouldn't have had a glass of wine with dinner. Zazen requires me to sit with my back straight, my head tipped slightly forwards and with my left hand sitting on top of my right, palms facing upwards. I am to stay in this position without moving a muscle. This is no easy task. I'm aware of how much I fidget, but even an itch or a tickle is to be ignored. It's taken a while to grasp that Zen isn't a practice I can switch on and off. There's no sitting down and "being Zen" for twenty-five minutes a day. Sitting is only part of it.

During the meditation, ideas dance inside my mind, vying for centre stage. The TM mantra sneaks in too when I'm not paying attention.

Not surprisingly, my counting doesn't go above a two or three, but given how active my mind is, I'm remarkably calm afterwards.

A week later I'm back at my second Zen class, scuttling to my seat with minutes to spare, bowing, I hope, in the right sequence. Relieved that I'm not the last to arrive, a petite woman wearing fashionable baggy trousers saunters in after me. The class sits in silence as she plonks herself onto a cushion with no bowing whatsoever. She has broken the rules and all eyes turn to Garry. "No," he says firmly, but not unkindly, staring at the woman. "There is a Form you must follow." She gawks as confusion, then embarrassment, colour her face. She's sent back to the door to re-enter the room, attempting the bowing three times before Garry is satisfied. I watch keenly, realizing I bowed in the wrong order earlier. When she is seated correctly, Garry observes the rest of us. A man opposite is wearing khaki shorts, revealing stocky legs. Pointing at his bare legs, Garry says that another, stricter teacher would ask him to leave as shorts are not permitted. The man nods his understanding. Garry's eyes travel around the room as he explains the importance of the Form. Bowing is not just a protocol to make Westerners uncomfortable (although it often does), it's as ingrained into the practice as the practice itself. Bowing is a physical act, allowing us to connect to our bodies in an intentional way. Any resentment or embarrassment is useful as it points toward something we can work on. Nothing in Zen is unimportant and at the same time nothing is important. There are lessons within lessons, and I am fascinated by the mixture of insight and confusion Zen evokes in me.

After the disciplining, Garry softens and relates another story. Several novice monks, undertaking strict Zen training in a secluded monastery, decided to test one of the more senior and seemingly imperturbable monks. The senior monk's job was to make the morning tea so at 4am, when the corridors were dark and cold, he walked along with a laden tray. As he turned a corner, the mischievous monks jumped out. Although startled, the old man did not drop his tray, but carried on until he carefully laid it down in an alcove, covering it with a cloth. Leaning against the wall, he then exclaimed, "Oh, what a shock." Garry deciphers the story by quoting an old Zen teacher: "You see, there is nothing wrong with the emotions, only do not let them interfere with what is being done."

Garry relates other stories too. One is about junior monks being pummelled by established monks to help them through their arduous three-day initiation into the monastery. He reassures us that this was simply a means to break up the monotony of the test. Chuckling, he explains: "The students were pummelled just enough to distract them and perhaps give a deep-tissue massage". Although these stories sound grim, Garry explains that Zen is anything but. In all cases, the monks were offered an opportunity to test and practise the "taming of the inner bull" – the reactivity they were seeking to contain.

Zen's strict hierarchy is explicit in these stories, as is the sometimes brutal treatment. Garry tells us that the mind is like carbon; by compressing and putting it under pressure, it eventually becomes a diamond, providing the light we seek. While I haven't yet experienced this illumination, I understand these stories are not about punishment, but about freedom. That said, Zen has its critics. Miguel Farias and Catherine Wikholm, the authors of *The Buddha Pill: Can Meditation Change You?*, get inside this more thoroughly and historian Brian Victoria's account, *Zen At War*, highlights how Zen doctrines were bastardized during World War II for Japanese militarism.

While Zen stories often centre around training in some form or other, the practice focuses on the same eternal problems most of us suffer: frustration, anxiety, sadness, feelings of isolation or failure. Zen could be considered a "system" with its group meetings, the daily practice, zazen and the stories collectively holding a mirror up to our lives. As a Zen student I must examine every facet of myself, not just the bits I want to observe. In this respect, Zen is a discipline and while that often incites defiance, acknowledging that is important. Garry doesn't end today's class with a zazen practice (as we've run out of time) but with chanting. We repeat the heart sutra *Maka Hannya Haramita Shingyo* in Japanese, a traditional Zen sutra recited at the end of every class. I try my best to keep up, but chanting is an acquired skill. Glancing away from the prompt sheet, I'm lost. Garry claps his hands at the end and I jump. Jeez. If I'd been holding a tea tray, I would have dropped it. As I start to chastise myself, I recognize the ingrained reaction.

This practice is hard on purpose. It provides challenges to identify how I judge myself. This is where the work lies. There are subtle parallels with loving-kindness here. Of course, they're both Buddhist traditions so that's not surprising, but being kind to myself is also at the core of Zen. Both practices force me to see, with utter clarity, not just the circumstances of my life, but how I live it.

The Angry Librarian

It's 3am and my heart is pounding. My unconscious mind, mid-dream, is waggling its finger, insisting that our local, rather mild-mannered, librarian will have me arrested. My crime is losing a book. While just a dream, my fear is real. This is the ridiculous storytelling my mind engages in during the night. Sweaty and panic-stricken, my thoughts collide: our son struggles to read; Ed stays up too late. The voice insists this is my fault. It's not, but the wrong part of me is awake. In *The Chimp Paradox*, Peters explains that it is our emotional "chimp" that's on duty at night, allowing our rational "human" to sleep. At this time, all reasonable thought flies out of the window and a chattering psychopath takes over. My chimp has created a catastrophic storyline that could compete with any thriller. Groping my way into our son's bedroom in the morning my tumultuous night is still here. It's only as my eyes adjust to the dark and I see the library book on my son's dresser that I see how ridiculous my nighttime fears were.

By week three I've shifted my evening schedule and arrive at the Zen class with time to spare. I've been sitting daily at home wearing the headset, mostly in the morning and sometimes in the evening. I constantly forget to be aware of what I'm doing, whether it's chopping vegetables or locking the front door. However, the ritual of zazen kicks in the daily practice of mindfulness and this has provided a heightened appreciation of small things.

I'm more comfortable at the class now and, taking my seat, I count twelve others, five of whom are women. There are new, anxious faces, but most I recognize from before. After the preliminaries, a man with a strong Spanish accent speaks up. I don't know him, but he has the self-assurance of a regular. He describes feeling constant panic, a deep concern that something terrible might happen: the old woman on the bus might collapse, or that man on the stairs might trip. His anxiety is all-consuming and weirdly infectious. He talks at speed, barely pausing for breath. Garry allows a beat before replying, explaining that the man is experiencing "the bull within" – the elevated sensitivity that many of us want to address. This heightened reactivity can take many forms and isn't always a bad emotion. It can be what we might consider to be a good emotion too – like passion or elation.

Bulls feature heavily within Zen vernacular. A series of famous drawings called the Ten Bull-Herding Pictures illustrate the stages of Zen practice leading toward enlightenment. These drawings show a man endlessly searching for a bull. Once he finds it, he learns to train it and over time the bull becomes gentle and so he rides it home. The last few drawings depict the bull and the man merging into nothingness and "re-emerging into a life of freedom". The premise is that during his search for enlightenment the man realizes the non-duality of existence (what the Buddhists refer to as "emptiness") and he then becomes at one with himself.

Garry reminds the Spanish man that the most important thing is to notice his emotions flaring and to hold these energies close. He must not deny his discomfort, but endure and embody these moments.

Moving his attention to the rest of the class, Garry asks how we're doing with zazen – the seated practice. He says we must also avoid getting tangled up in what is happening now – and to embrace emptiness, the focal tenant of Buddhism. It's in these moments that I experience a clash of continents, particularly as I inevitably view any Buddhist teachings through a Judeo-Christian lens.

Buddhism relies heavily on the Buddha's insight that there is no "I", no individual self. The Pali term used to describe this is "anatta", which means "substance-less". This came up during my Tantric training, but Zen is full of visual imagery to explain this further. Buddha taught that the self is fabricated – that it's just a mental construct. In some respects I get this as, try as I may, I cannot draw my "self". Zen scriptures have a saying for this: an eye cannot see itself, a tooth cannot bite itself.

There's also a useful ocean analogy: every wave is born in the midst of the ocean. Each is different from the one in front and the one behind, but all head toward the shore. As the waves crash and turn to foam on the beach, so the others will follow. This is the temporary nature of waves – they are not separate from the ocean, they are the ocean. Waves are analogous for our true nature – we may be changing shapes on the surface, but that just makes us the ocean.

These teachings contrast with Western beliefs born out of Christianity, philosophy and psychology. Where Buddhism believes our ego is the cause of most of our problems, the West places much importance on self-identity, self-esteem and self-love. "Who we are" is highly regarded within individualistic Western society. If I have no self, then who is the woman embarking upon this meditation experiment?

This existentialist dilemma ties me up in spiritual knots, but I'm not the only one. The psychologist Michael Washburn says that this disconcerting notion is created because we try to objectify the self without being able to see or describe it. All we find are the results, the outpourings of this invisible self in the form of confusing thoughts, feelings and images. We never see the source of where this seemingly disjointed content arises from.

The practice of zazen seems less about sitting still and more about continually cutting off extraneous thoughts, combined with withdrawing physically. When my mind is less magnetic and ceases to pull my attention, it becomes clearer. However, this still doesn't help me experience pure emptiness.

I asked Geshe-la, the spiritual leader at Jamyang, how Westerners can interpret this sense of no-self. Smiling, he answered, "I'm sure the Buddha said, 'I'm going to buy bread today.' We all refer to ourselves in the first person, so don't get too hung up on it." I suspect the more I consider this theory, the further I move away from understanding it which, of course, is the nub of Zen.

I have got distracted. Garry is telling another story, this time about two monks who come across a beautiful woman trying to cross a river. Struggling with the currents, the woman asks for help. The older monk immediately lifts her up and carries her to the other side. Several hours later, after considering the impropriety, the younger monk asks his companion why he carried the woman, when it went against their vows. The older monk simply replied, "Brother, I set her down on the other side of the river, why are you still carrying her?"

Of course, there are as many morals within this story as there are versions of it. Garry tells us that a good student can stick too much to the rules, unable to know when to break them. The older monk decided a compassionate act was more important than his vow not to touch a woman, in that moment at least. He didn't break the rules, his compassion bent them.

Garry is on a roll and cites a famous study called the Good Samaritan run by two behavioural scientists, Daniel Batson and John Darley, in the 1970s at Princeton University. Posing the question: "Why do people do good things for others?", they asked theological students, studying to be priests, to give an impromptu talk. Some were told to give a talk on the Good Samaritan (the Bible story that tells of a traveller who, after being beaten up, receives help from a man of different faith – a Good Samaritan). The other students were instructed to give a talk on a different religious topic. All students in the study were asked to walk to another building to give their talks. On their way they had to pass a man (an actor) lying in an alleyway needing help. The surprising result was that the topic of the talk made no difference to who stopped to help. Even though some of the students were thinking about the Good Samaritan, it did not encourage them to be one.

The implications of this study are enormous. We may think we are compassionate, kind or caring, but our thoughts and actions (our head and our hearts), are often split. Even the intentionally appropriate subject matter of the students' talks did not influence their actions. As Garry sums up, understanding and even preaching altruism doesn't mean anything if we don't act upon it. Intellectualizing isn't doing. If I want my children to truly understand what altruism is, it will not be from words, or stories. In some respects, I'm glad I came to Zen after loving-kindness, as it reinforces what I've already learned. However, before we leave the room, Garry is clear on one last point: we must not preach Zen or try to impose it on anyone else. This practice, he says gravely, is not to impart but to do. Clearly, he has been reading my mind.

The Zen Doctor

It's May and the days are getting longer. Today my zazen sitting sparks so many ideas I have to interrupt the meditation and write them down. A recent tube trip flashes up details I need to capture: a teen spitting onto the tracks, an old man clutching a Tupperware box, his breath smelling faintly of Marmite. These strangers morph into characters for a book I want to write. In the still of the meditation, my unconscious mind releases minutiae I didn't register at the time. This isn't unusual and was a common occurrence during TM. My mind, freed from the animation of life, is alive with inspiration. When I can't contain the deluge anymore, I tap the headset as a cue to Barbara that something has interrupted my meditation. Sometimes this is the doorbell, my children or, as today, my imagination.

It's week five and, as I bow my way into the class, Garry isn't here. Instead, an older statuesque man with a graceful air is standing in his place. Introducing himself as Desmond Biddulph, he explains

Garry is on a retreat. Desmond, it turns out, is a doctor as well as a Zen teacher but he eyes us in the same shrewd manner as Garry.

In keeping with the weekly structure, Desmond tells a well-known story about Ikkyu, an infamous fourteenth-century Zen monk. One day a wealthy patron invited Ikkyu to a banquet. Ikkyu arrived dressed in his usual beggar's robes, but the host, not recognizing him, chased him away. Ikkyu went home, changed into his ceremonial robe of purple brocade, and returned. With great respect, he was received into the banquet room. There, Ikkyu laid his robe on the cushion, saying, "Evidently you invited the robe since you showed me away a little while ago," and left.

I particularly like this story. It segues into the unrealistic expectations we have of ourselves and others, and how we judge based upon status, appearance and position. This peels back the perfect veneer we paint, revealing the flawed, unwelcome and decidedly normal person underneath. Will Storr's book *Selfie: How the West Became Self-Obsessed* (which I came across on David McRaney's excellent science podcast, You Are Not So Smart) sums this up succinctly. Storr says we are expected to be "an extroverted, slim, beautiful, individualistic, optimistic, hard-working, socially aware yet high-self-esteeming global citizen with entrepreneurial guile and a selfie camera". Clearly that person doesn't exist, yet we all desire to be it. Our self-obsession leads to obsessions about everyone else and creates the awful cycle of judgement that's present in modern society.

Making An Exhibition of Myself

It's the last Sunday in May and I'm meeting Genet to walk. Eight weeks on, the Zen perspective has infiltrated many aspects of my life. As a born analyzer and fixer-of-problems, I've had to relax my need for control.

Zen "koans" are useful for control freaks. These short phrases are sometimes used by a teacher as an exercise to challenge a student's intuition and their willingness to let go of analytical questioning and absolutes. These phrases cannot be solved by thinking or reasoning, and are only given when a student has settled into the training and their meditation is stable. My children would probably call them mind-benders, but the idea is to meditate on the phrase and present an answer to the teacher. The teacher will either accept or reject this, giving the student pointers for further enquiry. A classic example is: "Pull Mount Fuji out of a teapot". Thankfully, I am a long way off receiving a koan as part of my training.

Zen is not meant to wind me up, but to unwind some of my constraints. Things like letting go of what others think of me. Heading to the park, I tell Genet I'm considering only posting unflattering photos of myself on Facebook, but I'm worried it might backfire. Will I look like a pretentious arse? And, lo and behold, there's that judgement again. Genet just laughs – she's not on Facebook. Pulling my phone out I start to delete my profile, but freeze at the last minute. Seems I'm still a fully paid-up member of the self-sabotaging club. That said, talking about these concerns has shifted our conversation. Maybe it's not about removing these social vices, I suggest, but lessening the impact they have?

Having coffee later, Genet picks up the theme and suggests we make some changes in our lives. I'm in – I love a challenge. Genet wants to be more proactive in family decision making. I want to spend more time with my brother, having let distance and life get in the way. I suggest measuring our success, so we agree to check in on how we're doing in a few months' time.

Middle of the Road

This experiment has been rooted in a sense of seeking, present within all of the methods I've tried. The idea that I start in one place and travel to another is synonymous with spirituality, and Zen has a pragmatic, almost playful approach to this. The foundation of compassion, inherent in loving-kindness, has formed a useful basis upon which to learn Zen. In amongst my frustration and the inevitable head-scratching, I sense an emergence – an ironic freeing of my mind. With all of its strict rules, Zen has taught me to be kind to myself. The resilience I sought in the beginning has come by unexpected means, the ability to laugh at myself – my habits – my eternal "me-ness". Zen has injected a much-needed humour into my spiritual journey. I may not fully grasp emptiness or no-self, but I have peeled back yet more layers, revealing my knee-jerk reactivity and the nuances of judgement that lie beneath every act and thought.

There's a stripped-back honesty I wasn't expecting to find. Zen makes no promises. There's no marketing plan, no evidence-based rhetoric. There's no talk of de-stressing or becoming superhuman. It doesn't propose we employ mindfulness to increase productivity or "better" ourselves, but simply to notice the simple beauty of the world around us (even in the washing up). This is mindfulness in its true uncommercialized form.

I like Zen; but I'm not sure I would have a thousand years ago. It has survived and evolved because many of the core tenets make sense today. Yes, there are rules, but I was less bothered by the rigidity of the Form and the daily practice, than I was by TM reining in my curiosity. After all, Buddha told students not to take his word for anything, but to experiment themselves. Zen is simply about being the best, flawed, imperfect human being I can be. It's rather like a strict old aunt who scares you half to death, but at the same time is weirdly comforting.

Bedtime Tales

Reflecting on my Zen journey, it's the storytelling that has resonated the most. Life is just a collection of tales knitted together by time; it is only when I see it as such that the wisdom becomes visible. My children love books at bedtime, but they'll choose a memory from my past over any fictional tale. My stories transform humdrum events into mystical moments of untold delight.

My son's current favourite is The Art Gallery. In 1999, when I lived in Sydney, Australia, I visited the Modern Art Gallery. Arriving early, I was told to follow a guided route around the exhibits. Two men were ahead of me so we fell into a routine of looking at each exhibit, then moving on. After a while, the first man stopped to examine a small white sculpture on a stand. He seemed to hunt unsuccessfully for the plaque describing the piece, but nevertheless appraised the sculpture and moved on. As the second man approached, a security guard appeared and picked up what was, in fact, a white Styrofoam cup and drank from it. Realizing the mix-up, we all fell about laughing.

Even when I have suspicions to the contrary, I often allow myself to be guided by circumstance. The first man questioned the cup's provenance, but, because he too was on display, allowed himself to be bound by the constraints of polite society.

I toe the line all the time, regardless of what my instincts tell me. I fit in to maintain an image, but like the "sculpture", it's a facade. I can't remember a single piece of art I looked at that day, but twenty years on, I remember the cup.

CHAPTER 7

A SLEEP EXPERIMENT PART 1: HYPNOSIS

May 2018

Sleep and me have … history. While breathing exercises, self-hypnosis and visualization helped me manage the anxiety brought on by my sight loss − nothing allayed the insomnia I suffered at night. Back in 2012, insomnia taped my eyes open for four days. People often don't believe that I stayed awake for so long, 96 hours of panic-induced hallucinations. Insomnia is not a bad night. It goes much deeper than that.

Sleeplessness has plagued me much of my life. At the height of my career, I often couldn't sleep, or I'd wake at dawn dreading the day ahead, knowing exhaustion and self-recrimination would fill the hours. The times I did drift off, I'd jolt awake, dripping in sweat. Mostly triggered by the fear of a presentation or public speaking, insomnia has caught me out lots of times − before a training course I ran and a talk at a school. Regardless of what relaxation techniques I'd tried, or what my rational voice insisted, the unconscious part of my mind hadn't been listening.

Fear was at the root of it − that I knew. Fear of being exposed as incompetent − a failure. In 2012, I feared I'd never see again. I know the answer to my sleeplessness lies behind a door inside my rabbit-warren mind. Meditation has never reached that door, but I believe hypnosis might hold the key.

To be in keeping with my experiment I can employ a daily self-hypnosis practice utilising audio recordings, and wear the EEG headset in the same way I have done for the other modalities. As hypnosis is commonly used to target a specific problem, I need to approach this part of my experiment differently – sleep will be my goal.

The word hypnosis refers to the induction of a passive state of mind that allows a two-way dialogue to open up between the conscious and unconscious mind. It's important to distinguish hypnosis from meditation. Confusion comes from the associated language and the intersections between the two. Some guided visualizations can be both a form of self-hypnosis and meditation. A self-hypnosis track is likely to repeat targeted, affirming messages over and over, employing visual metaphors to reinforce the message. Often using naturalistic imagery, a listener feels as light and free as the field of daisies they are imagining walking through. Instructions to elongate the breath connect the listener to their body and music is a trigger. A gentle voice repeating "that's right" anchors the message to the corresponding hemisphere of the brain and rewards the listener's unconscious for relaxing on cue. Hypnosis recordings are intentional with deliberate, strategic pauses. The pattern, tone, and rhythm of those spaces allow the mind to travel or slip into different brain states. Hypnotic "suggestions" are the trademark of hypnosis and help direct and effect subconscious and autonomic transformations to meet the intended goals. This is part of what sets hypnosis apart from meditation.

Still the lines blur. A case in point is how Bianca Andreescu, who beat Serena Williams in the 2019 US Open, reportedly used visualization repeatedly, seeing herself winning and holding the trophy. In doing this, she created a specific reality that her unconscious mind believed.

Self-hypnosis is certainly a way to train my mind so is a legitimate technique for Barbara and I to explore within our experiment. It also helps that I already have some beneficial experience using this technique. Hypnobirthing (used during my pregnancies) is a specific kind of hypnosis and is pretty much what it sounds like –

inducing a state of hypnotic trance in order to expedite a calm and natural birth. My daughter's traumatic birth in 2007 had resulted in panic attacks and a fear of giving birth. I read Marie Mongan's book, *HypnoBirthing: The Mongan Method*, when I fell pregnant for the second time in 2009 and, even with my midwife unavoidably absent, went into a deep trance and surrendered to one of the most powerful experiences of my life. Just eight weeks of intensive self-hypnosis (also involving audio recordings) had rewired the terror I associated with birth and replaced it with a blissful serenity. I hadn't suppressed my fear – I just couldn't find it anymore.

Remembering how hypnobirthing had helped in the past, I had sought the guidance of a hypnotherapist when I was asked to give a TEDx talk in Belgium back in 2016. Terrified about speaking in front of 700 people, I arranged to see Jane Ellsbury, a local Quest Cognitive Hypnotherapist. Over three 90-minute sessions she used relaxation techniques and positive, suggestive language to help assuage my fears. In particular, an audio recording Jane made (using my own words from our hypnotherapy sessions) proved very effective at helping me nod off. Unlike talks in the past, I slept soundly the night before and, word-perfect, breezed through my TEDx talk with a smile on my face. It was the most confident I'd ever felt speaking in public. While Jane's hypnotherapy intervention had been a success, my insomnia returned. A sleepless night before I spoke at a conference in the USA earlier this year revealed it was still a problem.

Frustrated that I still haven't got to the root of my sleep issues, I make a suggestion to Barbara on my next visit to Cambridge. It's a bright spring morning when we chat in the lab.

"I want to use self-hypnosis as part of the experiment," I announce, "to target sleep."

"Great. I'd be interested to compare those experiences to meditation. Do you have poor sleep right now?"

"No, my sleeplessness is normally triggered by events – mostly the fear of public speaking. That's why I used hypnosis before the TEDx talk," I explain.

"Do you have any talks coming up then that we could use for an experiment?" Barbara asks.

"Yes – a school careers talk in July, and I'm speaking to the Cambridge University Mindfulness Society in November."

"Perfect. The school careers talk can be the control – don't use hypnosis before it. We can use the second talk in November as the 'active' part of the experiment, where you do use hypnosis so we can compare the results."

"But if I use hypnosis before the Cambridge talk – how should I prepare for the school presentation before that?"

"Practise a technique that's not specifically used for sleep. What about the mindful breathing you learned on the MBCT course?"

We agree that I'll ask Jane to help with some further hypnotherapy sessions and that I will wear the EEG headset during any self-hypnosis sessions I do at home. A week later, after explaining the project on the phone, Jane is excited to meet.

An Experiment Within an Experiment

It's a sunny afternoon when Jane and I have a coffee together. The hypnotherapy work we did before my TEDx talk was short and targeted. As such, it only focused on that event and my very real fear of going blank. It didn't target public speaking (or sleep) in general. My goal had been to deliver my talk confidently, to remember my script and to cope with the unexpected. Jane did this by suggesting "I had already completed the talk with aplomb". In this way, my unconscious mind didn't need to worry, as it was reassured that everything had already been a success. Jane had added a brief mention of "sleeping well" the night before, but this was an aside, rather than the focus at the time. Jane explains that is why some elements of the hypnosis hadn't transferred to other talks. "Hypnotherapy is very targeted," she finishes.

"One element has transferred though," I cut in. "Since the TEDx talk, I've had moments of 'utter conviction' just before I've given a talk. It's a strange, elated feeling that comes out of nowhere."

Jane smiles – she's not surprised. This is exactly what her audio recordings had suggested I would feel. This message is permanently embedded – which is good news. I no longer fear speaking in public, but my ability to sleep the night before is still a problem. These details are important as they will direct the focus of our future sessions. Sometimes, in hypnotherapy, it's good practice to focus on one issue at a time, as it's best not to unpack more than you have time to re-pack afterwards.

Jane and I book in some hypnotherapy sessions to start after my first talk (the control) in July to the Year Elevens at a local secondary school. Along with only practising a mindful breathing meditation each day for a month before this talk, I will record my brain data daily using the EEG headset and fill in the online diaries as normal. However, as we are specifically measuring sleep this time, Barbara has also given me a chart to log the number of hours I sleep, sleep quality, bedtime and wake-up times, and disturbances during the night. Wearing the EEG headset to bed (as well as during my meditations) will provide an indication of how my sleep is generally, along with how it changes on the lead up to the talk (the critical part). The assumption (our hypothesis) is that by only practising mindfulness before the school talk, I will experience my normal disrupted sleep the night before. If hypnosis works, I will sleep soundly the night before the second talk – to the Cambridge University Mindfulness Society. It all feels satisfyingly binary. The data will talk and I'm happy to let it do that. Of course, this is an experiment with only one participant, the talks are not exactly the same and there are other life and environment factors to consider. However, even with these limitations, I hope it will reveal something.

I've only ever had my own anecdotal evidence to support how powerful self-hypnosis has been. I don't need convincing, but I'd like something tangible to present to others. This time, science (in the form of the EEG headset) will be lying on the pillow next to me.

End of Term-itis

It's July and the kids are restless and suffering "end of term-itis". A friend has spent an hour in my kitchen bemoaning her daughter's tantrums, when I realize everyone is hot. I'm grumpy and hot too. The school holidays will be a blessed break from the monotony of routine. Thankfully my own meditation routine has been going well, practising mindful breathing meditations daily while wearing the EEG headset. This is preparation for my first talk to the Year Elevens, but while this practice is familiar and often relaxing, my nerves are building the closer the presentation gets.

My father's health is unsettling me too. As he endures gruelling radiotherapy miles away, I'm kept away by distance, shielded from his illness. A convivial man, my father is well liked for his humour and generosity. Several of my female friends had crushes on him over the years. Yet, while happy to discuss the cricket or bemoan his latest golf game, he rarely discusses his feelings. One of the most special times I recall was when my daughter was a baby and we took some day trips around Cape Town. Although we spent hours on dusty roads in silence, it was a companionable quiet. I don't remember what we talked about, so much as the gentleness in my dad's voice. The way that, when my daughter sicked up in a smart restaurant, he just smiled and found us a towel. The memories are precious but I'm resentful that, now finally home after 20 years away, my father is physically and emotionally unavailable.

Talk #1: School

Two days after my talk to the Year Elevens, Jane knocks on my door. Heading into our living room she draws the curtains to block out the sun and then perches on a footstool. I'm comfortable with her padding around and rattle on about how I slept badly before the school talk.

"It was as I expected – an awful night. I only slept for two hours," I explain. "I couldn't fall fully asleep – it was like I was lightly brushing sleep, like snorkelling in the sea without breaking the surface."

Scribbling notes, Jane hmms and asks for more detail. Without any self-editing, she wants to know exactly what went through my mind. She wants thoughts, colours, textures, smells, anything that helps build a picture. Even insignificant details could be important. I explain my mind was "naughty", it played tricks on me. I dreamt I was awake when I was asleep. It told me to "wake up to keep rehearsing". I dreamt the whole talk was a disaster and that something inside me wouldn't let me sleep.

"What wouldn't let you sleep?" she asks quietly, and I instinctively know our hypnotherapy session has started.

"There was a block…"

Jane is softly repeating my words and my eyes start to close. My mind shifts into a receptive state. "Thinking about blocks…" she says, "is there a shape to them?" Dipping inwards, my shoulders drop, my voice is distant.

"No, but the block is listening in."

"What's the purpose of the block?" Jane asks, her voice almost a whisper. "Is there a feeling that goes along with it?" Images fill my mind – a swirling wave becomes my childhood bedroom, filled with teddies and floral wallpaper. I'm reading with my finger poised, ready to flick off the light if I hear footsteps. I look across from the teddies guarding my bed to a shaft of light at my bedroom door. This light strip had to be 30 centimetres across (12 inches). The length of a ruler – no less.

When I was eight I was left at our neighbours' house as my parents were out for the evening. Their teenage sons were instructed to look after my brother and I, and to put on a movie. The boys had the choice of *Smokey and the Bandit* or *Spawn of the Slithis*, a low-budget horror movie. They chose Slithis, as they figured it would have less swearing in it. The nightmares started that same night and lasted for years. Even if someone pushed my door to in the night, I would wake and measure it back to 30 centimetres. Associations of protection and a lack of safety, suppressed for years, break the surface and I see how far back the strands of my fear go.

It's understandable why many people fear hypnosis – associations with stage hypnosis, of being vulnerable and out of control. Yet I feel safe with Jane, so I don't worry about getting stuck or revealing embarrassing secrets. The reality is that we go in and out of a trance state many times a day. I'm in a trance when I unthinkingly punch my PIN number into the card reader in Sainsbury's. I'm awake during this moment, but some cognitive function is switched off.

While I'm still in a hypnotic state, Jane suggests we revisit the memory of the film. There are associations with sleep and safety that we can re-program. We can, she suggests, rescript the movie. I agree, weighed down by the complex memories that have broken the surface. We focus on me watching the Slithis film, and I recall it was mostly set at night – a cheap trick for budget horror films. She suggests I pick three scenes and imagine them in black and white – a method used to distance oneself from the content. I fast-forward and rewind these scenes, altering something as we go. This doesn't change the original memory, but shifts the focus of emotion, jumbling up the brain code associated with it. Jane suggests I add in a detail that wasn't there before – a wide shot showing the director on his ladder. Then I make the monster just a cameraman in a wetsuit. Asking me to switch these new scenes back into colour, she suggests adding humour – a man farts as he runs downstairs and everyone laughs. In the water a piece of the monster's arm falls off. I am changing the associated feelings of fear with amusement, giving my brain an alternative version. A safer version. By rerunning this new movie in my head I overwrite history. I am changing what I feel now, by changing what I saw back then.

After our session Jane explains that my unconscious mind is not governed by logical thinking. This ever-watching overseer accesses an ocean of memories and stored experiences on a moment-by-moment basis. Sometimes my experiences have been filed in the wrong place, or perhaps weren't fully processed at the time. This misfiling of information and events can cause a bug in our operating system, triggering emotional responses that don't make sense in the present.

I need Jane to help me do this; I can't do it alone. In my twenties, I tried to confront my nighttime fears. Searching for Slithis on a movie database, I found a slamming review and a hackneyed film poster. Even though I knew it was just an awful B movie, I couldn't reach that eight-year-old version of myself who was still terrified. I needed hypnosis – and Jane's help – to reach her.

In a Daze

Before Jane left my house, I admitted that I was more nervous about the second talk to the Cambridge University Mindfulness Society, booked for four months' time. This wasn't a talk to teenagers, but to graduates at one of the best universities. Jane suggests that in order to prepare my mind I should listen to a daily self-hypnosis recording that targets sleep (while wearing the EEG headset). Thankfully, I have been given a comprehensive sleep programme by hypnotherapist Dr Dyan Haspel-Johnson. I first met Dyan in Los Angeles four months earlier, at the conference where I couldn't sleep. I'd delivered a speech that morning after a sleepless night, so when I attended her sleep workshop later that day, I knew it was serendipity. With over twenty years practising hypnotherapy and with a PhD in mind-body-spirit psychology, Dyan is a passionate advocate of self-hypnosis. Contacting Dyan about my plan to run a self-hypnosis sleep experiment, she'd agreed to help.

While some people are put off by hypnosis, fearing the unknown, I feel inspired by the possibility of change. And yet, my session with Jane was sobering. I hadn't appreciated how deep the process could go or how visceral the memories evoked could be. I'm glad I am not alone in this stage of my experiment.

With four months to wait until the second talk in November (the "active" part of our study), I cannot start Dyan's self-hypnosis recordings for another three months. Since there is time to spare before I complete the second half of the experiment, I have a gap to fill. In the meantime, Father John Pritchard, a priest at my local Church of England church, has replied to the email I sent enquiring about Christian prayer. I may have a new technique to learn.

CHAPTER 8

ON MY KNEES: CHRISTIAN MEDITATION

July 2018

I can't remember religious education at school; only one memory stands out. During a particularly boring lesson our RE teacher, a flaky-skinned man with leather patches on his elbows, lost his temper and slammed the door so hard, a pane of glass fell out. As we sat with our mouths in the shape of o's, he screamed, "Nobody cares!" over and over. As the deputy head led him away, I wondered what had caused his outburst. I've never forgotten the peculiar sense of guilt I felt at the time.

Religion played an insignificant role in my upbringing. My father wouldn't let me be baptized and we never went to church. Not ever. Not even when my mother pleaded to go on Christmas Eve. My father's antagonism meant that I grew up with few religious influences. We didn't have many church-going friends and our only churchy neighbours didn't allow their children to eat sweets or watch television. Not surprisingly, that created a distorted stereotype. Of course, Christianity shaped my life, the infrastructure by which I lived, but I had no personal relationship with it.

Then, when I was around fifteen, a school friend discovered God. She explained, in a very matter-of-fact voice, that God had come into her life and she'd been reborn. I was horrified. In my mind, this meant she wouldn't want to hang out and talk about boys and, for a while, I even avoided her. Looking back, I see how ridiculous this was, particularly as we're still friends 30 years later.

Heading toward the vicarage at Saint John the Evangelist, an Anglican church close to my home, I feel a sense of trepidation. I have put off meeting Father John Pritchard, my local vicar, terrified that my lack of religiousness would be exposed. However, Barbara and Tristan are both keen that I include a form of religious prayer so we have it to compare to the other secular practices. Over the last few weeks, Father John's chatty emails have reignited my waning curiosity. Maybe this won't be so bad?

Meditation, in some form or other, is part of most world religions. Christianity is no different and both Centering Prayer and Christian meditation are practised in silence, using a sacred word. The main difference between these practices is that the mantra is repeated continuously during Christian meditation and only when distracted (as a means to return) during Centering Prayer.

Thinking about this next stage of my experiment, my heart is pounding. I'm scared of The Things I Am Supposed to Know. Things like when to stand or sit in church, the Bible, and what all the rituals mean. I'm scared of publicly falling flat on my face, of getting it all monumentally wrong.

Wandering around the church grounds, I can't locate the vicarage. Eventually, I discover a pleasant nineteenth-century stone building with tall chimneys. As I raise my hand to knock on the door it swings open, revealing a gigantic man dressed in a polka dot bikini. I'm speechless as he towers over me, wobbling on four-inch heels. Sporting a black jumper and dog collar, Father John hovers behind. Grinning, the huge man swivels and says, "Thanks for listening, Father," and teeters away. John, appearing completely unfazed, ushers me in. There's a woman typing furiously in the corner and nodding in her direction, he asks if we need privacy. Still slightly wrong-footed, I say it's fine.

After offering me a cup of tea, Father John relaxes into a worn armchair and smiles. The room is cosy, decorated with overflowing bookshelves and fraying rugs.

After some chitchat, he asks what religious upbringing I have. Blushing, I describe my lack of Christian-ness, but John shrugs this aside. He's more curious to understand how I might take on a religious practice without faith. He's right to ask this question, as it could be a stumbling block. I'm hoping curiosity and a suspension of judgement might allow me a foot in the door.

All of the practices I've tried have fed into my life in some way or other. MBCT revealed a lifetime of (unhelpful) habitual behaviours I could change. Loving-kindness showed me how to connect emotionally to others. Tantric reignited my neglected femininity and introduced a spiritual aspect I hadn't considered. Zen brought with it order and a glimpse of unexpected humour into what I had (incorrectly) considered to be a draconian practice.

Dodging the faith question for now, I suggest any connection to Christianity will be via the community spirit that St John's propagates. Plus, I say, I quite like churches. John smiles at this, but I really do. I like the stone walls that history has worn down and the light that dances when the sun hits the stained-glass windows. I'm not sure it's enough. I'm not sure it replaces faith.

John suggests I try the Christian meditation group held on Mondays and Tuesdays, agreeing that I could wear the EEG headsets there. He also asks that I attend the daily 9am services, which he calls the Morning Office. These half-hourly sessions involve singing, prayers and some sermons which, he explains, are simply ancient spiritual stories. Even the upcoming school holidays aren't a problem as John says my children can come too.

I feel safe in the vicarage. I'm fairly sure the man in front of me is not a typical priest, but right now the Church of England seems far more relaxed than I expected. As I walk home, I wonder what coercion will be required to get my children into church.

Learning the Ropes

It's 8.54am so I'm hurrying to get to Morning Office on time. Even though I've made it most days this week, I'm still not familiar with the procedure. The church smells of cut grass and there's the motorized hum of a lawnmower outside. As I weave in amongst the wooden chairs, a circular-saw squeals somewhere in the distance. Four men, mostly middle-aged, stand in a line alongside me. Father Daniel, a member of the pastoral team, is here wearing khaki shorts and Birkenstocks. With his gelled hair he'd look as comfortable shopping in a fashion store as he is here in church. When the hymn starts, everyone sings beautifully – despite my self-conscious warbling. Father John, smiling briefly in my direction, reads a line from the Common Worship book containing the service and prayers for the day. Although the others murmur a reply, I don't know what to say. One man leans over and points out the page and while I mutter the replies, I wonder who wrote these Psalms.

After the office, I'm introduced to Tom, the retired priest who guides the silent meditation group. This is based on the World Community for Christian Meditation (WCCM) Christian meditation practice rediscovered by Father John Main in the 1970s. There's a class tonight so I agree to go.

Leaving my children with a neighbour, I eventually find the group up a steep wooden staircase at the back of the church hall. Tom smiles and introduces me to the five others there. He makes us laugh, regaling his angry reaction to being knocked off his bike – yelling at the driver until he remembered he was wearing his dog collar and cassock. The story reassures me that priests suffer road rage too. With the meditation about to start, I pull on the EEG headset and close my eyes.

Each session begins with a short prayer, though the aim of Christian meditation is not to focus on God, but to dip below our "thinking mind" and be with Him. The idea is to allow God's mysterious and silent presence to be within me. It's all a little mysterious, but I do my best.

The mantra we use is *Maranatha*. This is an ancient Aramaic word that means "Come Lord", and was one of the first recorded Christian prayers. The only instruction I have is to repeat Ma-ra-na-tha over and over. Listening to these four consonants gently undulating inside my mind is satisfying. Nonetheless, I am distracted. My mind wanders from topic to topic, regurgitating nagging thoughts. A friend who lives abroad is in London. I only know because she's splashed photos across Facebook. My chest tightens. Why didn't she tell me? The rejection is raw. Dragging my mind back to the mantra I remind myself to be tolerant, to be reasonable. Ma-ra-na-tha. Negativity is a flame illuminating the inside of my mind. A question Father John asked comes to mind: "Who's looking after you?" Time compresses and 30 minutes are up. Opening my eyes, I ease the headset off. Even though my mind has been popping open like a faulty Jack-in-the-box, I feel calm. And yet, Father John's concern over my welfare remains unanswered floating inside the watery cavern of my mind as I head home.

Whitstable

It's late July and, as Ed is away for work, Mum and I are taking the children to Whitstable, a small seaside town in Kent. To keep some kind of continuity, John is going to send me phone recordings of the Morning Office via WhatsApp and I've agreed to practise Christian meditation twice a day for 30 minutes while wearing the headset.

Sitting having a last-minute coffee in Victoria Station, a middle-aged woman clutching a clipboard approaches us. Spotting her, Mum and I turn our faces, assuming she wants to canvas us. There's something vulnerable about the woman so when she looks back, I ask how we can help. Her reply is unintelligible, but her eyes are bright and pleading. Asking for her clipboard, I see instructions to a centre nearby. She's lost. Relieved I can help, I point out the exit she needs and she ambles away.

Heading to our platform five minutes later, I mull over this small, seemingly insignificant event. It feels important. With a jolt I realize that my first instinct had been to avoid helping the woman. I'd had to override that reflex and it took effort. The children, of course, took in everything. "What did you say to that lady, Mum?" my daughter asks as we board our train.

"Oh, I just helped her find her way," I reply nonchalantly, hoping this will suffice. She seems satisfied, but I am reminded, yet again, that I am not just teaching myself what compassion looks like.

Christianity puts much emphasis on compassion and one of the office sermons the previous week talked about Jesus on the cross. While I shuddered at the gruesome image, the sermon focused on Jesus' attitude toward his fellow prisoners (most of whom were dodgy criminals). Jesus refused to judge these men and said they would join him in paradise. I didn't buy the paradise part, but while it was a horrific story, there was something uplifting about it. Even when faced with death, Jesus offered these men a way not to suffer. They found peace via compassion.

Here are parallels with Buddhism again: the underlying moral that any situation (particularly an unpleasant one) offers an opportunity to flex our compassion muscles. It may seem extreme, but compassion needs awfulness to bounce off. Jesus views his experience on the cross as a means to not just develop his own benevolence, but to unite his fellow men. I don't need to be tolerant of kind people, simply because there is nothing to be tolerant of. Paradoxically, I need conflict if I am to test this theory.

Compassion often lives in unusual places. During World War II, a German pilot called Franz Stigler showed extraordinary courage and compassion. During combat he was about to shoot a damaged American plane down, when he saw its occupants trying to save the life of one of the crew. Risking court-martial he flew alongside the damaged plane in order to guide it to safety. Both pilots kept this story of humanity secret until many years later when they eventually met and became friends. It's a heartwarming story, but theirs is not the only example.

Christianity isn't proffering a new way of seeing things – it's corroborating what I've already learned. Perhaps, weirdly, Candice wasn't the irritant I thought she was. Perhaps she was just tolerance homework.

A week after our trip to Whitstable, my phone rings early one morning. It's my mum and I instantly know it's bad news. "Your dad's had a massive stroke," she says softly. "He's in hospital. You need to go and see him."

Hours later we arrive at the stroke ward and are told that my dad is unable to speak. Standing in front of him, I don't know what to do – but my daughter does. Waving her arms, she looks Dad in the eye and insists he sing. Like a child, he smiles and follows his granddaughter's instructions. As his faint rasp fills the room, the nurses clap and cheer and I see compassion all around us.

Tower of Cushions

Back home again, I return to church. It's only 9am, but it's already hot and sticky outside. The children are unenthusiastic about accompanying me today, but I've promised them ice creams afterwards. John has the day off, so Father Andrew, another member of the parish team who I met previously, is taking the service and there are only two other parishioners here. Quickly updating Father Andrew on my father's health, I jab my finger at a miniature table surrounded by miniature chairs, indicating that my son should read his book. His sister is already seated, her knees up by her chin. When I glance back, I spot my son crawling away on his hands and knees.

Yet again, I don't recognize the hymn. I haven't known any to date. I murmur words, reminded of school assemblies, feeling awkward and uncomfortable. Thankfully, I can recite the Lord's Prayer without thinking.

We read Psalm 37, which advises us to avoid evildoers. Murmuring: "The wicked plot against the righteous and gnash at them with their teeth", I wonder how this translates into modern times. My attention is diverted when I hear a muffled thud. My son isn't reading his book.

After the Psalms, I'm reminded of the place this church has within the community. Father Andrew reads from a list of people that need our prayers: Peter, waiting for his hospital results; Muriel, who's had an operation on her knee; Terry, who lost a loved one last Monday. Father Andrew mentions my dad's stroke and my chin wobbles. Even people abroad suffering earthquakes get a mention. I find it surprisingly moving. It's so easy to get caught up in my own small life. Here on my doorstep are people suffering real loss, who need me to think about them. I don't believe in God, but I do believe in the need to have people around me who care. I'm participating in something important as I pray for the wellbeing of people I don't know.

After nodding my thanks, I head back to the miniature table, but neither child is there. A squeal draws my attention to a mountain of prayer cushions, with a beanbag balanced on top. I spot my son the second he throws himself at it, whooping in delight.

"I told you God would tell you off," his sister announces smugly. Hiding my smile, I start picking up cushions. "It smells nice in here," she continues, drifting past, not helping.

"Grab some cushions, can you?" I ask as I scrabble around on the floor.

"I didn't put them there," she replies archly. "I didn't want to come in the first place. It's child abuse making us go to church." Rolling my eyes, I turn to see my son back at the little table, pretending to read his book.

Holiday Baggage

We're on our family holiday in August, so meditating is taking a back seat. I've only managed 30 minutes here and there in amongst long car drives and trips to the beach. Father John sends recordings of the Morning Office again, but it's strange listening to the shuffling feet and tinny organ.

Ed takes the children out, promising to text when 30 minutes is up. Sitting on our balcony, my mind is turbulent as I slip on the headset. I'm worrying about the scratch on our hire car and where we're going for supper. I repeat *"Maranatha"*, but the word gets lost in amongst the mental clutter.

My phone buzzes with an apology that 35 minutes have passed. I'm surprised, pulled out of my meditation with a sense of levity. I feel smoothed out. While I am still struggling to find a connection to God, the mantra itself has spring-cleaned my mind. Scoring the meditation afterwards, my finger tracks my experiences on my phone screen. Surprisingly, emotion is high, but the words I write are "contentment" and "clarity".

John Main pioneered the mantra element of Christian meditation, insisting it was a daily practice and not a technique to pick up or put down. He learned meditation from an Indian monk when he was working in Malaya in the fifties. Experiencing the benefit of silent contemplation, he incorporated this into his own Christian practice. It was only when he was asked to give this up, after becoming a Benedictine monk, that he discovered Christianity's meditation ancestry. From the third century onwards, groups of Christians known as the Desert Mothers and Fathers began to separate from society to live in the deserts of Egypt, Palestine and Syria. Practising kindness and a form of silent contemplation called "Hesychasm" (also considered a "way of life") they lived frugally. Main was encouraged to set up the first Christian Meditation Centre in Ealing Abbey in London in 1975. The WCCM (World Community for Christian Meditation) itself was then founded in 1991 in Washington, USA by Laurence Freeman, John Main's successor.

Silence is at the core of Christian meditation and, indeed, Centering Prayer. My days are full of noise – buses trundling past, the whoosh of a tap, the scream of a coffee grinder. Pure silence, I am starting to understand, is much underrated. This isn't the lull between conversation, or an early morning somnolence. This is a different state entirely, an utter stillness going beyond awareness of thought to a place where I hear myself.

Reginald is Dead

Having dropped my son off at a friend's house with a cursory hug, I'm greeted at the church door by John. He's dressed in traditional long black robes and looks rather dapper. I'm a little on guard as he appears to be standing on some kind of ceremony. All is revealed when I spot a coffin behind him. This is not normal. A coffin. Following my gaze, John explains that Reginald will be joining us today. I know my jaw is slack, so I pull myself together.

"Is he, you know, in there?" I ask in a small voice.

"Oh yes," John replies, whispering back. "That's the point. He'll be part of the office. We're wishing him on his way. The funeral is this afternoon."

My heart is beating. We have a dead person in the room. I have only ever seen a coffin once before and that was awful. Death scares me.

Yet when the singing starts, I'm less distracted by Reginald in his wooden box. I'm glad he's here and that we're looking after him. I'm comforted by how much people care. I'm happy to be part of – whatever this is.

After the office, I pull John to one side, confiding that my request for my children to help scatter my aunt's ashes is being met with resistance. He nods, sighing that many people think death should be hidden away and, waving at the coffin, that it's old-fashioned to allow the deceased to spend a night in church. Recalling my earlier reaction to Reginald I feel a nub of shame. John's right.

My family believe scattering ashes would be too upsetting for my children. I think they fear their own reactions more. Explaining grief to a child is complicated, but that doesn't mean we shouldn't do it. My son had a beautiful relationship with his great aunt. The day she played football in the park, tackling him with a fervour that had her dog yapping in delight, is a memory he'll never forget. She was nearly eighty years old, but she said it was the most fun she'd ever had. I don't think anyone in my son's life has impressed him quite like she did that day.

Death gets treated like an adult secret, not suitable for the eyes and ears of children. Ed and I have a responsibility to allow our children to know death fully, to look into the discomfort death brings and talk about it. I don't want my children to be scared of sadness, of tears, of showing emotions they can't label. They should have the opportunity to say goodbye to my son's football-playing pal, but I know I will lose this battle.

Harvest Festival

None of us got to scatter my aunt's ashes in the end, but my frustration propelled me to open up to my dad. Because of his stroke, he struggled to speak, but his eyes told me he heard every word. While one door closed, another inched open. Mortality is tracing a finger over our lives, reminding us of our frailty. Illness is once again forcing us to reach out to each other in new ways. Worry has been taking a toll. My sleep is disrupted with 5am wake-ups most mornings. I don't admit this to Barbara, worried it might affect the second part of our sleep hypnosis experiment, due to start in a month's time.

And yet, in amongst the high emotion and confusion, Christian meditation has provided space to breathe and a new arena in which to think. Even though thinking is not the goal. The Ma-ra-na-tha mantra is melodic and slow, evoking the same feelings of expansion and creativity I experienced during TM. At times, it's felt liberating.

The school holidays are a unique time. Time for family and activity, but fraught with spiralling routines. Bedtimes got later, so evenings got shorter. Child-free time became scarce. The 30 minutes of calm I've snatched in hotel rooms, by poolsides and at home have been a gift.

Now, routine has been put back in place, like a police cordon. School has resumed, along with homework and the shortening days. Aware that this phase of my experiment is coming to an end, I feel the need to try harder. I know I have avoided going to the Sunday services, legitimizing my absence by the erratic nature of the holidays. With our weekends freeing up, I find some time.

It's a grim September Sunday morning when my daughter and I arrive at Saint John's. There's an air of joviality and, I notice, a strange proliferation of leopard skin and black patent boots. Picking up the order of service, my daughter is outraged when she reads that the proceedings will last an hour. A procession of priests arrive, wearing white and green robes. I spot John as he traverses the rim of the church, swinging a metal globe spewing smoky incense. I'm fascinated by the pomp and ceremony and realize this is a special event. Harvest Festival, the leaflet says quite clearly on the front.

A party of ruddy-faced priests (visiting clergy perhaps as I don't recognize them) start the proceedings. Looking at the gold objects and the huge open Bible on the altar, I start to sweat. I know I am going to Get Things Wrong.

We spring up with everyone else and sit down at the rustle of clothing. My daughter frowns at all the singing and looks embarrassed when asked to shake hands with the ladies behind. "Peace be with you," they say, looking her squarely in the eye. I wonder if I have a sign on my back saying: "Not a Bloody Clue". Yet for all the confusing rituals, the atmosphere is friendly and the sound of song uplifting. When it's time for the Eucharist, we watch the congregation line up.

"Mummy, I think we should go up," my daughter whispers, nudging me.

"No," I growl.

"Why?" she persists. "We're the only ones who aren't!" She's right, but I am frozen by the fear of Doing The Wrong Thing. I stand rigid until she pulls my hand, dragging me into the queue. Father Daniel is handing out little wafers and looks bemused to see me.

"Can you?" he whispers. Can I what? Are the wafers not gluten free? I don't understand and people are fidgeting, so rather than duck out, I mumble "Yes?" After taking the wafer and then a sip of wine, I hurry back to my seat.

When everyone has sat down, a rustling of plastic carrier bags fills the room. I groan. Sainsbury's Bags for Life sit bulging with tins and packets of biscuits underneath the altar. Another thing we didn't know about.

We scarper as soon as the service finishes, jumping straight onto a bus outside. I'd promised that my daughter could spend her pocket money afterwards, convincing myself this wasn't bribery – which of course it was. On the bus, I mention the sermon. The theme was our obsession with wealth and consumerism and our desire to constantly seek more. The question posed was: can we be happy with the basics? The priest had cited a passage from the Bible: "Why are you anxious about clothing? Consider the lilies of the field, how they grow: they neither toil nor spin, yet I tell you, even Solomon in all his glory was not arrayed like one of these." (Matthew 6:28–29)

It was a simple question, but given we were on our way to spend money on glittery, overpriced tat that my daughter didn't need, the sermon niggled me. My daughter has other ideas. This money represents freedom. The tat may seem meaningless, but for her, it's wrapped up with choice, independence and street-cred.

Helping a ten-year-old recognize over-consumption is a challenge, given the consumer-culture we live in. We're encouraged to crave things. We want novelty. We want the stuff we buy to prop up the image of who we believe we are. It's an endless cycle. I got the sermon, it segues beautifully with an article by Rob Walker, former "Consumed" columnist for the *New York Times* on how Buddhist teachings can help us see this craving and realize, like all things, its impermanence. In an online dialogue with Bobbi Patterson, a professor at Emory University, whose research encompasses both Christianity and Tibetan Buddhism, they agreed that Buddhism and the act of mindfulness offer a circuit breaker. The sermon today has done the same thing. It's given me time (and space) to consider not what we were about to buy, but why. It's making me think differently. Seeing the anticipation on my daughter's face though, I know she didn't go to church to earn this shopping trip. She went to church to spend time with me.

Piling into the house three hours later, my daughter regurgitates the mornings events, interspersed with what we had for lunch and what she bought.

"Church was boring. I love these sparkly headphones; they're going to be so useful. Then at church we had a biscuit and Mummy had wine, but I just had juice," she rattles on, as everyone tries to keep up.

"What?" Ed says sharply, interrupting her flow. Something inside me dies.

"Nobody tells you what to do – or what not to do!" I bluster.

"You only take the sacrament if you've been confirmed," Ed says slowly. "And I don't think you have been?"

"No," I admit weakly. And then Ed is laughing. "Don't worry, love," he chuckles. "I'm sure they'll let you back in."

Saving Grace

My daughter and I try church again two weeks later, this time armed with more knowledge after Father John filled me in on some of the protocols. Hurrying in, we plonk ourselves down. It's a large, seemingly older congregation today, with a number of formally dressed women wearing colourful headscarves.

A visiting Father from Africa delivers a fierce sermon, explaining the message is metaphorical and not to be interpreted literally: "If your right eye causes you to stumble, gouge it out and throw it away. It is better for you to lose one part of your body than for your whole body to be thrown into hell." (Matthew 5:29)

Wondering if the topic is alarming my daughter, I'm relieved to see her faraway expression. The visiting Father explains this text simply means we should notice if we are thinking sinful thoughts and nip them in the bud.

He tells the story of a woman who'd asked him why she still prayed, when her prayers hadn't been answered (a reasonable question, I thought). To this he responded that she should keep praying, because the answer may not come in a form she expected. I find myself agreeing. Sometimes the answer doesn't come in a form we welcome either. At the beginning of this meditation experiment, I had a set of questions too. Some of the answers (or rather, the insights) I've received were not what I wanted to hear. My impatience is one – and that sneaky judgement (that hides behind justification) is another. Then there's the sense that "I'm doing okay" (just as long as someone around me is doing worse).

The counter to these unwelcome insights is knowing I am not alone, and compassion, as always, is the remedy. If nothing else, this experiment has shown me I can do something about these very human quirks. Shame researcher Brené Brown sums this up in her book *Daring Greatly: How the Courage to Be Vulnerable Transforms the Way We Live, Love, Parent and Lead:* "... research tells us that we judge people in areas where we're vulnerable to shame, especially picking folks who are doing worse than we're doing".

Through this meditation road-trip, I'd hoped to gain mental calm, reduce my reactivity and feel more connected to others. Yet for my hard work, all I've got are uncomfortable, if honest, truths. Truths that had I not discovered for myself, I would have rejected outright.

So I understand this Christian message, but it's the delivery that bothers me. I don't think you can tell an insight to another person. We have to peel back the layers and expose it for ourselves. Perhaps that's what the process of praying is all about. This makes me want to understand how praying differs to meditation. In an interview with Oprah, Deepak Chopra, the well-known spiritual teacher and author, says: "Prayer is us speaking to God and meditation is allowing the spirit to speak to you." Chopra explains that meditation, in different forms, exists within all religions, but does not interfere with or negatively influence those religious beliefs.

My resistance to praying comes from the belief that I have to buy into the concept of God. God implies an external focus and a kind of exchange. If you ask God for certain things, you might get them, if you're chosen or lucky. Meditation, on the other hand, appears more internally focused and non-transactional. I'm not asking anyone else to help me; only I can take responsibility for my life. While perhaps this oversimplifies things, it does highlight why I chose Christian meditation (and not formal prayer) as my in-road to religion.

Interestingly, Cynthia Bourgeault, an American Episcopal priest and writer, has another view of prayer, suggesting there is no form of exchange at all: "Prayer is not a request for God's favours ... Genuine prayer is based on recognizing the Origin of all that exists, and opening ourselves to it."

This sounds closer to my own experience of meditation, which makes sense as Bourgeault is an advocate of Centering Prayer – with its many similarities to Christian meditation.

The sermon over, it's time for communion. My daughter and I don't go up this time, but sit while others pass by. Even though John has explained there's a way I can receive communion without being confirmed, I wonder if other church newbies know this.

And yet, all that aside, I do like it here. Behind the glances is a warm curiosity. If I dig deep enough, I see that by just being here, I am doing work. Good work. I recognize how perfectionism has been in the shadows, covert in amongst my irritation and defensiveness. I have to show my daughter that it's okay to get things wrong – that we can laugh about it and learn something new.

In Good Faith

When I dialled in to Christian meditation, I ran the risk of separating "technique" from belief. Would Christian meditation only be effective if I engaged on a deeper level – as a life practice (as John Main suggests)? This is back to Father John's original question: "Can I follow a religious practice if I don't have faith?"

The answer is yes, and no.

Did this technique calm my mind? Yes. Could it, with time, bring me closer to God? Perhaps, but only if I reframe what I believe God to be. If God is something in me, rather than out there, then maybe.

Any unity I've experienced has come from the holding space of silence. In silence, the truth echoes and cannot be ignored. In this way, Christian meditation has provided a positive experience, but has provoked difficult questions. I've learned that discomfort is my signpost. Eight weeks following a religious practice ignited fears, but at the same time connected me to my community (as I suspected it would). But it also opened up debates about death and life that I wouldn't have otherwise had. In Buddhism, the Sangha is a spiritual support network that keeps Buddha's teachings on track, providing guidance for practitioners. Stephen Cope writes, in his book, *Yoga and the Quest for the True Self*, that we all seek "transformational spaces". While these don't need to be explicitly spiritual, they do need to offer refuge and safety with opportunities for experimentation. In this chapter of my experiment, that support system has been my local church. While at times this has felt unfamiliar, the church and its pastoral team have been utterly supportive. I wasn't expecting that.

The bottom line is that I put more effort in and got more out of a practice that was offered within a supportive framework with regular meet-ups. By traversing these different spiritual paths, I have come to see the importance of those around me and how vital a spiritual foundation is for any meditation practice. Christianity overlaps the teachings of loving-kindness and has reminded me of the importance of people. It forced me to confront my own fears and biases in order to open up to myself and the two small people who watch every move I make.

CHAPTER 9
A SLEEP EXPERIMENT PART 2: HYPNOSIS

October 2018

It's my daughter's eleventh birthday, so I only Skype Dr Dyan Haspel-Johnson (the American hypnotherapist I met earlier this year) after the well-wishers have stopped calling and Ed has shooed the children upstairs.

Dyan has already sent me her online sleep package – a series of seven recordings designed to combat issues such as waking in the night and getting back to sleep (sleep is one of her specialist areas). I will follow these recordings daily while wearing the EEG headset for the second half of the self-hypnosis sleep experiment (the "active" part), due to start in two weeks' time. As Barbara and I expected, a month of mindful breathing meditation did not stop me having a sleepless night before the first school talk back in July (the "control" part of the experiment). We are all curious to see how Dyan's self-hypnosis programme might impact my sleep now. Dyan and I have decided to check in today before I start using her recordings, but also for a friendly catch up.

Jumping from Christian meditation back into self-hypnosis has left me unsettled. Ping-ponging from technique to technique for nearly two years has become stressful. I don't want to admit it, but I am sick of wearing the headset. With each practice uncovering more and more insights, I am feeling overwhelmed. Finding time to process the truths I am discovering about myself is proving difficult at a time when my family is dealing with serious illness. My sleep is worse than ever right now, having deteriorated during the first part of our hypnosis experiment. When, twenty minutes into our call, my voice has risen and my legs are shaking, I admit my poor mental state. Pressure for this sleep experiment to yield successful results is putting me under enormous strain.

"I see that," Dyan says kindly. "The researcher in you wants results, but your welfare is more important right now."

Welfare. There it is again. I hear Father John's question "Who's looking after you?" loop silently in and around our conversation.

"I'm exhausted, but I want to finish the sleep experiment. How will I prove self-hypnosis can help me sleep better before the Cambridge talk if I give up?"

"Here's the thing," Dyan says slowly. "You clearly have a lot on your plate, but I also think your unconscious mind is getting a different message from your conscious mind. These two parts of you are in conflict. Your unconscious mind is thinking that the worse your sleep is before the night of the Cambridge talk, the more significant the results will be."

"But why would I sabotage my own experiment?"

Dyan laughs. "Why does the unconscious mind sabotage our sleep in the first place? It may not make sense to your rational, conscious mind, but it may make complete sense to your unconscious mind, which is more concerned with your desire for success and achieving the results you want." And there it is. That is exactly what is happening. My unconscious mind, driven by emotional impulses, is skewing things. As acceptance dawns on me, I realize that along with the need to succeed, there is that old familiar fear of failure. Combined with worry about my dad's health and my lack of opportunity to process everything the different practices have uncovered, it's not surprising I feel this way. As my unconscious mind's priority is safety, these old fears have been triggered. This time I am fearing I will fail the sleep experiment.

Dyan is an expert on diagnosing sleep issues, so it's not surprising she can see the mental quagmire I am in. It's only now, talking about it, that I can see how complex sleep problems can be. Even my "assumption" that the first experiment wouldn't work was a form of hypnotic suggestion in itself. I encouraged my unconscious to rebel. The horrible irony that an experiment designed to help me sleep has potentially caused sleeplessness is a smack in the face. It is also enlightening.

At the end of the call, Dyan and I decide sleep is more important than any experiment. I'm starting her sleep programme now and will spend the next two weeks calming my nervous system and getting back on track. As Barbara and I are investigating sleeplessness triggered by the fear of public speaking, it is the quality of my sleep during the week before the Cambridge talk that will provide the most important data. Getting my sleep back on track now won't impact that.

Going Under

A week after my call to Dyan I'm sat on my sofa wearing the EEG headset and following her sleep hypnosis programme. I'm not exactly sleepy, but my focus is high and somehow more animated – like a fleeting out-of-body moment. Listening to Dyan's recordings, I hear the mechanics – the spaces between words into which my mind dips. Dyan's sleep recordings employ descriptive language that follow the architecture of sleep, how the brain operates within this relinquishing state. They are deeply priming, bridging meaning with resonance. Like Jane, Dyan's words are her work.

"You have nothing to worry about," her voice soothes. "Nothing to fear." My attention zones into vibrations, a certain syntax within the syllables. Whoosh, my mind curves back, releasing again. Hypnosis is a language within a language.

Each session varies. In some, I transition quickly into a deep trance, losing sense of space and time. The sessions often end without me knowing, but even if my conscious mind drifted, I sense deeper parts of my psyche were listening.

Talk #2: Cambridge University Mindfulness Society, November 2018

I'm sitting in the EEG lab at Addenbrooke's Hospital with Barbara in mid-November having just finished one of our meditation marathons. During this session (the fourth we've done) we have recorded my brain data as I practised each meditation method one after the other. The purpose of this exercise, which has taken six hours to complete, is to capture high quality EEG data in a lab setting. This means Barbara has complex data to compare alongside the more abundant, but less detailed, headset data.

"Oh God," I moan. "I look like I've been attacked by an octopus."

"They'll go," Barbara mumbles, peering at the sucker marks the electrodes have left on my forehead. I'm less convinced. I feel spaced out and I'm wondering why I agreed to schedule this EEG marathon on the day of my talk to the Cambridge University Mindfulness Society (the second and active part of my sleep experiment). Thankfully, self-hypnosis has proven a reliable ally once again. Using Dyan's sleep hypnosis programme not only improved my sleep over the weeks following our call, but helped me sleep the whole night through last night too – The Night Before The Talk. In the past, the night before an event was always my Achilles heel of sleep – often resulting in no sleep at all. While my hypnosis intervention has been a success, it feels an anti-climax. The sleep experiment has supported our hypothesis that self-hypnosis is more effective than mindfulness at avoiding sleep disruption brought on by a nerve-wracking event. Yet somehow I feel flat.

A few hours later at the talk itself, I am battling a projector that won't work while feeling tired from meditating all afternoon. Sweating a little, I'm out of my comfort zone. There are around

30 people in the audience, ranging from graduates through to faculty professors. Cracking a joke at the restless audience, I try to regain my composure. When the slides finally pop onto the screen the familiar feeling of "utter conviction" kicks in. Jane was right, this element of our original hypnotherapy has transferred to all talks. I feel a surge of confidence as I describe my project and the adventures I have had to date. It's the first time I have talked about our meditation experiment in public and questions come in thick and fast. I might be preaching to the converted (my audience is the mindfulness society after all) but they are excited to hear about my experiences using other techniques. Suddenly, one question catches me off guard.

"What's the third most impactful thing you've learned about yourself?" a mature student asks, somewhat impishly. Opening and closing my mouth, I consider the various answers I'd rehearsed, but my mind is blank. I blurt out an awful truth.

"During loving-kindness, I discovered I didn't love my kids enough." The silence that follows is devastating. Endless. I have just told a room full of strangers that I'm a bad parent.

Thankfully, a researcher approaches me after the talk explaining that her PhD focused on the use of loving-kindness as a therapeutic intervention. "What you said about your children mirrors my research. Many of our participants found it difficult to admit they felt disconnected. The fact you are aware of this is huge and probably means you got more from the practice then you realized."

Suddenly I see how far I have come. That one truth has cracked open the Teflon veneer encasing me. My defensive armour hadn't just stopped things getting to me – it had stopped things getting out. Having a glass of wine with Tristan afterwards, he looks pleased.

"An hour of questions after a talk is good, Potter. They like your project – and you."

"I guess so," I reply absent-mindedly.

"Did the self-hypnosis help?" he asks more gently.

"Yes. I slept really well last night. I didn't wake up once."

"This is good," he says, a statement rather than a question.

"Yeah, but you know, what's more important is that I've learned why my sleep became disrupted in the first place. Self-hypnosis helped me get to the core of the problem, how my fears impacted what was happening, and that's far more useful."

The End in Mind

This "experiment of two halves" has taught me more than I expected. While it corroborated how effective and targeted hypnotherapy can be in tackling specific psychological problems, such as poor sleep, it also highlighted the unpredictable nature of my unconscious mind. The work I did with Jane revealed fear as a powerful and complex emotion. I thought I was only fearful of speaking in public, but it turns out I was fearful of failure too.

The process of hypnotherapy peels back the strata of the unconscious mind, revealing buried beliefs that can cause conflict in our lives. Triggers are not always obvious and, even if I uncover one, it may disturb another, buried more deeply below. Throughout this sleep experiment I was both on the couch and in the therapist's chair. By allowing the quieter, unconscious part of me to speak I discovered a way to override the fear that was at the root of my sleeplessness. While not everyone is hypnotizable to the same extent, hypnosis can be immensely powerful if used correctly and with a qualified professional.

The hypnosis work I have done may not stick. I may have to top it up, or tweak the message in the future. I may need it to work with and clear suppressed trauma, as I did with Jane. Or I may need a different self-hypnosis programme to treat a problem without a therapeutic framework (as with Dyan's sleep self-hypnosis recordings).

Hypnotherapy has helped me understand (and respect) the unconscious parts of my mind. This home-spun experiment revealed how sensitive that can be and how I had unwittingly agitated it.

Meditating might be therapeutic at times, but self-hypnosis has been the real deal. Meditation generally activates relaxing Alpha brainwaves, yet hypnosis seems to bring about slower Theta brainwaves which occur in the deeper stage of sleep. This could be why it stands out from the meditation techniques I've experienced to date. Whatever the reason, hypnosis offered a practical application – a real tool to help combat my sleeplessness.

During this experiment, I have conditioned myself to notice – to listen in to my thoughts and feelings more keenly. However, using hypnosis as a means to access the unconscious mind is a two-way street. We must listen first – then reassure. Humans are subtle creatures and the unconscious mind needs time – and space – to tell us the stories we need to hear. It requires precise targeting and exactly the right, non-directive words to penetrate. And still, the process can be smoke and mirrors with the truth often hiding in plain sight. I have a new respect for my emotionally driven psyche. I know It Is Always Listening.

CHAPTER 10

THE SERPENT: KUNDALINI YOGA

November 2018

Through a London Kundalini Yoga Facebook group I've been introduced to Prakashjot Kaur, a teacher in South London. Kundalini Yoga (also known as KY) is a movement-based technique that binds the spiritual with the physical. Barbara and I have agreed to include a gentle movement-based practice as we can capture EEG data as long as I don't move too energetically and keep my eyes closed. She's interested to compare my experience traces from a physically challenging practice with more static, inwards-focused practices.

On a rainy November day, a tall, smiling woman wearing jeans and a white jumper arrives at my house. Prakashjot, whose real name is Patrycja Stawicka, was born in Poland, and trained at Amrit Nam Sarovar Kundalini Yoga School in London. She teaches Yogi Bhajan's streamlined form of KY, introduced to the West in the late 1960s.

Like Zen, KY can be considered a lifestyle system, rather than a physical practice. This is where yoga isn't "yoga". This word, dating back to the Vedas (the early Indian scriptures), implies an all-encompassing programme incorporating breathing, physical movement and contemplation. I'd always seen high-street yoga as a lifestyle choice – a form of exercise that increases flexibility and tones the body. While I've felt smug after a class, I've never found it particularly spiritual. KY seems different. This yoga system puts as much emphasis on the internal manifestations as on the physical effort.

Yogi Bhajan, born Harbhajan Singh Puri in Pakistan in 1929, had an unusual childhood. Educated at an all-girl's Catholic school, he became a spiritual master by sixteen. A keen athlete, he studied economics at university and used yoga as both a spiritual and physical strengthening tool. It was on a visit to California in 1968 that he saw how ancient teachings might benefit American disenfranchised youth. Bhajan established the 3HO Foundation, the Healthy, Happy, Holy Organization, melding Sikhism and the once-secret practice of Kundalini Yoga with a drug-free, healthy-living ethos. His movement took off and spread across Europe and beyond.

I don't admit to Prakashjot that I have a hangover. My mind is thick as she explains how KY has been shown to be effective in treating depression, anxiety, addiction and physical pain. I hope it'll ease the thumping in my head.

Prakashjot sits cross-legged as we talk about chakras. We have seven main auric hubs, ranging from the crown chakra at the top of the head to the base chakra at the bottom of the spine. I've always found the concept of energy centres ambiguous, mainly because chakras are not physical entities. However, I did follow a daily hour-long chakra meditation shortly after my illness. During this guided meditation, which required me to visualize each chakra in turn, I felt a unique flow of vibrations. The earthy red of my base chakra and halcyon blue of my throat chakra (experienced only within my mind's eye) had a symbiotic connection to my health. At a time when my colour vision was still recovering, I felt connected to myself in profoundly new ways.

Prakashjot suggests she teaches me the Ten Bodies – a philosophical system that targets the body and psyche in an interconnecting way. Yogi Bhajan taught that we have not one human body but ten, made up of the physical body plus three "mental" bodies and six "energy" bodies. These are the:

1. Soul body
2. Negative mind
3. Positive mind
4. Neutral mind
5. Physical body
6. Arcline
7. Auric body
8. Pranic body
9. Subtle body
10. Radiant body

Prakashjot asks if I'm feeling strong. Does she know I have a hangover? Rolling my mat out, she suggests we try the arcline today. I put on my EEG headset and show Prakashjot how it will record my brain's activity during the practice. I'm actually trying out a new headset today as my old one stopped working. After a call from Barbara, the guys at Dreem have sent me an updated model.

The arcline is the energy body that represents the sixth chakra (the purple third eye chakra or "Ājñā", located in the middle of the forehead). This represents inner wisdom and the connection between our ability to see the inner and outer worlds. This is manifested by a halo that reaches from ear lobe to ear lobe. In KY the arcline is believed to connect to the pituitary gland, regulating the nervous system and is associated with intuition and perceptivity.

Prakashjot chants the Adi Mantra (one of the core KY mantras), *Ong Namo Guru Dev Namo*, then recites, "I bow to the creative wisdom, I bow to the divine teacher within," three times. This is the tuning in that precedes all KY sessions and is believed to link us to Yogi Bhajan himself.

I sit cross-legged in Easy Pose ("Sukhasana"), raising my left arm out to the side, slightly bent, with my hand facing down and level with my heart. My right arm is raised to 60 degrees, in a kind of salute. This is why I need to be strong. Locking my stomach muscles to keep my back straight, I wait. Prakashjot instructs me to breathe in and out for equal counts, then to increase the out-breath over time.

The pain starts almost immediately, intensifying into a fiery ball. Thirty years ago I was kicked in the back by a horse and I can feel the exact spot right now – a corkscrew slowly winding into my spine. It's unbearable. I let a long breath out, loosening the knot, but can only muster a short breath back in. My ribs refuse to expand. After around three minutes I wonder if this is some kind of test. I can't see Prakashjot, but tinny music is playing from her phone. My mind is empty, save for a huge red flashing light of pain.

When I can bear it no longer, the pain lets up – as if the light ran out of battery. The second I acknowledge this release, the pain returns. *How long will this last?* Prakashjot's alarm bleeps and I slump gratefully to the floor.

"Eleven minutes," she grins. I hated every single second yet I instinctively know it was good for me. Flexing my back, it seems to have held up better than I thought. And I've totally forgotten my hangover.

Next, Prakashjot teaches me the Root Lock. This term refers to the "mulbandh" which is used to switch on the muscles from your perineum to your navel. This powerful contraction of muscles is commonly applied at the end of exercises and meditations to "seal in" the healing effects of the practice. We breath in and out three times together, releasing our breath after 20 seconds.

Kundalini Yoga is strange, otherworldly even. This is not the yoga I was expecting. We haven't finished – we have another "kriya" (the Sanskrit word for the poses). This involves me sitting with my palms together, my left thumb over my right, pointing forwards – like I'm shooting a gun. I am to whistle my favourite tune. I haven't whistled in years. Floundering for inspiration, I choose Happy Birthday as my son is learning to play it on the piano. I feel silly whistling. Really silly. A few minutes in, my lips turn to rubber. Whistling is meant to stimulate my sixth chakra, but I feel self-conscious and want to laugh.

I'm aware of how my body is kept rigid all day long – stooped over the sink, hunched over a computer, bending to hold my son's hand. I never move into these unusual positions, let alone stay in them. My body feels different. I am being forced to examine my relationship to my corporeal self – to pain. My mouth is dry and puckered – I think about which parts of my lips and my tongue are making me whistle. If Prakashjot wanted to make me sensorily aware of every part of my body, then she's succeeding.

Kriyas are meant to do this. Each sequence of moves is part of an encompassing system pulsing energy through the body. A kriya can be an individual pose or a combination of poses. They are about creating angles and tension, and aim to purify or readjust the balance between the five elements. Karta Singh, Prakashjot's teacher, says, "If kriyas provide the alphabet, then the body is the expression of the language that it creates. We get locked in an emotional cave, so when we move through a kriya, the energy opens the door of that cave balancing the body and mind."

After a blessed ten minutes of "Shavasana" or Corpse Pose lying on my back, we are done and I remove the headset wondering if it captured the pain I felt. Thanking Prakashjot we agree I will wear the EEG headset to practise the poses each day this week along with scoring each meditation. For the next two months, we'll work our way through the Ten Bodies, seeing the effects each has upon me.

Snakes and Ladders

Hatha yoga influences the physical practice of KY; however, the kriyas also employ breathing exercises (pranayama), mantras (repeated phrases), "mudras" (hand positions) and contemplation. Along with regulating our nervous system and improving wellbeing, this practice can also evoke a Kundalini awakening. Although rare, this involves a serpent-like spirit, or inner female energy known as Shakti, unfolding from the base of the spine and rising up through the body. Kundalini can rise at any time, not necessarily as a result of a spiritual practice. Anecdotal descriptions describe people being taken over, spontaneously moving into unusual yogic poses.

Hannah, a German researcher, experienced an awakening during a yoga teacher-training course. Lying on the floor, she dissolved into the ground. "I was everything and nothing," she says. "I heard voices, but I was at one with the universe." When Hannah "returned" to her body, she felt newborn, and highly sensitized with no negative thoughts. Kundalini awakenings don't happen to everyone and there is much unknown – but this a powerful phenomenon.

A Pain in the Neck

Dragging out my mat several days after meeting Prakashjot, I can't hold the first arcline "salute" pose for more than seven minutes without dropping my arms. This kriya is pushing me toward my limits.

Moving on to the whistling pose, I'm bored of Happy Birthday so I try a Christmas carol instead. Jingle Bells proves considerably easier than Silent Night. Having practised these poses for four days, I'm fed up. I stop whistling mid-flow and thoughts rush into the gap. *Has Ed booked the roofers? Did I take chicken out of the freezer for dinner?*

I'm distracted today. My back aches, I've got cramp in my knees, and behind the roar of my thoughts I can hear the washing machine bleeping to be emptied. I don't want to empty it as that means walking past the cupboard door that's hanging off its hinges. Another thing to do. My mind is rejecting this practice because of the physical discomfort it's provoking. It would be much easier to give up – but I don't.

The next morning I wake with a stiff neck. After showering, I can't lift my arm high enough to put my towel on the hook. This is annoying, but I don't dwell on it. I'm tired. My sleep has improved after using self-hypnosis, but it's still up and down and easily triggered.

I have an aversion to the physical requirements of this practice, and that aversion is making me irritable. Yet I don't have to feel hacked off. KY is forging a bridge back to what I learned in MBCT and how I reacted to my injured foot, nearly two years ago. Back then, I was irritated by every spasm of pain. Now I am less distracted by it. Dave was right; pain can be interpreted as a sensation − a form of energy and not a thing. Kabat-Zinn, who pioneered MBSR, believes we all have huge biological capacities, not just within our (possibly limited) cognitive framework, but in ways we don't always understand. This other form of intelligence is a kind of awareness that goes much deeper than what we consider to be our anatomical body. As a Westerner, I haven't experienced much awareness-training and I now understand just how much of a training it really is.

Regardless of higher forms of intelligence, scientific studies have investigated the use of KY to treat specific psychiatric disorders, such as OCD, phobias and learning disorders. One paper suggested the kriyas could be used prescriptively as a form of treatment (though it is worth noting that the study was run by a student and devotee of Yogi Bhajan).

Back to Front

I'm glued to *Killing Eve* on BBC One. Ed and I have been following this series avidly, but he's out tonight. As the credits roll I realize I haven't moved in hours. Trying to get up − I can't. My back has seized up. Closing my eyes, I know what this is. When my back goes, it goes, leaving me immobilized for weeks. Inching my bottom toward the edge of the sofa I attempt to get one knee onto the floor. Every move sends shards of pain up my spine. Why is our sofa the most dangerous place in our house? Forty minutes later, Ed finds me on all fours, an arthritic gecko, stuck on the bottom stair.

"Oh dear," he says, chuckling and smelling of beer.

"Bloody help, will you," I snap, but Ed is laughing at my ridiculous pose and his humour is infectious. But laughing hurts.

"Your back hasn't gone in years," he points out, helping me up the stairs. "Why now?"

I know why. This Kundalini Yoga and its impossibly hard poses. Lying in bed, I wait for anti-inflammatories to kick in, mulling over what appears to be horrible déja vu. Is this a physical injury or is my body reacting in an extraordinarily rebellious way? Is my body both assailant and healer? I imagine how unscientific this all sounds, but there's so much going on beneath the surface that I just don't understand.

Eastbourne

A week later we decide to have a weekend by the sea. My frozen back only lasted two days, easing up almost immediately. This was a surprise as it has never recovered this fast before. Quizzing Prakashjot, she believes the freezing was a psychosomatic event with unconscious issues manifesting into the physical world. Part of me believes her.

Battling the winds, we drag our suitcases through Eastbourne's drab town centre reaching our hotel on the beach front. The children want fish and chips, but I can't miss my practice so I banish them downstairs with iPads first.

Prakashjot has taught me the awakening of the Ten Bodies. Slipping on the EEG cap I start what is a very physical practice. There are fifteen different kriyas, which can be held for up to three minutes each. I opt for two minutes. Sitting in Ego Eradicator Pose (with my arms held out at 60 degrees) my mind travels. I'm on edge, tired at the end of a long week and worry takes over my body, making my legs tremble. As I hold each pose, the physicality of the practice soon separates my anxiety from me. Forcing my attention onto my body distracts and soothes my mind. I've discovered a space that exists between an event and my reaction to it. That space is elastic and can be stretched out. KY helps me squeeze into that gap and see my worry as it occurs in real-time. Of course, the notion of "pausing" came up in MBCT, but actually finding my pause button has taken effort. Intellectually understanding this was one thing, living it is another. Connecting to my body in the KY practice helps me link everything I have learned together.

After dinner, we trudge through the damp streets, ignoring premature tinsel and cardboard Santas. At the pier, the children play the penny arcades and buy colourful sticks of rock that I know they won't eat. I'm not fazed. I recognize my previous elevated state of anxiety only because now, anchored to the present moment, I am no longer in it.

Range Rover Rage

It's late November and my son and I are driving home from football in heavy traffic. Pulling out in front of a white Range Rover, it looms behind us. We tut tut at the car's unnecessary revving, but it doesn't let up. Turning into our road it follows us, staying dangerously close. As I slow to manoeuvre into our driveway, the Range Rover roars past sounding its horn. I hit my horn too, inflamed by this obnoxious behaviour.

"It was a mum," my son says pragmatically, as I turn the engine off. "There was a kid in the back."

"Oh," I say, considering my next move carefully. My son is quicker. "You used your horn, Mummy. You've got anger issues."

As my mouth opens and closes, I am furious that I'm in this situation. She was the one driving dangerously.

"You're meant to sound the horn as a warning," I say unconvincingly. My son doesn't buy this. On the walk to school the next morning, it comes up again. This time I admit to my anger, my uncontrolled reaction – telling him I was wrong. I need to be responsible for my own reactions if I am to teach him how to control his own. I feel ashamed and annoyed that I have not come as far as I had thought.

A Higher Bar

I am learning Laya yoga kriya this week. The word "laya" refers to a suspension from the ordinary world, which I hope will remove me from my living room into some kind of distant, pleasant state of being.

The purpose of this kriya is to access one's higher consciousness – that ambiguous state that many spiritual teachings talk of. On a day-to-day basis, we all operate within our lower consciousness. This is necessary in order to get things done. This part of the mind is responsible for our reactivity, behaving aggressively, blaming others and for seeing the world through a self-absorbed lens (amongst other things). Most of us have rare moments, normally when we have time on our hands, when we experience a quiescence. Here we catch a glimpse of our "higher minds", the realm of imagination, empathy and impartial judgement, where our ego is sleeping and we can approach life with a ubiquitous perspective. In this state we're able to stop seeing the world in terms of how it affects us. We see, with clarity, how others are often victims of their reactive, unconscious and conscious minds. The idea of a higher consciousness dates back to Vedic spirituality, but it's also a recognized scientific state (seen as a heightened state of self-awareness, deeper insight and increased metacognitive abilities). Finding an in-road to my own higher consciousness is basically the modus operandi of my project. This, I realize, is the place where compassion lives.

In the middle of this pose it dawns on me that by focusing on my body, my attention is drawn to parts of myself that are normally hidden. The wounds, the injustices of the past spark when I touch them. I'm getting a wider perspective, an increased meta awareness.

Breath practices are integral to Kundalini Yoga. The Breath of Fire is one, but I've found this difficult to learn, although the benefits are believed to be many. It can release toxins, expand lung capacity, rebalance the sympathetic and parasympathetic nervous systems, increase endurance, reduce addictive impulses and boost the immune system. Breathing practices help reduce emotional reactivity and the Laya meditation has breath at its core. By blocking my right nostril with the thumb of my right hand and breathing long, deep breaths through my left nostril, I focus on my third eye chakra for two minutes. Found in the middle of the forehead, this is believed to be a gateway to these higher states.

A week later I meet Prakashjot again. With Christmas around the corner my worry levels have spiked. I haven't ordered a turkey and the roof still isn't fixed. I hope this new kriya will calm me.

Prakashjot is teaching me the kriya for the negative mind. This is the part of the brain that cannot stop itself reacting negatively to everything it encounters, as its goal is to protect. The negative, positive and neutral minds work together, but when they're out of sync, we become anxious, fearful and self-doubting. The negative mind (also known as the "second body") relates to the second chakra, representing creativity and sexuality. This meditation should clear my mind of unwanted negative thoughts and rebalance things.

We go through a number of kriyas until we get to the meditation. Prakashjot explains that I am to allow my thoughts to flow. Any statement that comes up must be reversed. Thoughts can be prescriptive to begin with – for example, I am Vanessa, I am not Vanessa. I'm sitting on my mat, I'm not sitting on my mat, and so on. I love this! My mind latches onto this theme immediately and carries itself off. Five minutes later when I stop, I feel woozy, but strangely still.

The nagging voice inside my head was very loud today, repeating things in the hope I would believe some of what it said. We all have a self-referential part of our mind, but how much we hear depends on our level of self-awareness. Meditating today has helped me see this voice for what it is. A barometer, and a guardian. Most of the phrases I reversed today were negatives that became positives.

A Roof Over Our Heads

It's the week before Christmas and the roof repairs are finally underway. Even though they were warned not to, the children couldn't leave the scaffolding alone and my daughter has hurt her back.

At the hospital she snuggles up, unsettled by memories of my illness six years ago. When we leave after being given the all clear, she's subdued. "Thanks for not being cross, Mum."

"These things happen," I smile. "Am I less cross these days?"

"Yes," she replies slowly. "Not like when you bought the gingerbread man."

I know what she's referring to. Two years ago, we'd been late for a hospital appointment and struggling to park, and I'd shouted at her. Afterwards, I'd felt so bad that I'd bought her a gingerbread man to say sorry. I squeeze her hand now and say sorry again. This experiment doesn't just impact me, it impacts her too.

Next morning my daughter joins me for a practice. This is a trade-off. If she does these exercises, I will look at cellphones with her later. We both know she isn't getting one, but it's part of the deal.

Prakashjot, has taught me Nabhi kriya, which focuses on strengthening the abdominal area. Wearing her pyjamas, my daughter is floppy, putting in minimal effort. I explain that the third exercise requires us to clasp our knees to our chests. This is supposed to eliminate gas and relax the heart. We giggle, which of course has the predicted effect. This makes us giggle all the more. I'm not sure if it's the practice, or the fact we are practising together, but my heart is bursting. Our legs bump into each other and I squeeze her arm. As I make contact, I'm reminded of how soft her skin is. This is time together, but it's also closeness. Suddenly I see. These practices haven't just highlighted what I'm doing wrong, but what I am doing right.

When we chant the Adi Mantra at the end of the session, we are out of tune, but our feet are touching. "If that's meditating Mum, it's lovely." She smiles. Of course, in her next breath she mentions the phone. Cuddling at bedtime later, she's disappointed I didn't buy one. "You don't trust me," she says. "You're too young," I reply. Downstairs I replay the conversation. A year ago I would have left this, maybe talked again in the morning. This time I go back up and in the darkness, lightly touch her cheek. "There's something you need to know," I whisper. "I do trust you completely. I just need to protect you."

"I know, Mummy," she sighs sleepily. "I love you."

Compassion is always at my fingertips. The bonding I've just experienced felt like a lifetime collapsed into a few seconds. Similarly, when I lost my sight, my consultant had to get used to me reaching out for him. The dry warmth of his hand transmitted more emotion than anything he said out loud. I don't need research to tell me how vital touch is, but Dacher Keltner, director of the Greater Good Science Center in California, explains more in an online video.

Keltner says that what may appear to be an inconsequential touch on the shoulder, is "our primary language of compassion". Studies even show that we are more accurate at communicating by touch, than we are by facial expressions. Like much of this project, I figured this out for myself.

Meditating has given me the ability to delve into my psyche and find my own evidence. The touch research told me what I already knew, but my inner wisdom is reinforced. This is where science and I meet head on.

A Turn for the Worse

When Christmas is over, Prakashjot and I squeeze in one last set of kriyas before my next adventure. She knows I have a Vipassana retreat starting in a month's time. "Can you take your headset with you?" she asks after we finish our lesson.

"Nope," I reply. "No devices are allowed. You can't even take a notebook and pen!" Wishing me luck, she promises to stay in touch.

In the supermarket later with Ed, a WhatsApp message bleeps. There's news about Dad and it's not good – he's had a fall and everyone is panicking. I feel helpless, left out of this slowly unfolding tragedy. As frustration bubbles, I close my eyes and breathe. If meditating is a bicep curl for the mind, then I'm bench pressing weights. As my thoughts veer this way and that, I reach for Ed's hand. Breathing in and out, the bullet train slows and I return to my shopping and the warmth of my husband's hand.

Anger is tiring. How many extra breaths have I just wasted? Slowing my breathing relieves the pressure on my autonomic system, helping me cope with these unpleasant moments. It doesn't remove the cause – I can't change what's happening to Dad – but I can remember the space that exists between this news and my reaction to it. I'm sure this is the "now" the author Eckhart Tolle talks of.

I wasn't sure I would like Kundalini Yoga, but I do. It's been hard work, but whenever I practise now, I am committed. This surprises me because I still avoid getting my mat out for as long as possible. When I do, I feel an unusual calmness like I'm coming home to myself, even if just for a second. I've had to accept that times can be challenging – there will always be ups and downs, but KY helps shoo the worry away. This practice links my body to my mind, allowing a connection that (at times) is deeper than a static meditation. The MBCT body scans were the closest I had come to this.

It took a while, but I came to understand the feminine aspect of Kundalini Yoga too. It's customary to employ a Root Lock and deep breathing for many of the kriyas, to not only support the spine, but to ground the practice. I started feeling sensations – a heat rising up through my pelvic floor. It wasn't anything as exciting as an awakening, but it was a sense of my own femininity. Once again, like Tantra, I'd found a practice that reminded me of my own womanhood. I'll never know if my temporary back pain was the result of an old injury or stored up emotions manifesting. I don't think it matters.

CHAPTER 11

FIDGETS BEWARE: VIPASSANA

February 2019

It's February half term and I'm at Mum's with the kids. Busy putting dinner on, she offers me a gin and tonic.

"No thanks," I reply, as ice clinks into a glass.

"Here," she says, handing it to me anyway. "I'd already made it."

I want to cut down alcohol. The habit. That cold glass of wine at the end of a day. One of the drip, drip effects of intense introspection has been a brutal assessment of my life. I rely on alcohol for many things – a stimulant when I'm tired, a boredom crusher, a transition into the weekend. A social disarmer. After two years of meditating regularly, my relationship with myself has changed. That means my relationship with alcohol must change too. I figure a good place to start is on the Vipassana retreat I have coming up in a month's time.

Vipassana March 2019

The 1960s were a fertile time for Eastern spirituality. S N Goenka, a Burmese-Indian businessman turned spiritual teacher, taught a technique called Vipassana, purportedly from the Buddha himself. Like TM and Kundalini Yoga, here was another school offering enlightenment for the Western consciousness, spearheaded by a charismatic leader. And Satya Narayan Goenka was engaging, with his neatly combed hair and cheery smile.

Vipassana, from the Theravada Buddhist tradition, translates to insight or "seeing things as they really are" in Pali. It is an intense form of concentration meditation that claims to offer "a universal remedy for universal ills". It describes itself as "self-transformation through self-observation", which sounds like something I'll have to experience to understand.

Vipassana is intriguing, particularly the all-faith, non-sectarian approach. The retreats are offered for free, relying on donations from past students. My eyes widen when I discover that all courses are residential and students new to Vipassana must complete the standard 10-day retreat (which is, in fact, 11 days long) before booking further retreats.

Vipassana is a bit trendy these days. It even made an episode of the Netflix series *Black Mirror* when a new-age tech CEO of a social media company is interrupted on his silent retreat to deal with a hostage situation. Jack Dorsey, the CEO of Twitter, also famously tweeted that he'd visited a Vipassana retreat in 2016.

According to Goenka, "Everyone seeks peace and harmony, because we lack this in our lives." He's right. I wouldn't be doing this experiment otherwise. After twenty-six months of full-time meditation, I feel frustrated that these eight techniques haven't significantly (and obviously) improved my life. Of course, there have been moments of clarity – of jaw-dropping self-awareness, but it hasn't been an easy ride. I'd wanted the positive impacts of meditating to be big, hat-waving changes, not the small incremental shifts in my awareness and behaviour that they have been. Annoyingly, the effects of a meditation practice are not clear cut. I still find myself out of kilter – meditating hasn't changed that. If anything, my introspection has attuned me to these moments, although they are less intense than they used to be. Negativity still gets passed around, like an unwelcome pass-the-parcel. Goenka would call this "the gift of misery", suggesting this is not a skilful way to live. For social creatures who coexist in a tribal setting, we are pretty awful at living well with each other.

Recognizing and managing reactivity is a learned skill. It requires unlearning a lifetime of bad habits. According to Goenka, Vipassana offers not only the key to understanding why we feel so damn miserable, but a way out of that misery hole. I'm wondering if Vipassana is the holy grail of meditation.

Day One

Planning this lengthy trip has been a military operation. The online application for the Dhamma Dipa retreat was thorough. While I expected some medical screening (due to the trauma I suffered during my sight loss), I hadn't expected the level of detail requested. After some toing and froing, I was deemed psychologically fit. I'm not permitted to take the headset to the retreat – or use my phone to score each experience – so Barbara and I have agreed I will record my brain data when I practise back at home, having learned the technique.

I've spent months stockpiling favours, pre-arranging friends to collect and drop the children to fit in with Ed's schedule. Even his (potentially disastrous) overnight work trip has been resolved. Grannie, in her indomitable spirit, is coming to cover the gap.

With the kids ensconced at school, I have a leisurely hour to get to the coach station. This would be fine if my visual fuse-box hadn't just tripped. It's not unusual for me to become disorientated – a legacy of my sight loss. Standing in the train station, once familiar buildings meld seamlessly into each other. I know the coach station is a short walk from here, but spinning wildly I am lost.

Ten minutes later, I'm standing in Costa Coffee with my eyes closed and my heart rate subsiding. All of a sudden, I hear a voice so magical and pure my eyes fly open. A young man with blond dreadlocks, wearing a colourful woven jacket, is singing to himself. Catching my eye and grinning, he asks, "Vipassana?" Gawking at how he could possibly know, I nod as he guides me onto the coach for Gloucester.

Dhamma Dipa is situated in a remote area of Herefordshire, accessible only via a single track. Before his death, Goenka had taught the technique to over 1,300 teachers who, in turn, have taught hundreds of thousands of students. Over 170 centres like this one exist around the world.

Trailing like inmates into the purpose-built building, all 128 students are channelled into a large dining hall. After a communal lunch, men and women will be separated for the entirety of the course. Tucking into a bowl of soup, I meet a tall woman from Oxford. Her bouffant hair and Alice band contrast the ethnic garb of Western dreads and harem trousers that many are wearing. Alice band is over-animated and chatters about her stressed-out friends on Prozac. She's looking for a lifestyle change. A petite older woman sits quietly, listening in. Her grown-up daughter booked her onto this course so she could discover "who she is". This startles me. Should I be asking this question too? The petite woman explains this is the question she has been asking her whole life.

The centre is highly organized and I am assigned a tiny single room with a bed, side table and shelving unit. It's plain but warm. As men and women live in separate areas, signs delineate the Female Course Boundary in case we stray too far. The only time we'll see the men from now on is inside the hangar-like meditation hall situated at the top of a small slope, or through the hedges separating the walking areas.

We are expected to live a monastic life as genuinely as possible. This includes what Goenka calls "noble silence". The schedule is strict. Wake-up is at 4am, with the first meditation at 4.30am. Breakfast is at 6.30am, with more meditation afterwards at 8am. Lunch is a simple vegetarian meal at 11am with rest afterwards. A group sitting is at 2.30pm, followed by more meditation and fruit and a cup of tea at 5pm. The evening is, yes, another group meditation, followed by a video and Goenka's instructions for the next day. Bedtime is 9pm. Silence is strictly imposed and this includes no eye or physical contact. We quickly learn to hold the doors for each other while staring at the floor.

The cavernous meditation hall is the main focus. Accessed by men via a segregated entrance, it is an architecturally designed structure of wood and glass. Inside, four instructors, seated on padded stools, reside over the proceedings. The head female teacher is a well-dressed woman in her sixties, with a younger, dark-haired assistant by her side.

Although Goenka died in 2013, audio recordings play his drawling voice through speakers in the hall. His first instruction is that we all agree to be bound by the five moral precepts that govern his teachings: not to lie, kill, steal, take intoxicants or indulge in any sexual activity.

He starts by teaching "anapana sati", which I recognize as mindful breathing. I can do this. Goenka instructs us to observe our breath as we breathe in and out of our nose. This is to sharpen the mind's focus. Buddha chose the breath as it is a portable function that can be controlled both automatically or consciously.

Sitting cross-legged on my blue mat, I'm surrounded by the smells of my fellow students; coconut shampoo and Olbas oil mingle in the heavy air. There's a lot of coughing going on, so I try not to breathe too deeply. With cream blankets pulled tightly over our shoulders, we resemble human pyramids. Out of the corner of my eye I spot Alice band, her head hung low.

My mind is already wandering, but Goenka reassures us this is normal. What I find less normal is sitting still in this huge space hemmed in by strangers. My mat is located three rows from the front and two rows from the invisible line that separates the men from us. Having loaded cushions and blankets onto a sloppy pile, I have created a mini fortress. And yet, after ten minutes of sitting immobile, my back is playing up. Damn. Sighing and opening my eyes a crack, I watch our teachers. They don't move a muscle. I wonder if they are even breathing. Maybe they're avoiding catching a cold too. Closing my eyes, I sense the seriousness of the proceedings. This is not going to be fun.

Monotony

Surprisingly, time goes quickly as I settle into the routine. I jump when I hear the gongs to get up, go to the hall or go to bed. My plan to use exercise to punctuate the day is working well. Walking after meals makes it easier to people-watch. This is a distraction from the tsunami of thoughts flooding my mind. As I head up the path, my mind is an angry time-traveller, dragging the past into the present. That catty remark about my hair ... being ignored on the school bus. Lengthening my stride, my armpits are sweaty. Why is this voice so bitter? "Go away," I hiss, ignoring all the damn nature I'm supposed to be mindful of.

Breathing heavily, I overtake a tall older woman who's also striding purposely. I wonder if she's raking up old wounds too. Spying out of the corner of my eye, her neat-cropped hair and hand-knitted scarf make me wonder if she's an artist. Or yoga teacher? Either way, she lives rurally by the look of her robust footwear. City dwellers don't invest that much in Wellington boots.

As my interest wanes, the voice jumps back in. *You were treated badly!* It's so loud, I wonder if the other women can hear it. I remember Rumi describes thoughts as "visitors". My visitors today are not welcome – I wish I had a thought-bouncer to escort them away.

The worst is not knowing what has triggered this outpouring. I force my attention onto my breath, but the voice is still there, crouched in the shadows.

In the next meditation, Goenka instructs us to focus our attention on a small area between our nostrils and upper lip. After twenty hours of mindful breathing, I'm relieved to have something new to do. The air flows in and out, creating tingles on my upper lip. There's a mild throbbing above my nose, an itch on my cheek. Goenka says the repetition of this exercise will help us develop a pin-sharp awareness. I almost wish I'd sneaked the headset in. This stage of the Vipassana training would score really high in terms of effort and concentration. My meta awareness (how aware I am of my thoughts) is also off the scale. I may not welcome my "thought visitors", but I am acutely aware of their presence.

Afterwards, trailing out of the hall, I notice the utter uniformity of this place. Designer pebbles and succulents surround the hall, mirrored I suspect, on the men's side. Even the pots of flowering pansies are equally spaced. The gardens are immaculate, with a double row of silver birch standing guard. Everything is in its place. It looks like nature has been curbed.

Walking into our dormitory, Alice band tries to catch my eye. As the soft-close door shuts behind her, I realize she was saying goodbye. It's not unusual for students to leave a Vipassana retreat. Some even flee in the middle of the night. Perhaps the silence became too loud.

Dreams

On my second night I have a dream. I am walking around our house, but it is not our house. I approach a yellow door desperate to open it, but instead I wake to the 4am gong. The yellow door travels with me through the loose tiers of sleep. Even fully conscious, the colour is still present. This isn't the insipid dishwater of dreams; this is real. Stumbling out into the dark, I wonder if anyone else had the same dream.

Dragging my feet around the dining hall, I slop stewed prunes and yoghurt into my bowl. I'm not hungry; my appetite has shrunk and one meal a day is enough. While the food is delicious, I grimace at the prunes. Like the boxes of tissues in the dorms; nothing is here without a reason.

My mind isn't in the dining hall. It's stuck in the past again, plucking out memories: the disco in the village hall when I did the twist with a boy I didn't know. That scene in *Breaking Bad* when Walter White fingers the lily of the valley plant and we know he's the killer. Experiences from my childhood play on a mental showreel, one after the other: falling into a rose bush aged three, being dragged beneath a horse at the age of ten.

Later I sit in line, waiting for my five-minute appointment with the head teacher. After constantly trying to train my unconscious mind not to react to any stimuli, whether with craving or aversion, I want to understand how my mind knows the difference. In other words, how will it know to react joyfully to stimuli I want it to react to – like the warm sun on my skin or the pleasure of seeing my children again. The teacher laughs off my question and repeats Goenka's instructions to practise equanimity. Her reply isn't so surprising as I understand Goenka's teachers are given little flexibility to translate his teachings. Feeling fobbed off, I slope back to my dormitory, frustrated at what felt like an automatic and somewhat robotic response.

Back in my room I hold my breath, listening to myself in a way I haven't done before. There's a tremor running throughout my body, a low-level hum that's taken days to manifest. Goenka said we are "performing surgery" upon ourselves. He warned that by cutting off our habitual reactions at the root, we might uncover emotional abscesses.

Along with this emotional purging, I am also guilt-ridden. We were told, twice, to hand over any notebooks or pens at the welcome talk. I broke this rule. I handed over my notebook, but I kept a biro. It sat in my bag for a day before I gave in. There's no paper on site, only laminated signs, but I found a solution. Tiny scrawled sentences now cover one side of my ticket home. Fear of a room inspection, or worse, being spotted through my window, means my illicit scribblings are hidden inside my sock.

Day Three

Seated in the hall for the 8am meditation, I'm as skittish as the wind. My face is cool, yet my feet are hot. As I make myself comfortable, mint tickles my nose. Has someone got gum?

Periodically the rain pelts the metal roof creating a violent tattoo. The wind hurls itself against the outer walls, slamming doors and shaking windows. I know a student has got up when I hear her feet crack as she pads across the carpet.

I focus inwards. This has been getting easier, I can feel tiny sensations on my face, pulses, twitches and even the pinprick of an individual hair follicle. Goenka calls these subtle sensations. The more obvious ones, like an itch or the burning pain in my back, are gross sensations. We are to observe our bodies with a neutral mind, putting no labels on sensations and treating them all equally. This, Goenka explains, will develop our equanimity.

While Goenka doesn't say this, it occurs to me that we are deactivating our reactivity. By removing emotional labels, I can accept that everything I feel will pass. But this is not easy and I'm still attaching lots of emotion to everything.

Goenka has been talking about impermanence, or "anicca" as he calls it. I remember this concept from the Buddhist practices I've tried, but I still struggle to live it. Buddha taught that everything in life changes, nothing stays the same. Goenka says it is our desire for things to not change that causes us pain. If happiness is reliant upon us never getting old or a child never leaving home, then we're nosediving toward misery. Accepting impermanence means our happiness is no longer reliant upon things we cannot control. Goenka repeats anicca over and over. I think he is trying to hypnotize me.

During the midday break, the women creep around. In the bathroom, Crocs squelch on the floor and two cubicles down I hear a woman burp. Unwrapping a forgotten packet of biscuits, I worry that the crackle of the cellophane is deafening.

Heading out for my second walk, the wind roars like an ocean above. Battling the gusts, I know why Alice band fled. My mind is so boisterous, I swear it has a microphone. I am going insane. Yet there's a clarity too. I am introspective in a way I couldn't be at home. This retreat – my cell – is a golden cage. Vipassana is my kindly gaoler. For the first time ever, I can see myself. And, I am not my mind.

Vipassana Day

Finally, it's "Vipassana day", and it seems fashion has gone out of the window. Trousers are tucked into socks and faces are bare. My old jumper feels frumpy, but I really don't care. The schedule has changed and I feel a flutter of excitement. Today, we learn the true skill of Vipassana. The reason we are here.

Back in the hall, I'm ignoring the agony in my back, telling myself it is just a sensation. If I focus long enough, the pain splits apart, disintegrating into a kind of hot buzzing. I am amazed at how many sensations I can feel here. An itch on my scalp, a pressure on my chest, tiny spiders running up and down my shins. By removing all emotional labels, I relate to my body in an anatomical way. I'm not sure it's objective as such, but I am certainly curious. With every sensation, I repeat the phrase "it will pass". And, the really weird thing is – it does. I shouldn't be surprised, as the same thing happened when I experienced extreme pain during Kundalini Yoga. Yet every time my body behaves in a way I'm not familiar with, surprise shows up.

Vipassana is basically an elaborate body scan, and it inspired the body scans Dave taught us on the MBCT course. By harnessing the pin-sharp focus I've spent hours cultivating, I can fluidly and methodically examine my body. Starting at the top of my head, my attention moves from my scalp to my ears, my cheeks and gradually my whole head comes alive. It's a strange awareness, particularly when I manage to somehow sweep this focus up and down my face. I feel a pulse move from my forehead to my eyelids, down to my chin, like a stream of vibrations. Excited at my new party trick, I repeat this over and over, desperate to tell Barbara about it. My torso is less forthcoming, but my shins and feet offer fertile territory as I shift my attention from foot to foot.

That evening, as on previous days, Goenka offers his insights. Even filmed back in 1991, these amateurish videos, complete with camera wobble, are eerily on the ball. They've answered almost every question I've had so far. Goenka talks directly to camera, dressed in the traditional meditator's outfit. He's often sat next to his wife as she stares into space through Coke-bottle glasses.

Tonight, Goenka smiles and asks, "So you think you might believe what I say now?" Nodding to himself, he continues. "Perhaps, you think, I am responsible for your reactions, maybe fifty percent? Yes, you think, fifty percent sounds okay. I'll accept that much."

As I watch the video, I nod with Goenka.

"No!" he exclaims, making me jump. "No! You are one hundred percent responsible for your reactions!"

Oh my god. And the penny drops again. Clearly, I cannot be told this fact too many times.

Day Nine

It's nearly over, only forty-eight hours to go. I've continually scanned my body, enduring the tussle for attention with my habitually reactive mind. The "strong determined sittings" (introduced on day five) have nearly broken my spirit. During these group sessions we are encouraged to remain as still as possible. Even with burning hot feet, shooting pain in my buttocks, and what sometimes feels like ants crawling in my hair, I haven't wavered (much).

Nearing the end, we are introduced to metta bhavana (loving-kindness) as a means to end each Vipassana meditation. This short instruction felt a little unsatisfactory – possibly because I have studied compassion in some depth already. Goenka only brushes over this topic, omitting several stages of the loving-kindness practice.

It doesn't bother me though because I am counting the hours left. I understand the technique and I'm prepared to "give it a chance" as Goenka asks. I see how Vipassana is compatible with any religion and, while I have been subjected to a very prescriptive environment here, I believe everything Goenka has said.

It's strange, but my sense of acceptance is very strong, and I wonder if my belief system has been hacked. I've had a shift in the way I see myself, which is both exciting and unnerving.

I'm desperate to write more – words are trapped inside my head, but my coach ticket is covered with scribbles. Padding into the toilet block, there isn't even an old tissue box I can rip up. Then, inside a cubicle, I spot sanitary bags. While shiny on the outside (no good for writing on) they are matt inside. Grinning, I stuff three down my leggings and scurry back to my room. Coughing to cover the ripping noise, I tear each bag into perfect sheets of paper.

Day Eleven

Fully packed and with one group sitting left, I wonder what real life will feel like. I haven't missed my phone and I haven't worried about the children. I've even forgotten what wine tastes like.

Thankfully, my inner voice has quietened and my body scans are flowing well. Sitting in the last session, I feel like a gnome, scanning my body up and down. I am not distracted. I am actually here, in this room, doing this. I long for the session to end and for what Goenka cheerily calls "noble chatter" to start.

The sun is out and light dances across the room. The metal roof contracts, cracking like a pistol shot. A few rows behind a woman stirs. My inner clock tells me we have ten minutes to go. The room is so still the air has stopped flowing. The woman fidgets again and I hear a loud Achoo! followed immediately by an enormous Prrrrrrrpt! All I can picture is an exploding frog. I'm both horrified and amused that, minutes from the meditation finishing line, she has succumbed to the prunes. Not surprisingly, the blanket next to me starts to shake. My neighbour cannot contain her mirth and snorts with laughter. This sets off the woman next to her and within seconds the pyramids are crumbling. A booming voice calls out for calm and the giggles subside. I remain smiling, my eyes closed, quietly enjoying this moment of humanity.

Home

"How was your day?" I ask my son when I pick him up after school, a week after returning home.

"Fine," he mumbles, before launching into a story about a boy who was mean to him. I'm listening intently, when I slam on the brakes. A parked car has pulled out nearly causing a collision. Hoisting ourselves back into our seats, we gawp at the miscreant car. The driver simply waves, then drives off. As I change gear and continue on, my son is staring at me.

"What?" I ask, catching his eye.

"You didn't honk the horn," he says slowly. "Daddy would have." Smiling, I don't respond. "And you didn't shout," he continues.

"Yup," I say, feeling just a little bit smug. His next question catches me off guard.

"Why, Mummy?"

He is genuinely interested and it's a good question. Why was I so calm, especially when it was the other driver's fault? Of course, we're both remembering the Range Rover incident only months before. My first reaction then was to sound the horn and yell like a banshee. This time is different; those wild emotions aren't here. Am I really more present? Ugh; that word. But, it's true. I am present. I am living in this exact moment now, chatting with my son. The car pulling out was just that – a car pulling out. No horn, no shouting, no anger.

Deep down, I know I've discovered a kind of weird truth. The fact is that I couldn't react to that car pulling out. I would have shouted, if I'd been able to, but the anger that normally lives quite close to the surface was just not there. In fact, it's not anywhere. Frustration and annoyance are still here, but there's no anger.

Vipassana has waved its magic wand. Even though I followed Goenka's instructions, I didn't expect it to work. I'd worried that on my return I might feel tempted to exaggerate any serenity I felt in order to justify the ordeal. Yet I have deactivated the knee-jerk reactivity that lurks beneath the surface. I have communed with my unconscious mind in some kind of mystic chat room.

Unfortunately, the serenity doesn't last. Goenka recommends that to maintain the benefits, meditating twice a day for one hour at a time is required. Oh, and husbands should join in too. That's not going to happen. Hourly meditations were fine for the first few days, the residue of a nun-like existence lingering in the discipline I employed. It wasn't hard to creep downstairs and slip on the headset to meditate. I'd never got up before everyone else before – I like sleep, I like my bed. However, the thought of losing control over my emotions was enough to drive me from my duvet. I didn't manage the full hour's meditation (more like 45 minutes) but I kept doing it. Likewise, in the evening I eschewed Netflix (or rather, talking to the side of Ed's face while he watched Netflix) to meditate before bed.

Meditating at home, my skin comes alive, zinging and pulsating with surges of electricity. What's really fascinating is that this pinprick awareness stays with me. Making a cup of tea, I ignore an itch on my arm; sitting at my desk I notice a feather-like tickle on my neck. I don't need to react, so I don't.

Two Weeks On

Putting my daughter to bed two weeks after the retreat, she's upset. She's terrified about a swim gala she's competing in tomorrow. Lying on her bunk bed, I ask where she feels the worry. She points at her tummy. Can you describe it without using emotional words? I ask. Wrinkling her nose, she says, "Ouchy. Like tummy ache."

"Okay. Does tummy ache last?"

"No," she replies slowly. "But I won't sleep tonight because my teacher says I have anxiety."

"Anxiety is just a word. You don't have to keep it. You can hand it back if you want. The feeling in your tummy is no different to tummy ache. It'll go if you say it is 'just a sensation'." She's not convinced, but we do some breathing exercises and her eyes start to close.

The next morning she crawls into my bed wearing her swimming costume. Nuzzling my neck she kisses my cheek. Slithering out of bed, she's gone.

After the swim gala my daughter is excited. She'd told her friend that anxiety isn't anxiety at all – just a tummy ache. "She was so relieved, Mummy." She grins, flushed with the pleasure of helping someone else.

Uncoupling emotional labels from physical sensations has been a vital lesson. I had to unlearn the habitual response to label pain or discomfort, which has rippled out to my children. But Vipassana hasn't made me a better parent. The next day my son has an almighty screaming fit. I still respond to his outburst in a predictable way: cajoling, reasoning and then threatening in order to manage the situation. What's different is that I can hear myself. Rather than waiting for the post-tantrum comedown and inevitable guilt, I can see the situation as it plays out. That means I can stop it from escalating. I don't have to try to be reasonable, I just am. I'm still frustrated by his unruly behaviour, yet there's less potency in my response. He needs to be in my sightline and I understand that with a new clarity. Children are a great measure of the effects of a meditation practice, and my children are experts at testing me.

In the short term, Vipassana has improved my ability to deal with the challenges of family life. The 5am gut-punch of worry that has plagued me so much in the past is a distant memory. By pointing my attention toward my discomfort, I remind myself it's just a physical manifestation. This uncouples the anxiety that would normally leave me restless and wide-eyed. I have an emotional dial I can turn down which is immensely freeing. This mindset shift is supported by the hypnosis work I did – these practices are working in tandem.

Recording my EEG data dutifully each day, I add notes to Barbara explaining how different the technique now feels, having suffered the arduous task of learning it. Meditating on the retreat took enormous effort, often leaving me exhausted afterwards. Now in the safety of my living room, the practice feels easy and my senses sharp. The experiences I score now would be the opposite of what I would have recorded (had I been able to) on the retreat.

That said, the maintenance is hard. The twice-daily sittings require family coordination. There are meet-ups offered to old students (which I am now) on the dhamma.org website, but most require a half or full day's commitment, which is difficult to swing. Finding time to meditate for two hours a day is becoming a chore.

One Month On

Before I went on the Vipassana retreat, Ed was concerned I would be brainwashed.

"Sleep deprivation, silence, isolation?" he listed gravely. "Sounds like a cult to me."

Smiling, I consider the emotional purging I experienced was more akin to mind washing. Like everything else, Goenka has a word for this: purification. This is perhaps where our Western desire to simplify and label spiritual practices as techniques falls down. Vipassana is indeed a form of purification that goes beyond practical methodology.

I understand Ed's concerns. When I initially returned, I claimed the retreat hadn't been cult-like at all and that everything had been transparent and open – which it had been. Over time, I realized I'd edited the stories I'd shared.

My response to my own rule-breaking was undeniably heightened. Hiding scribbled notes inside my socks was hardly criminal, yet I'd feared consequences. Other women broke the rules. Several admitted to hiding food and one said she'd been so bored she'd applied and removed full make-up several times a day. While they'd laughed at their antics, I'd feared reprisal. Of course, this reprisal was imagined, paranoid even, but at the time it had felt real.

Mine wasn't the only over-reaction. On the last day, many women hugged each other and wept. The friendly woman I'd met on the first evening attempted to hug an old student, but at her touch the old student jumped in the air shrieking, "No contact!" The reaction shocked many of us at the time and the memory has lingered.

In acknowledging my psychological state, it's important to separate out the technique from the conditions in which it's taught. For many, a monastic life is difficult to comprehend, let alone follow. Lack of sleep, restricted food and long periods of isolation create a prison-like environment. I often felt like I was locked up with a raving lunatic. Realizing that the lunatic was me was the worst part. It was a terrifying truth that, in the absence of human contact, my own mind was my foe. We all have inner critics and Sharon Salzberg suggests we give them a name. Dan Harris suggests the same in his funny book, *Meditation for Fidgety Skeptics*. The practice dredged up the worst chest-thumping outrage my inner critic had to offer. Had it occurred to me on the retreat, I would have named mine Cruella de Ville. At these times, the only weapon I had was self-awareness – and equanimity.

Given my dislike of Vipassana's cell-like routines, it's ironic that it has been taught in prisons. In 1985, Goenka established the Vipassana Research Institute to focus on teaching and researching the benefits of Vipassana. One study in 2002 reported that inmates at Tihar Jail in Delhi who participated on a Vipassana course felt it improved their wellbeing, gave them better self-control and made them less likely to break the law.

Goenka repeated many times that Vipassana is not a cult. I hadn't gone on the retreat thinking it was, yet his persistence on this point made me wonder. Certainly, there was a level of conditioning going on. Any phrase repeated monotonously has a hypnotic effect. Plus, Goenka's references to Buddha's teachings didn't bother me, however, some women felt the terminology he used gave things a religious slant. Of course, I'm also wading through my own resistance as, ultimately, Vipassana was a rude awakening.

Goenka's retreats are not the only way to learn Vipassana. Mahasi Sayadaw, another Indian teacher, used concentration meditation that focuses on the abdomen and inner organs. Whilst a different approach, the intention to combat reactivity is much the same. There are online debates as to which technique is the most beneficial.

Vipassana is a valuable tool, although it may not suit everyone. The organization has a stringent filtering system, recommending those with a serious mental health problem don't participate. I think that's good advice. That said, I got a lot from the retreat and there's a part of me that won't be quite the same. Ed noticed changes, saying I take things more in my stride. My writing was positively affected too. The day after my return, I wrote ten thousand words in one sitting, achieving a state of "flow" I'd never experienced before. I felt invigorated, with a deepened love for my family. Relating the story about the exploding frog, we laughed so hard Ed had to pull over. Whilst not unimportant, I felt that the paranoia I experienced during the retreat was more to do with the monastic environment than the technique itself.

With nine meditation modalities under my belt, I can see the accumulative effect. All of these practices have helped me make sense of my journey. With the effects of Vipassana now fading, I head toward the biggest challenge of them all – psychedelics.

CHAPTER 12

TRIP: PSYCHEDELICS

May 2018

I don't do drugs. I never have, so I was shocked when Tristan brought up psychedelics back in 2016. "Like magic mushrooms and LSD that hippies took in the sixties?" I questioned.

"No," he laughed. "Not now. There's encouraging research from Imperial College, London using psilocybin to treat depression. Plus, psychedelics allow you to experience a completely different state of mind, and isn't that what your project is all about?" I kept quiet at the time, there was no way I was doing anything illegal. However, my views on a number of things have changed over the last three years.

Throughout this experiment I have worn two hats. One of the eye-rolling sceptic, the other of the open-minded believer – prepared to accept an experience at face value. After all, exploring my inner landscape has been the nub of this experiment. But psychedelics are another beast entirely, so rather than conduct research after my experience (as I've done up until now), I decide to arm myself with knowledge before I venture into this unknown.

"Just Say No!" was drilled into me when I was fourteen years old by the chart-topping cast of *Grange Hill*. This popular children's drama featured the hard-hitting storyline of teen drug addiction. Even in 1986 the war on drugs, launched as a backlash to the counterculture, was still rumbling. It left me suspicious of all drugs and, if I'm honest, scared witless.

Psychedelics are often associated with religious ceremonies and festival-goers. These psychoactive compounds trigger otherworldly (albeit temporary) thought, visual and auditory changes. In other words, a user "trips". The term trip (from acid trip) was coined by the LSD community. Andy Roberts' book *Albion Dreaming: A Popular History of LSD in Britain*, chronicling the history of LSD in Britain, contains a useful glossary of psychedelic terminology.

These wild and sometimes extreme experiences augment a user's perception of time and reality, uncovering parts of themselves they didn't know existed and challenging precepts of nature and the universe. Author Aldous Huxley's classic 1954 book *The Doors of Perception* narrates his experiences taking mescaline. Here, tables and chairs took on a hyper-real, painterly quality and time was "in abundance".

By 1971, the British government had taken action. Psychedelics, including LSD, magic mushrooms, mescaline, DMT (the active part of ayahuasca) and MDMA were re-classified as Class A drugs. This made them illegal to supply or take. Unfortunately, widespread prohibition halted promising research in this field until the early 1990s, when a DMT study by Rick Strassman and a later psilocybin study by Roland Griffiths ended the hiatus, easing the counter-culture associations with these drugs and offering opportunities for therapeutic applications.

Prohibitions and media hysteria had done nothing to decrease drug use. In fact, it grew. In 2018, a UK Home Office report estimated that 8.7 per cent of young adults aged 16 to 24 had taken a Class A drug in the last year (around 550,000 young people).

To the uninformed, these drug statistics sound disturbing, but I've never fully understood what a hallucinogen does. Nobody ever explained that. The word "psychedelic" derives from the Greek word "psych" meaning mind and "delein" meaning manifesting, which provides the first clue. Recent studies have brought these molecules back into the public domain (minus the demonization) as a potential therapy. Public opinion is shifting, due in part to encouraging results, along with the "Pollan Effect". Michael Pollan, an American author and plant-loving journalist, makes an important distinction about psychedelics in his book, *How to Change Your Mind: The New Science of Psychedelics*. Entheogens, he explains, are the centuries-old ceremonial psychoactive substances used within a wellbeing framework. Plant medicine is taken reverentially, for the purpose of spiritual gain. These, he says, are not recreational drugs.

There's no denying that psychedelics have a colourful past. Albert Hofmann, the unassuming Swiss chemist who discovered LSD, did so by accident. He originally discovered LSD-25 (lysergic acid diethylamide) in 1938 – created from the ergot fungi – but it was revisiting this chemical compound in 1943 when he accidentally came into contact with the molecule and unwittingly took his first trip. Three days later he famously ingested 250 micrograms of LSD in his lab (a normal dose is 100–250 micrograms – a millionth of a gram) and then cycled home on his bicycle. Hofmann's LSD bike ride is celebrated on 19th April each year by the spiritual community as the birth of acid.

Hofmann knew he'd stumbled upon something bigger than himself. In his book *LSD, My Problem Child*, he muses how a promising psychiatric medicine sparked such a public outcry.

The Bike Ride That Changed My Mind

It's midnight on a cool August evening in 2019 and I'm balanced, somewhat precariously, on the parcel-seat of a "Boris bike", laughing wildly as Barbara freewheels toward Oxford Street. It's been a lively evening as scientist friends provided an encyclopaedic breakdown of psychedelic research.

Psilocybin (the psychoactive ingredient in magic mushrooms that is transformed inside the body to psilocin) has been used to successfully treat alcohol dependency, and has proved an effective treatment for end-of-life cancer patients. It occurs naturally in more than 200 species of mushrooms.

There's a study looking into treating anorexia at Imperial and an ongoing "Ceremonial study" in collaboration with a number of legal retreats in the Netherlands. This study is investigating the psychological effects of guided psychedelic experiences. Whilst psychedelic-assisted psychotherapy (PAP) isn't yet available to the public, scientists hope this will be in the future.

I've also discovered intriguing similarities between tripping and meditating. Scans have identified that the brain's default mode network (DMN) is deactivated during both meditation and psychedelic experiences. The DMN is the set of networks that underwrites the self-referential part of the mind – that voice that obsesses over what to wear in the morning, or what your partner really meant by that remark. Studies have shown that this inner narrator (likened to our ego) quietens during a trip, mimicking the same brain activity observed in long-term meditators. It's not surprising then that many of the acid-dropping counterculture took up spiritual practices.

Whatever the similarities, I am still a scaredy-cat. Throughout the early 1990s, I avoided the rampant Ecstasy use of my peers. I was one of the few who didn't drop an E most weekends at university. It was only on an American road trip in 1993 that I was introduced to pure weed. As popping cannabis seeds singed a hole in my T-shirt, I experienced something new. Staring at a television, the broadcaster had a parrot on his shoulder and was wearing a loincloth. It wasn't the biggest trip, but it was the first time I knew that reality was subjective.

Perhaps not surprisingly, it's the visual changes that interest me the most. Hallucinogens can evoke beautiful and sometimes grotesque images, even in those with no or limited vision. This is because we see with our brains – not our eyes. A 2018 study reported that a congenitally blind man experienced visual hallucinations when he took LSD.

This is fascinating for someone like me who suffers low colour and low contrast-sensitivity (a legacy of my sight loss). This means colours are muted and blend into each other – gold coins look the same as silver and forests are a sludgy-green blur. Could psychedelics allow me to see dazzling colour again? Even if only for an hour? With legal retreats springing up in Amsterdam and my misguided view of psychedelics overturned, it's time to change my mind.

I Am The Music

It's January 2020 and the beginning of a new decade. I can hardly believe that my project has nearly finished – taking double the time we thought it would. Standing in the drizzle at Centraal Station, Amsterdam, I'm approached by a couple. "You for Synthesis?" they ask, smiling with the effortless confidence Americans imbue. We're soon joined by five others as we wait for our ride to the Lighthouse, the architect-designed location of our retreat. Given we range in age from late thirties to mid-fifties, we're a bang on target audience for this psilocybin retreat.

From the conversation, we've all done our homework. With a number of legal retreats offering "magic truffles" as part of a ceremonial weekend, there are varying options available. These range from group to personal retreats, run over a weekend, a week or longer.

Synthesis Retreat is the brainchild of Myles Katz and Martijn Schirp, and was set up in 2018. Since then, over 700 people, from priests to CEOs, have attended their medically supervised ceremonies. Their curated "set and setting" allows the curious to expand their consciousness, find meaning and inject verve, connection or creativity into their lives. Chatting to Myles on the phone, he's excited to hear about our experiment and is happy for me to bring my headset along. He also mentions the Ceremonial study that Imperial are running and that some retreat participants choose to complete.

Everyone in the cab has undergone phone interviews and medical screenings. The Pollan Effect has been at work. Most of us have dabbled in psychedelics, with one woman listing 40 trips.

My sight-loss trauma yet again caused a temporary blip. Suppressed trauma can be triggered during a psychedelic experience, so protocols are in place to protect participants, along with medical waivers. Whilst the retreat is certainly therapeutic, psychedelic-assisted therapy is not offered.

Driving through suburbia, we arrive at the converted church. Ushered inside a magnificent atrium, we meet the rest of our group. There are eleven of us in total, supported by nine staff, most of whom are wellbeing or spiritual practitioners. We have the same adult to child ratio as toddlers in a nursery.

Natasja, one of the lead facilitators, hugs me. "Welcome," she beams, squeezing my hand.

I'm allocated an apartment in the basement with two roomies. Amy is married, in her forties and, while she lives in France, is originally from Texas. Robin, who's a little younger, is a self-confessed nomad, running wellbeing businesses from Bali. Like teenagers on a school trip, we unpack our bags and giggle whilst making Lion's Mane mushroom tea (a reassuringly non-psychedelic brew).

Flight Instructions

The focus of the weekend is The Ceremony, which will be held tomorrow at 1pm. Today's activities are to prepare us for that. Led into a white-walled studio, mats and meditation cushions are laid out in a circle. I feel hot – I know what's coming. Introductions are necessary, but these group things always stress me. Both Natasja and Tessa (another facilitator) provide a strong female presence and the energy they emit is palpable. Unlike previous groups, we have more women than men, which is strangely reassuring. Sitting cross-legged wearing a bright red shirt, Natasja introduces the "talking stick" which we'll pass around when we speak. We are to show our support for each other using finger snapping rather than clapping. As the stick travels around the room, it reveals many are looking for connection, transformation and, in some cases, resolution. When it's my turn, I babble. Speeding through my sight-loss story, I casually mention I'm writing a book. Staring at the floor, I pass the stick along.

Natasja offers reassurances, without imprinting any expectations onto tomorrow. She reinforces the importance of intentions, asking us to write three down. Dad is at the top of my list – I want to value the time we have left. Taking notes and journaling is encouraged. We are consciousness explorers and how and where we navigate tomorrow may have positive ramifications in the future. One word scribbled in haste can hold much weight.

Natasja is reinforcing the importance of "set and setting". This is a primary difference between a recreational and therapeutic experience. Set is short for mindset, the psychological and physical state of the tripper. Setting is the environment within which the entheogen is taken. Controlling and being sensitive to these two factors is key.

After lunch, we re-enter the studio to get our "flight instructions". This covers dosage and how to make truffle tea. We'll be given truffles rather than mushrooms tomorrow, following law changes in 2008. Legislation changes didn't cover the underground part of the plant, hence truffles are still legal.

Along with detailing the stages of a psychedelic experience and the shamanic framework within which our ceremony sits, Natasja outlines some practicals to watch out for. The possibility of nausea, vomiting and diarrhoea add to my stress load, along with the knowledge that some participants believe they are dying. Natasja explains this is often a fear of letting go. Breathing through resistance can help. "Lean into the experience," she says. Trust your body.

Guides, which some consider a higher form of oneself, can appear in human, animal or plant form, but there's no prescriptive journey or landscape. "Ask yourself – what am I learning?" Tessa says. "Be open to what you're teaching yourself."

We're introduced to anchor points. The breath, smell, touch and music are all integral to the ceremony and can ground the body. They can also trigger insights. We are all "students of ourselves".

Questions come up – one man asks if he might regress into childhood. Natasja replies, somewhat enigmatically, that "the truffles will give you what you need, not what you want." At the end of the session, we're asked not to compare our experiences and, more kindly, not to judge ourselves.

The team then remove the mats and we're each given a "mind-fold". These are foam masks that allow us to open our eyes while they are covered. Totally blacked out, we walk around with our arms out, bumping into each other. For the next exercise, music blares through the speakers and we are instructed to move with the sound. Whilst these exercises are designed to build trust with and connect me to my senses, I am hunched with embarrassment, fearing everyone is laughing at me.

After a stint in the sauna (conveniently located opposite my apartment) and a light supper, my roomies and I climb into our single beds. None of us sleep well; unfamiliar surroundings and jittery minds keep us awake.

After a light breakfast (including ginger tablets to combat nausea), Sven, a smiling Dutch guy with a man bun, takes us into the studio. He's introducing us to a form of breathing similar to Transformational and Holotropic breath. These are both forms of "breathwork" involving consciously controlling the breath to induce mental, physical and spiritual wellbeing.

Our breath is our life force, Sven explains. We can survive without food or water for days, but rely moment to moment upon our breath. Our breathing changes to accommodate the immediate needs of our bodies. Waiting for something to happen, we inhale, holding air in a suspended state of alertness. We gasp when startled, or pump out air when we laugh. Clutching our diaphragms, we obediently mimic laughing and crying.

Sven describes how he was suspicious the first time he tried breathwork and encourages us to remain open. I'm not concerned. I enjoy yogic breathing, so whatever he's teaching, I expect to be relaxed. At least it's not dancing whilst blindfolded.

Lying down we cover our legs with blankets and pull on our mindfolds. I'm grudgingly grateful for the exercises yesterday as the black-out doesn't bother me now.

Sven explains that we should take two breaths in and one breath out in a continuous circular motion, oxygenating the blood. Because I'm lying down, I can do this without getting dizzy or lightheaded. I struggle to keep the breath going and soon my mouth feels dry. Within minutes, a lump of emotion starts to form. Mildly horrified, I suppress it yet drums are beating inside me, like a primal heartbeat. A huge sob is making its way up my body, building like steam in a pressure cooker. My hands are tingling and a pulsing tremor, that I know is my nervous system, shakes my body. Warned that emotions might arise, I'd brushed this aside. Yet tears are leaking out of my mindfold. The pressure is like a cannonball, threatening to crack open my chest. A comforting hand touches my shoulder. My distress has been seen.

This is terrible. I can't cry in public! My neck is aching from holding it in. Like a somatic conductor, Sven leads our breathing toward a climax. We "tantrum" by stamping our hands and feet. *This is ridiculous!* The room is buzzing. As I pump my breath, pure energy – like touching a soft blanket – fills my hands. Reaching my arms up, invisible waves burst from my fingertips. *Have I trapped a nerve?* A part of me knows what this is. Holding my hands above my body, the energy swoops and surges like a beautiful bird. *Holy shit – I can control it.* The realness – the force of what is happening – is incredible. I let out a small cry, but it's drowned by the noise of the others. Poised at the precipice of something life-altering, I'm scared to let go. Then, at the last tantrum, the room is lifted by shouts and yells and my cries are heard. I am no longer mute.

Calming our breathing down, Sven guides us back to the studio runway and my emotions subside, like a tap being turned off. Sitting up, I remove my sodden mask and stare at the floor. *Did that happen?* I can't look anyone in the eye. Passing the talking stick, Sven asks us to share. "Holy shit," I say, this time out loud. "I think I might be a bit less English. What did you do to me?" Sven laughs, he knows exactly what happened.

Whilst the session only lasted an hour, it was an inexplicable experience. Like the Starship Enterprise, I'd travelled at warp speed, hurtling through a black hole into another way of being.

Stumbling back to my apartment, I finally get it. Spiritual awakenings were real – I had just signed up to the believers' club. Non-ordinary states of consciousness can be achieved without drugs.

Time for Tea

It's ten to one and I'm flustered. With minutes to spare, I've just filled in the Imperial College Ceremonial study. The data I provide will help to advance the scientific understanding of psychoactive plant medicines and how these compounds might induce psychological change. This in turn could help develop future studies on psychedelics, including clinical trials.

There are more questionnaires to complete over the coming weeks, but at least this one is done.

Sitting at the trestle table in the Lighthouse, I follow Natasja's instructions on how to grind up my 30mg of truffles. Pouring boiling water onto the paste and adding ginger and lemon, I've made truffle tea.

Mattresses and gravity blankets are laid out in the studio as white-robed staff waft smoking sage over our bodies and hug us. Stepping over my mattress, a participant places a trinket on a small altar in the middle of the room. When we're all settled, we're instructed to drink as much tea as we feel we need. "What does that mean?" I whisper to Tatiana, a facilitator squatting behind me. "Follow your body," she whispers back. Shit. My body doesn't know. Nervous about vomiting, I drink a small cup and lie down.

The ceremony is accompanied by an eight-hour curated music track created by Mendel Kaelen, a former psychedelics researcher at Imperial. As guitar strings fill the studio, I wait. Psilocybin is meant to dull the talkative part of my mind so after ninety minutes of incessant chatter, I know the truffles aren't working. With the option of a second dose (and with no nausea), I drink the remainder of my tea. I won't be the only tripper not tripping.

Ten minutes later, I blast off. Strange things are happening inside my brain. The psilocybin has activated my serotonin receptors, prompting "cross-talk" between different brain regions. There are well-documented stages of a psychedelic experience – ego dissolution is one. Pollan quotes one study volunteer as saying: "I didn't know where I ended and my surroundings began." There are no surroundings for me. I soar into the stratosphere, except that I am the stratosphere, which is very funny. I am completely aware of this, yet my mind still tries to peer around the edges – to stand back from this sense of non-being. These molecules can outwit my overactive mind with their weird, god-like intelligence. Natasja was right, they are cheeky. Like scrolling scenes from *Prospero's Books*, reality warps and unfolds. Although I am particles inside an unveiling universe, it's a non-visual one. After a while, I lift my mask to take a swig of water. Tatiana whispers, "It's kicked in?"

"Yes," I sigh. "I'm the universe." She touches my hand and I lie down.

Visuals, which are often sacred geometry, fractals and vivid colours, are known as the pinta – the painting. Straining to see something, I stretch my mind's eye but there is no light show.

Suddenly, I hear laughter close to me. Grabbing ear plugs to muffle the noise, a strange thing happens. The music intensifies. Even though I've blocked out sound, I can hear a cello. No, I feel a cello – a symbiotic vibration. My mind whirrs, I want visuals not sound, so why is this happening? Then I understand. We get what we need, not what we want. I can't control this. The web of reality has unknitted – the strands that connect me to this world, this body, have relaxed – I *am* the music.

This is hilarious. Swaying my head, I direct an invisible symphony. A piano chord ripples the fabric of my universe, revealing the words: There are no miracles, only healing. My smile drops. Insights often appear like this; Natasja called them gifts.

I have been seeking miracles. I realize I've spent the last seven years searching for my lost sight. Tears spill out of the corner of my mask and Tatiana takes my hand. I don't even like music.

Yet that's just a story I tell myself. An illusion. It's all an illusion. Embrace what you have, the Universe whispers. And suddenly I remember a "sound bath" I experienced at the end of a Kundalini Yoga event last year run by the Psychedelic Society. The vibrations from the singing bowls sent me spiralling into another stratosphere. Sound cut my body in two. I laughed it off, said I fell asleep. Gongs are nice, but music doesn't heal you. Yet I knew it had. And just like that, I understand and my heart cracks open, like a fortune cookie.

Later on, a female hand takes mine. Natasja sprays a scent and whispers, "What do you see?" Rose. I'm at my grandmother's funeral thirteen years ago, pregnant with my first child. "She never knew I named my daughter after her," I weep, my heart splitting open again.

Time sweeps without restraint and suddenly I feel a heat in my abdomen. It takes a while to realize what it is. "Tatiana," I whisper. "How does the universe pee?"

By nine o'clock, most of the group are back in the Lighthouse. I am still dust. Eventually, they return to the studio and I sit up. "When does the music finish?" I ask.

"In five seconds' time," someone replies. Of course it does. I laugh.

When it's time for the closing circle, the man next to me looks dazed, his mask pushed up onto his forehead. Having heard his moans, I know he's had a rough time. "I died over and over," he says bleakly. "I don't love myself. My family love me, but I have to learn to love myself." We snap, snap, snap and he passes the talking stick on. Others had joyful experiences, expressing a deep connection and love. Some suffered darkness. Yet even in those depths, the gifts were there.

I got what my body was prepared to release, not what my mind dictated. This is typical. It is the infinite (if mostly unrecognized) wisdom of the psyche. It cannot be bossed around. I spent hours trying to navigate this inscape, only to realize that it guided me.

Integration

The next day is taken up with workshops and my second one-to-one meeting with Natasja. She asks about my father. Connecting with him had been one of my intentions.

"There was nothing," I admit. "Nobody I knew appeared."

"That's not unusual," she smiles. "Sometimes it's just about you."

Yet I'm unsettled. Guilty. "The rose made me remember my gran," I mutter. "I'd never grieved her. I couldn't process death because I was creating life."

Natasja nods and hugs me. I can contact her whenever I need. I say nothing as I leave.

Later, Sven guides another, gentler, breathwork session. My legs twitch, but that's all. Then we listen to one of the curated music tracks and an invisible trapdoor slides open. I am returned to my aural cosmos. Time stretches and fifteen minutes feels like two hours.

The team are gentle. They talk quietly, slowly. They say: "Take it easy. Insights can take weeks. Years sometimes. You have a lot to unpack." No kidding. I arrived with one rucksack, but I'm going home with five.

My psychedelic voyage was shaped by the emotional legacies of my past. Every unravelling scene was created out of the substance and content of my life. Both the life I knowingly live, and the life I unknowingly live. This is the past I can't speak of, because a somatic footprint has no words.

I discovered an inner tautness, an invisible hand gripping the pain my body carried. I resisted. I fought the process, asking why and how. I didn't lean in or accept. I received the same insight over and over, before I understood. The repetition was a message too.

It was only when exhausted that I succumbed, and the hand relaxed. I hadn't known I could confer with myself in this way. I know the real insights are still here – hiding in plain sight. Insights are like the annoying cellophane you get on a new phone. It's only when you peel it off months later, that you realize it'd been there all along.

At 4pm I'm still befuddled when our taxis arrive. This is not how I imagined our goodbyes to be. There's so much left unsaid. Even after the workshops, I'm tightly coiled, honesty hiding behind humour.

I find myself in a cab with the same people I arrived with. Now we have an arcane connection. We've put ourselves through the ultimate test, knowing we couldn't control the outcome. We were warriors and worriers.

An hour later, secreted in a quiet corner in Starbucks, I ring Ed. It's strange talking to him. I want to connect, to share insights that will make him understand me a bit more. Instead, we talk about the children and parents' evening. I shouldn't be surprised. Describing this experience isn't as hard as asking someone else to hear it – to accept there are realities they have no experience of.

I arrive at my friends' flat in central Amsterdam where I am to stay the night. I cook them dinner and tell them stories, but I'm depleted. Tired from holding back. I fall into bed, not even considering the warnings we'd been given about vivid dreams.

At 5am I'm fast asleep when my room suddenly lights up. There's a new three-dimensional glass wall at one side. A group of clowns stand behind it, wearing purple costumes. Paralyzed by sleep, I can only move my head. The clowns cluster, pawing the glass, trying to get in. Their faces are gnarled and bloody, but they're more curious than creepy. I don't trust them. They're so real I could touch them – or worse, they could touch me. As one curls its fingers around the glass, I try to call out. No sound comes. With a surge I hiss and they retreat. Hauling myself into consciousness, I sit up drenched with sweat with eyes like saucers. Staying awake until daylight, I'm too scared to sleep.

24 Hours Later

I've only been home a day before I'm on a train north to see Dad. A scan has revealed his cancer is back, and it's spread. The doctor is kind – he looks Dad in the eye when he offers palliative radiotherapy. Dad nods. I'm not the only one without a voice.

We have so little time left. I sit on Dad's bed, holding his hand. Words have been taken away and I see pleading in his eyes. He wants to explain – after five attempts I realize he's saying sorry. I shake my head and talk for him. I make him smile – that night in the rain – my daughter in her crib – the vegetable garden you built for me. I stroke his papery hand and when he tires, wish him goodnight.

Upstairs, my tears are silent. I want to shout and scream, but my voice has gone.

One Week On

"You can't say ineffable," Ed frowns, when I mention Amsterdam again. "It's a cop out." He's late for work, so he doesn't want to hear this. As the front door bangs, I boil the kettle for tea. My son has dragged two laser guns out. He puts one on the table for me.

Ineffable means indescribable – too extreme to be expressed by language alone. I can't force words into the shape of nuance, they're too loaded with meaning I don't mean. Superlatives only scratch the surface of a psychedelic experience. Decoding the experience requires spectacular language, so it can be uncomfortable to hear. It sounds too far away, or "far out". It's not surprising that psychedelic forerunners, such as Timothy Leary, the demoted Harvard psychologist who preached "turn on, tune in, drop out", were dismissed as evangelists. This language doesn't connect others – it separates them.

Psychedelic scenery is just that – scenery. The backdrop to the experience. I was deprived of beautiful visuals to stop me hiding behind descriptions of them. I had to go backstage, step over props and rigging to see who was pulling the strings. Turns out, I had a guide all along. I just hadn't noticed the child-like form – the younger version of myself. Now I remember how she'd laughed gently. "Sorry, there are no pictures in this movie. You have to learn to listen instead."

Psychedelics take you all the way − which is why it's taken so long for the memories to float back. I couldn't process it all in one go.

Sitting at the kitchen table, the truth drips into my consciousness. It was here all along: muteness in the face of injustice. The pain of being overlooked. My fear of failure − of Getting It Wrong. My inner child has been my guide all along. All seeing. My sight was my protection − and that was gone too. And with an almighty cascade of knowing, I understand. "I hear you," I whisper, as my son nudges me with his laser gun.

"Will you help me make a playlist?" I say, turning to him. "I think it's time Mummy had one."

"Sure," he grins. "Alexa, make Mummy a playlist!"

The truffles gave my body a voice. My memories are no longer compartmentalized, but appear as a linear map, linked together in a way I had never understood.

Yoga

I decide not to disclose my psychedelic experience a few days later when I'm at my Friday yoga class. Whilst this is a safe space, integration hasn't been convenient or controllable. I'm standing in Tree Pose listening to my teacher's instructions, when her voice cuts out. My body might be in the room, but my awareness has shifted elsewhere. Confused for a moment, I wobble on one leg. Her mouth is moving, but her voice has been replaced by a man's gravelly chant. Rattled by this eerie transfiguration, suddenly I get it. The truffles are listening in − I am the music again.

Scrolling through her playlist at the end of the class, my teacher reveals the voice I'd heard was Ram Dass and East Forest playing softly in the background. "Why?" she asks, eyebrows raised. I don't tell her I am the music. That would be silly.

Exit: 31 January 2020

My dad toasted my birth with a single malt, but was absent for much of my childhood. We only met properly in Sydney in 1998, when he came to visit me in Australia. We drove to the Blue Mountains to stay in a cabin with a tree growing out of it. Fit in my twenties, I kept up when we hiked and drank as much red wine as he did. I knew how the American button-lock on the door worked. "You're a clever know-it-all," he said, as I pulled the door shut.

"Chip off the old block," I grinned back. It was the first time he saw me.

Sitting by his hospital bed two weeks after my retreat, my dad can't see, but I know he can hear. His hand, a bony weight, is limp in mine. His fingers flicker when I remind him of the lock on the door. That trip changed everything, I tell him gently. It brought us back together. He doesn't regain consciousness, but he knows I'm there.

He left this earth just as Britain exited the European Union. An uncomfortable uncoupling that has left a Dad-shaped hole in my world.

The Nether-lands

No one comes with you on a psychedelic trip. Like death, it is solitary. Science didn't get a look in either. The EEG headset sat in my suitcase, somehow irrelevant. Others had attempted to record brain data during a trip in the past. Unfortunately, the headsets proved a distraction – in some cases impacting the experience, so I'm glad I didn't try. Tristan wasn't bothered – EEG is only part of the study. It's my lived experiences we're measuring.

Nothing has come close to psychedelics in terms of weirdness and boundary-defying experiences – apart from breathwork, perhaps. Of course, there's talking therapy, but I'm not convinced that reveals this level of truth either.

There's no doubt that the mind-training this experiment has provided laid the foundation for this last adventure. The amount of self-awareness, truth or insight I gained was directly related to how receptive I was to the experience. I hadn't acknowledged that somewhere deep inside me, I'd hoped to somehow reclaim my lost sight. The truffles helped me understand how I craved a miracle. As Albert Einstein said, "We cannot solve our problems with the same thinking we used when we created them." Sometimes, we need a new kind of reality – a different way of being to really see.

I've always found other people's epiphanies unsettling. Stories of revelation and awakening sounded so unreal. So unlikely. Without my own experiential interface, I'd had no relationship to these, quite frankly, annoying transformations. I'd been envious, but now I'm open. I am no longer a human pie chart missing a piece of pie.

The truffles didn't change me. I didn't hear anything I didn't already know. Yet I have a new way of perceiving myself and the world in which I live. My brain accessed data it might otherwise have discarded, allowing morsels of insight to dislodge, helping me understand myself a little better. As one Synthesis Retreat testimonial puts it: "I was slapped in the face by my own bullshit."

This experience has rammed home my need to relinquish control. Even control over what I learn. Trying to direct a psychedelic experience is counterintuitive. Interacting with my mind had to be about understanding the nature of it, not forcing it into a corner to behave in a way society tells it to.

The truffles didn't give me the script of my life – they gave me the ink with which it was written. That experience is only ever as real as the listener allows it to be.

CHAPTER 12 ¾

A MAGICAL ENDNOTE: BREATHWORK

It's fair to say that breathwork was a shock. I hadn't expected something so simple to be so powerful. As Sven at the Amsterdam retreat explained, sometimes truffles integrate a breathwork experience, not the other way around. I hadn't planned to include it – but it's an area I felt compelled to explore.

Dr Stanislav Grof, a Czech psychotherapist and researcher, is perhaps the most well-known pioneer of "non-ordinary states of consciousness" (what those in the business call this state of weirdness). His career spans sixty years studying psychedelic therapy and altered states of consciousness. Grof was one of the researchers who received a parcel of LSD from Sandoz, the pharmaceutical company Albert Hofmann worked for in the 1960s. That parcel changed the course of his career. Grof went on to develop transpersonal psychology and believes this field of study offers therapeutic, global and even evolutionary potential for the human race.

Along with his wife Christina, Grof developed Holotropic Breathwork as a non-drug alternative to psychedelics in the 1970s. Integrating consciousness research, transpersonal psychology and Eastern spiritual practices, Holotropic means "moving toward wholeness" (from the Greek "holos" for whole and "trepo" or "trepein" meaning moving toward something).

Transformational Breath is a similar technique to the one I was introduced to at the retreat. This was developed by Dr Judith Kravitz, a doctor of metaphysics and author of *Breathe Deep, Laugh*

Loudly. In the 1970s, Kravitz had been introduced to "rebirthing", a technique designed by Leonard Orr to release deeply buried traumas caused during birth. Employing "conscious connected breathing" (the umbrella term for this kind of breathwork), body mapping (hands-on acupressure) and affirmations, Kravitz developed this into a global self-healing network that is taught worldwide. By flooding the body with oxygen, combined with appropriate music and a safe setting, Transformational Breath can induce a sort of mild trip. These experiences can be sensory, relaxing, autobiographical or evoke unfulfilled memories.

Sven also teaches the Wim Hof Method which was devised in the 1990s by Hof, a sixty-one-year-old Dutch extreme athlete. Hof's rather unusual method involves withstanding freezing temperatures and a variety of breathing techniques, including controlled hyperventilation, exhalation and breath retention.

All of these breathing techniques offer profound approaches to self-exploration. Our breath mimics how we live. The rise and fall of our chest, abdomen or belly reflects the speed at which we live life, the way we view ourselves and others. In the same way grief draws a line down the side of our mouth, our breath paints its own picture, inside and out.

Breath has been staring me in the face the whole time. My use of Golden Thread breathing (along with hypnosis and visualization) in the hospital in 2012 kick-started this journey. Exhaling long deep breaths while imagining a golden thread spinning and looping in the breeze calmed my nervous system and grounded me. My curiosity to understand my mind and the extraordinary states it can achieve is why this book, and this experiment, exists. I've gone full circle – my breath top and tails this journey.

Whether you call it "prana", "chi" or "qi", it doesn't matter, breathing is central to life. Most meditation practices use the breath as an anchor. In meditation the breath is less about technique, than it is about focus. In most cases, the aim is not to change or manipulate the breath, but to harness the most regular and reliable function we have. Our breath happens whether we want it to or not.

It makes sense this function underpins many meditation practices, aside perhaps from some mantras.

All of the practices I've tried have whispered the same message: I am my own healer. Breathwork just shouted it. Intellectually grasping this fact wasn't enough – I had to somatically experience breathwork to believe it. And so it was that an introverted English woman lay on the floor with a bunch of strangers and sobbed. I was more grounded and more free in that moment than I have ever been.

There are many ways to train the mind and many ways to achieve different states of being. It turns out I had to try a bunch of methods before I discovered how I could let go. It shouldn't come as a surprise then that I have already successfully pitched a breathwork experiment to Tristan to further explore this exciting and transformational tool. The journey has not ended.

CHAPTER 13

FAMILY MATTERS

Wearing a fluffy cropped top and distressed jeans, I am sitting astride a small elephant inside a red house. My elephant keeps falling into a swimming pool. Why there is a swimming pool inside this house, God only knows.

"Mummy!" squeals my daughter, delighted at my ineptitude at playing Roblox. I hate this computer game, with its avatar characters and over-bright worlds.

Over the last year, we've had a new thing in our house. Ten minutes of uninterrupted, child-led, one-on-one time every single day. We're following an online parenting course from Positive Parenting Solutions and it's the game-changer it promised to be. I'd never choose to play Roblox, which is why we're playing it now.

Time (and the perception of it) is the point here. When I started this experiment, I was often too busy to consider how busy I was. Even though I knew how powerful slowing down could be, I had to remind myself that pausing was more than not moving. It required practise. Any pausing was pointless if my mental movements carried on. It's easy to dismiss this "time" element and suggest we all just need more empathy or compassion. The thing is, neither emotion gets a look-in if we don't nudge busyness to one side and make time for the people in our lives.

This experiment has taught me that when I'm self-conscious and squirming in discomfort, I'm doing good work. Work meaning identifying my need for control (like for my Roblox avatar to not be wearing skimpy clothes). For ten minutes I have to give up these things and, following my child's lead, be silly, roll on the floor and jump on the trampoline, shrieking that my pelvic floor can't take it.

Meditating hasn't just affected me – it's had a beneficial impact on Ed too. We wouldn't be the team we are now without all of these practices bleeding into our lives. While Ed hasn't been inspired to take up a meditation practice, he has recognized himself in some of what I've learnt – the numbing effect of television and this need for "quality time".

Mindful parenting is everywhere (and would have had us eye rolling in the past) yet it's so easy to undervalue. Mindfulness, I have learnt, is the launch pad for compassion – it's actually the launch pad for pretty much everything. Learning to drum with my daughter, drawing pictures with my son – and the body scans at night – are all mindful practices. And they're fun. Fun needs to be at the heart of a family. I hadn't equated fun with a meditation practice, but it's already there.

Ed and I live on a very dangerous freeway called modern life. At times our children have been stuck on the hard shoulder, the attention they've craved replaced by the parent-chant: "Just a minute", along with screens that glow. I cringe to admit it, but we've learnt to pause. Ed and I relate to each other in a kinder, more meaningful way. These aren't monumental leaps in our relationship, just small but vital shuffles. We still get stuck on the hamster wheel, but now we know when to look up and how to jump off.

It's ironic then, that technology is connecting me to my daughter now. "You were rubbish," she says happily when we stop playing Roblox. It was actually fun being appallingly bad at this game. It was important that she saw me fail and that I was okay with that. That it was normal. I'm learning to release my grasp on perfection – but I can't say it's easy. I'm desperate to direct, correct or, at least, make a suggestion. My daughter needs this attention-fix more than I need to be right. When our ten minutes is up, she's the one who flicks the iPad off.

Connectivity

I may have started this adventure as a human guinea pig, flying solo on my meditation mission. Yet the practising of meditation involved others.

I hadn't realized it at the start, but looking my son in the eye when he asks a question or stopping myself from hollering upstairs are also part of a meditation practice. Connecting to my family has underpinned everything I've learnt — mindfulness, self-awareness, self-compassion, even spiritual gain. Connection was an outcome I actively sought, desperate to shrug off a sense of numbness and dis-ease. Sometimes considered a "benefit" of meditating, this can be a red herring. Benefits (such as feeling calm or relaxed) are often positive outcomes, but they mostly come on the back of insights — which is code for "horrible little truths". Truths like the fact I berate myself when I Get Things Wrong. Connection never came as a by-product for me — I worked hard to develop it. It was worth the effort when emotional connection spilled out into my wider family too.

I hadn't expected death to accompany me on this journey — yet it did. After a lengthy illness, my aunt's passing was inevitable, if infinitely sad. At a time when I felt disconnected, the loving-kindness practice plugged me into my emotions helping me support those around me.

Dad's death was not expected. The shock is still here, simmering beneath the deadline to finish this book and the COVID pandemic. In the hours we had left I was present in every sense of the word. Stroking his hand and whispering in his ear, I was rooted in the moment. Synchronizing our breathing, I breathed his last breaths with him. Time ran out, but I felt calm in amongst this amplified awareness. I hadn't expected a meditation practice to help me deal with death, but meditation crept into every aspect of my life.

Dad's funeral was an upbeat affair, tinged with poignancy and commemoration. As Ed held my hand our twelve-year-old daughter stood up and spoke. Sad, but not fearful, a female wisdom visible in the tilt of her chin and the strength of her heart.

My brother Dan and I said our goodbyes, reconnecting at an unexpected time. There'd been no bridges to mend, busyness and apathy had just got in the way. Determined to maintain regular contact, to not let other things get in the way, I phone more regularly, reminded that connection isn't effortless. It requires commitment.

My ability to cope with (and even grow) during this time was a result of the practices I've learnt, reminding me to be mindful of how I was feeling. With the absence of regret, grief had a space to fill. I welcomed it with a sigh and a small smile. I have more resilience to entertain this visitor now. Letting go and not holding onto "coping" or "being strong" allows my suffering to release. It doesn't matter if it was the Buddha or Christianity that allowed this wisdom in – it's here.

Compassion School

Loving-kindness provided a breakthrough and once I "broke through", I could never go back.

Compassion was a slap in the face. The practice felt preachy and uncomfortable. If I tried to explain it to anyone else, I sounded preachy and uncomfortable too. I didn't want others to think I was taking some kind of moral high ground. It's a conversation we don't like to have. And yet, the practice I follow most days now is compassion.

The way I see it, it's mathematical. If you love more, you get more back. Compassion sometimes gets a bad rap – seen as soft, inconsequential or "bolted onto" other practices. Yet kindness is listening, rather than fixing. It's picking up the phone when you don't want to.

However, I had to understand what compassion felt like before I could exercise it in my personal life. If meditation is like prodding the unconscious mind with a stick, then the loving-kindness stick was a very pointy one. I was shocked that I had to be taught how to be kind – even to myself. Unpacking that became part of the practice and I was grateful for those around me. Discussing these insights with Genet on our weekly walks, we've examined our lives beyond the drudgery of homework and dinner-table rows. The need for compassion was always at the core.

I'm not a different person living a different life. I'm just a slightly better version of who I was before. I've stopped spreading myself so thinly, putting my energy into a few friendships, rather than spray-gunning time across too many. I don't have a smaller waistline or any fewer wrinkles, and my wardrobe still needs clearing. I think I smile more – Ed tells me I do. My liver is a bit healthier too – I rarely have that glass of wine now.

I've learnt to say no. And, not just to others, but to pressures I impose upon myself. I still have to-do lists, but they're shorter. I consider these side effects of my practice, rather than the focus they were at the start.

The effects of compassion play out every single day. My children know I now keep a stash of one pound coins in the pocket of my coat. Passing a man sitting outside our local station, my son takes one out and trots back. It's not much; we aren't changing the world. If my pocket runs out of coins, he tells me off. I'm still working on it, but my son has learnt unconditional kindness. Kindness, I've learnt, is infectious.

Tell-tales

Through self-analysis, I have heard the stories I tell myself. This helped me hear the stories I tell others too. Unravelling some of my childhood narratives illustrated how I was repeating the same messages to my children – and to Ed. Labels come in many forms – the "trouble-causer", the "funny", "capable" or "lazy" one. "You're good at English," or, "You're better at maths." Introspection has revealed how these labels can stick. I was told I was strong, that I came from stalwart stock. This pushed me to be successful and to fight for what I wanted. It also meant I never allowed myself to be vulnerable. Striving for success built up the protective veneer this project has peeled back.

And yet, however mindful I am, I still nag my daughter to brush her hair and I get cross when my son plays football in the kitchen. Now I see my anger arrive, which means I can bat it away quicker. I hug more.

Hearing these stories doesn't stop me from repeating the same mistakes. I still haggle, coax and threaten. Meditating doesn't remove conflict or hurt, but it does limit the impact. Every day I start over again and try to reward the effort my children put in, not the people they are. I reward myself for noticing the cycle too.

This experiment has helped me see what is right in front of my nose. Sometimes, our children say things that are incredibly profound. Sometimes they even write these things down.

Last Father's Day our son made Ed a card. He'd drawn a beautiful picture and wrote in his best handwriting: Thank you Daddy for always letting me get my own way. There it was in black-and-white. It was a shock for Ed. His jaw sagged. Like many working dads, he only sees the children at nighttime or weekends. It's not surprising that he takes the path of least resistance. Guilt, compensation – it's not uncommon. If he'd needed a written manifesto of why our ten minutes of one-on-one time was so important, there it was.

Bouncing Back

"Oh!" I say, timing my words with my bounces. "I. Need. To. Get. Off."

"Mummy's going to wet herself!" my son squeals with unchecked glee. And on the next bounce, sure enough, I feel a drip. Yet as I soar into the air, I see into the gardens beyond. The world looks different up here – the world looks different through the eyes of my children. The higher I jump, the more they feel safe – and seen. Loving is seeing. John Lennon sang it, and a thousand poets have written it. It took a crazy meditation experiment for me to understand that love is always the answer.

Whether Ed and I want to teach our children empowerment over helplessness or compassion over selfishness, we can only do that by exposing our own flaws.

These days they see me less worried about what others think, more patient, less quick to judge. That old knee-jerk reactivity is no more than a twitch. Falling off elephants and bouncing on trampolines shows them that "perfect" doesn't exist, that silliness and laughter are as important as reading and eating broccoli.

I didn't win or achieve a goal – there's no "end of the line" with a meditation practice. That sense of dis-ease still pops up from time to time, but like the other visitors, I welcome it in with a new clarity. The difference is I now know what to do.

CHAPTER 14

INNER SCIENCE

When I mooted the name for this book, Tristan shot me down.

"I know, I know," I countered.

"It's a neuro-myth," he growled. "You will be perpetuating it."

"It's a joke. A play on words."

I need to explain.

There is no evidence to support that we are either left- or right-brained. It's not that simple. Much of what we know about the functional differences between the hemispheres comes from the split-brain studies in the 1960s. The myth grew from the findings that the right hemisphere controls motor function for the left side of the body, and vice versa. The reality is that many regions in our brain "dance" simultaneously (to use Tristan's word) when we undertake any computation. It's too limiting to attribute personality traits to specific regions of the brain. We say someone is "left-brained" as shorthand for a person who is logical in their approach, leaving right-brained people to free-flow in their creative, big-picture thinking. Notions of left- and right-brain-ness are widespread, but they're over-simplistic. "Finding my right mind" was about finding the right way to live.

A New Scientific Story

It's been a little Jules Verne-like, descending this far into the centre of myself. The headset and the traces drawn on my phone have recorded every beat of my inner experience, and by climbing inside my mind, Barbara's study is telling a new scientific story.

As science moves away from behaviourism, the individual's internal experience (their inner narrative) becomes more valuable. Behaviourism traditionally believed that human behaviour could be explained in terms of external conditioning and circumstance (what was happening "outside") and not by their "inner" thoughts or feelings. The movement suggested that all behaviours are learned through interaction with or stimuli from the environment.

Barbara's study has been taking a new, interior perspective. She hasn't been looking for what *causes* my brain to behave in the way it does – she has been translating *what* it does. The relationship between our brain's activity and our thoughts has fascinated scientists ever since we understood that the brain was the seat of consciousness. If Who We Are is housed within the brain, how can we match its activity to the thoughts and feelings that make us uniquely us? Would doing this offer greater insights into human consciousness? These were the questions that Barbara asked at the beginning of her study.

It's difficult to articulate what we're thinking at any given moment, and there is no scientific method to mathematically represent this. It's almost impossible to express the annoyance, worry, frustration or sudden moments of elation that occur during a stream of consciousness *and* accurately time stamp them. As we can't peer inside our heads and "record" this vital information, Barbara needed to find another way to systematically capture it.

To date, meditation studies mostly recorded single sessions in a lab (or retreat) over a few months using scaling metrics (like scoring how relaxed a participant felt on a one to ten scale). This was crude and didn't capture nuances or a participant's fluctuating mental content during their meditation. Data had never been collected in a home setting or continuously over longer periods of time. Barbara's study aimed to test an ongoing monitoring method that she hoped would capture, test and analyze the brain's dynamics.

Meditation provided the perfect testing ground. Many styles are practised for the same length of time each day and evoke specific, categorizable thoughts and feelings. Meditators are trained in self-awareness, so make reliable human guinea pigs. As a single, committed participant, I provided Barbara with over 600 hours of data spanning the widest range of techniques ever recorded, over what ended up as a three-year timespan. I was the ideal participant to test her innovative model.

Drawing on Experience

Barbara chose to use EEG as it is cheap (in comparison to other brain scanning methods), portable and records high quality data, particularly when meditators sit motionless. EEG doesn't capture changes to my brain structure, the hardware if you like. It records changes in brain signature – the patterns of activity reflecting my different states of consciousness. On its own, EEG can't tell Barbara if I was feeling irritable because my daughter took my phone charger – or feeling a surge of love for her. It can only measure the *level* of emotion I felt.

Barbara could have just recorded my brain using EEG, which would have provided a stream of mechanical data demonstrating the functioning of my brain. However, that data wouldn't allow her to isolate or measure that surge of love or tell her when it occurred during my meditation. It's misguided to assume quantitative data, such as EEG, will be more informative than the internal experiences of others. On its own, it only tells half of the story.

Barbara's study is unique because it provides a bridge between the *contents* of my mind and the *workings* of my mind. Her model provides a new common currency for science.

For the last three years, my brain has been the source and EEG the signal representing that experience. By comparing my wiggly lines of EEG data alongside my wiggly drawn lines of experience data, Barbara can finally match brain activity with mental content. I might "see" my thoughts arrive, but until now we couldn't see how my brain behaved *when* those thoughts arrived.

Barbara's model offers a fuller and more detailed map of my inner landscape and the means to enhance the personal insights I have gained.

This is very exciting. But Barbara's model won't be able to tell me what any of my data *means*. This question of meaning keeps coming up. Barbara is looking at what the EEG tells her about my brain – inevitably, I want it to tell me about myself. EEG technology is alluring because I expect it to give me answers – answers that are simple, cogent and that support what I already believe. It's not the limitation of EEG that sometimes causes confusion, but the interpretations I'm seeking within that technology. Looking for meaning is called "reverse inference" and is considered a weak practice. This is when researchers impose meaning onto the data they've captured that could be explained as a functional or mechanical process. Any personal insights I gain will only come from what I interpret myself.

The EEG Top Line

It's February 2020 and I'm in the lab with Tristan and Barbara. Opening up her laptop, Barbara shoots me a grin.

"I've got something to show you," she says, moving so I can see her screen. "I've had a first look at your Alpha power."

"That's the EEG frequency bandwidth – the level of the brain's electrical activity – associated with meditation, isn't it?" I ask.

"Yes," Barbara replies. "Alpha waves occur around ten times every second. It's a useful frequency to start with because it's easily identified."

"Imagine tapping a drum stick ten times in one second," Tristan interjects, mimicking a drumming action.

"Exactly. Alpha waves appear in the occipital area of the brain — at the back of the head — when you close your eyes. I've looked at the first seven techniques you tried. If you remember, your headset stopped working so you recorded Kundalini Yoga and Vipassana with an upgraded model so that data isn't directly comparable." Barbara draws a wiggly line with her finger in the air. "I'll compare your traces – your hand-drawn wiggly lines – alongside the wiggly lines of the EEG's Alpha."

An EEG Alpha Wave

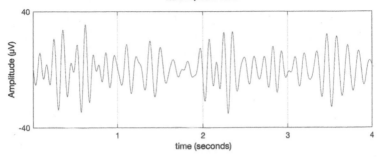

EEG Alpha 8-12Hz

One of my 'Awareness' Traces

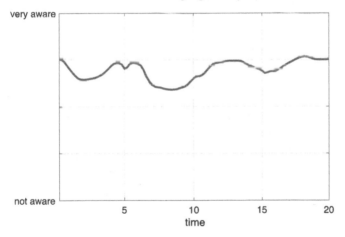

Awareness

How aware was I of what was going on in my mind, in the moment?

"These are just top line results," Barbara says, pointing at graphs illustrating the mean (average) Alpha data.

"Electrical impulses are picked up by the headset's electrodes via four channels, capturing the 'voltage' in different regions of the brain." Next, Barbara reveals another graph containing "mountain" shapes that incorporate the meditation sessions for each technique and the intensity of the Alpha (how strong it was), represented by a horizontal x axis. The vertical y axis shows how frequently this level of Alpha power occurred. The shapes of each meditation mountain clearly vary for each style of meditation, with different degrees of height and gradient.

"Each technique evoked a different EEG signature in your brain," Barbara explains, pointing at the graph. "Different mental processes were at work when you practised Christian meditation in comparison to hypnosis or loving-kindness. In other words, meditating trained your mind to behave in identifiable ways that were noticeable whether you were counting breaths in Zen or repeating your mantra in TM. This is great because, even though meditation is a subtle art, we'd hoped we might identify differences between this many techniques. The point of meditation is to achieve a stable practice – to repeat the instructions consistently and reliably. We can see that you did that neurally from pretty early on for each technique, and there was often a level of consistency. This could be very useful for meditation researchers in the future. If meditators follow the same instructions, researchers can compare the different experience states that occur during each technique alongside the correlating neural dynamics. They can examine if, like you, others achieved these states quickly and were consistent over time, and if this varied between beginner or experienced meditators."

"What's really exciting is that hypnosis is an outlier – an oddball in terms of the data," Tristan adds. "The 'peak' of the hypnosis mountain is much higher than all of the others. Like a rolling wave in the sea, the Alpha 'waves' were more regular during hypnosis than in other modalities, telling us that we picked up the same signals each time. Hypnosis has a narrow base too, suggesting these Alpha waves were very consistent and concentrated during your hypnosis sessions. The Alpha power (intensity) was highest in TM and loving-kindness, as seen by its distribution along the horizontal x axis. You were doing something very different inside your mind when you used hypnosis and, whatever that was, it was the same each time. There was a level of accuracy going on."

This means I consistently went into the same "state" during hypnosis (whatever that was) and stayed there throughout every session. The huge variability in MBCT, on the other hand, suggested my mindfulness meditations were inconsistent each time. This is perhaps not surprising as MBCT incorporated three different mindful practices.

Tristan is clearly excited about this. "If you were to close your eyes and wear the headset right now, we probably couldn't tell which meditation technique you were using, but we'd know straight away if you were using self-hypnosis from your brain activity."

"Differences are good," Barbara clarifies. "Now I can look at what other EEG brainwaves like Theta indicate and map your meditation experiences in relation to each other."

"It's an excellent start," Tristan smiles.

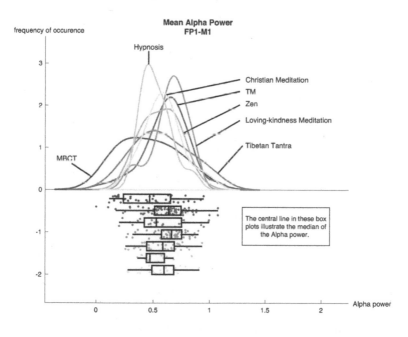

The concentration and regularity of Alpha power for hypnosis on the horizontal x axis is visible by its high mountain peak (higher than all the other techniques). In contrast MBCT shows the least consistency of Alpha waves recorded.

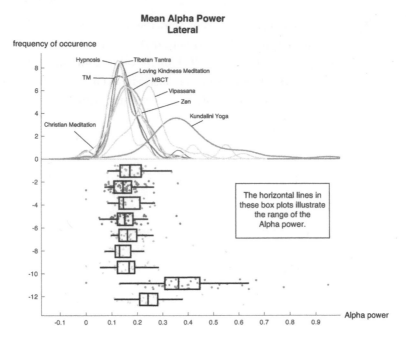

Mean Alpha Power
Lateral

Including all of the modalities in one graph changes the data because the replacement headset captured brain activity via different EEG channels. Comparing this data is like comparing apples with pears. By selecting a channel from each headset that was the most similar in their scalp location, Barbara could present all the techniques together. I recorded no data for psychedelics.

A Bright Future

Alongside looking at my Alpha data, Barbara has clustered my experience traces into separate "states". This simply means that she has organized the experience categories into five different sets of data. One set might contain high focus and emotion, another might contain low wakefulness and high boredom. This is so she can identify the different characteristics of each technique. For example, a quick look told her that my traces data for Zen showed particularly high emotion and changeable levels of focus.

Barbara will now analyze all my data and decide what questions to ask. Directly contrasting styles might not be efficient. Normalizing or stabilizing each technique will differentiate the high levels of focus I reported in Tantra in 2017 from the high focus recorded in Vipassana two years later. This will help qualify what "high focus" really means. She can examine which experience categories score high or low, but also which ones fluctuate over time.

The meditation marathons at the Cambridge lab allow Barbara to compare all of the techniques on a single day, eliminating some factors like the three-year time span and my dad's illness. However, analyzing this much data is a huge endeavour.

It hasn't all been plain sailing. When Barbara designed our experiment in 2016, we didn't know what issues would arise. For example, the "experience categories" evolved over time as we learned more. Barbara tried to predict what I might experience, but bouncing ideas back and forth provided data in itself.

Thankfully, it has all been worthwhile. Barbara's project has far-reaching possibilities both within meditation research and beyond. By running group studies, she can examine the commonalities and differences between meditation experiences. She can examine differences between people and differences between meditation styles. As she has data on twelve different techniques (more than any other study we know of) she can identify and categorize the "states" for each technique. Future meditation studies can use her model to collect far more detailed data, opening the door to new insights into the private and previously untapped experiences of meditators. Barbara's model doesn't have to be limited to meditation research either. Any psychological study could employ her model to gather data from participants.

In the future Barbara's approach could positively impact mental health evaluation. Psychologists and psychiatrists could supplement their existing diagnostic processes with a more continuous and intricate method of monitoring a patient's anxiety or depression. By capturing a patient's moment-by-moment thoughts and emotions, neural signals associated with feelings of anxiety or depression could be identified. Comparing this to moments when patients didn't report feeling anxious provides more diagnostic power for treatment or referral. In five or 10 years, Barbara's model could be used throughout multiple areas of medicine, including treatment for long-term conditions like diabetes that require extended monitoring, along with pain management. As healthcare moves toward a more patient-led experience with bespoke treatments, a model that provides an individualized blueprint could have a wide range of applications.

The scientific paper that Barbara, Tristan and I plan to write is in the pipeline. If you want a window to the future, you can read more about Barbara's research and our new breathwork project here: vanessapotter.com.

What the Data Told Me

While Barbara's study investigated "state changes" (the different states of consciousness a meditator experiences), my diaries and the traces I drew on my phone allowed me to observe my own "trait changes", how, and if, meditating changed my inherent behaviours and the way I now see myself and others. Analyzing the traces data alongside my diary enables me to see if a technique evoked the changes I believed it did, or whether my memory is playing tricks on me.

I am often asked which method was "The Best". That is impossible to answer. Annoyingly, that's how science (and meditation) works. However, I can answer some of the questions I asked myself at the beginning of this journey. While I cannot completely assign an outcome to a particular practice, some traces data stood out.

KNEE-JERK REACTIVITY
Several techniques have stopped me shouting on the school run, albeit in different ways.

The MBCT traces contradicted what I remember. The high introspection the course required, along with my steep learning curve, created much conflict. The more I understood how habitual patterns of thinking impacted my behaviour, the less negatively I felt toward mindfulness. Learning to pause and take stock reduced angry outbursts and made me less cross.

Vipassana caused the most emotional distress and was the hardest to learn. Yet it lowered reactivity efficiently – and speedily. The adage "no pain, no gain" springs forth. My diary says I could no longer "find anger", which supports the claims of the Vipassana movement. Lowering reactivity was both the *goal* and *outcome* of this practice. However, a monastic existence was a struggle to endure and the practice required too much commitment afterwards.

LETTING GO OF NEGATIVE THOUGHT PATTERNS

The relinquishing of negative thoughts was helped by the cognitive behavioural elements of MBCT. Recognizing negative self-talk relaxed my desire for control and perfection.

Both mantra practices, Christian meditation and TM, were effortless to learn and the easiest to practice. I experienced a profound *letting go* as my mind dropped into a deeply relaxed state. While my emotions were sometimes high during Christian meditation, it was mostly positive emotion.

It's worth noting that psychedelics, hypnosis and breathwork were remarkably powerful in allowing me to let go emotionally, releasing old traumas and self-limiting beliefs.

CONNECTION TO OTHERS

Although compassion and altruism underpin many practices, loving-kindness provided the greatest breakthrough in alleviating the numbness I'd felt. This isn't surprising as the practice hinges on a wish that ourselves and others will be well and happy.

Connection came as a by-product from other practices too, notably Christian meditation, Zen and Kundalini Yoga, possibly because they followed loving-kindness. Psychedelics and breathwork connected me to myself the most.

CURING SLEEPLESSNESS

Our sleep experiment suggested hypnosis was more successful at helping me combat talk-related sleeplessness than mindfulness. During hypnosis I experienced the least amount of distracting mind-chatter. It was the least effortful, least emotive practice and I was the least "awake". This makes sense as hypnosis is a passive practice.

While hypnosis was a clear winner in the sleep stakes, I often use the MBCT body scan to induce a deeply relaxed state at bedtime.

Outcomes I Didn't Ask For

This project provided added bonuses. While not on my wish list, my ability to focus on one thing without getting distracted skyrocketed. This skill improved over time, regardless of the technique I was using. Barbara was right: I did become more proficient at meditating.

Creativity was the other unexpected dividend. Both TM and Christian meditation sparked ideas and pent-up insights. The week following the Vipassana retreat produced a state of 'flow' unlike any other. I also now regularly employ a walking meditation to clear creative blocks and stimulate my imagination.

While these insights help construct a picture out of the experiences I've collected, they are unique to me. Ultimately, the aim of every meditation technique is to improve our wellbeing. What I have discovered is the different ways in which they achieved that for me.

CHAPTER 15

SCIENCE CAN BE SPINACH

I dreaded writing this conclusion chapter. What if three years of meditating hadn't made me calmer, wiser and nicer? I battled the urge to "big up" any changes, fearful that subtle shifts wouldn't be enough.

Science didn't give me The Answer. There is no new secret to success – or happiness. I can't tell my sceptic friends that if they meditate for twenty minutes a day for six weeks they'll be cured of being human and flawed. Because, nobody is flawed, but most of us are human.

According to Dr Paul Offit, author of *Bad Advice: Or Why Celebrities, Politicians, and Activists Aren't Your Best Source of Health Information*, science doesn't speak for itself and can't always proffer "easy answers". It can appear chaotic and confounding, and becomes easily misunderstood by a science-naïve public. Results don't always fit into the neat, sweet-toothed narratives the public requires. They're like spinach. The results might not be to everyone's tastes, but if they're evidence-based, they're much better for us.

Life is messy and learning to live with the mess is what meditation is for. If we try and tidy it up into some sanitized, plastic-moulded version of ourselves, we get into trouble. Buddhism tries *so* hard to explain this to Westerners, but I'm not sure we understand the message. We want to compare and manipulate the results to fit with how we already live our lives. True change is first knowing I probably need to start thinking another way. *Darn it.* No scientific data can tell me how I feel – I feel how I feel. There *is* only what I discover for myself. My sceptic friends won't be happy.

The solutions to life's ills doesn't exist inside a bottle, packet or on a smart phone, which is annoying, because society tells us they do. Every time I panicked that "meditating wasn't working", I saw my need for "transformation" to be instant – and conspicuous.

So much conspires to make life quick and easy – wrapped up nicely. Algorithms streamline what I see, cutting out anything distressing or unexpected. The creases of life are ironed out, the mavericks suppressed. I'm trapped inside my own personalized web with invisible overseers directing and persuading me, feeding on past information and predicting my future. Shrinking my view. Meditating helps me embrace my quirks – the clutter that is real human life. It takes away my need for a predictable storyline. This project has not been about looking away, but about confronting what is awkward and staying with it. Meditating is not the easy choice. It wasn't designed for a machine-driven world.

By the Book

Science didn't provide an epiphany, but I did find wisdom in a number of meditation books, articles, podcasts and interviews, which I've listed at the end of this book. Some of these provided insights that complemented my own experiences in a particularly fine-tuned way.

If Professor Peters' *The Chimp Paradox* provided under-the-hood explanations that reduced the blame I put upon myself, then Daniel Kahneman's *Thinking, Fast and Slow* was the brain bible. Understanding the different ways I processed information helped me understand the insights that meditating brought up.

While my experiment wasn't about happiness per se, it's hard to avoid this when you're trying to improve your life. Aspirations of what I expected happiness to look like shifted in size and shape. As I learned from my Buddhist teachings, happiness is not something I can consume or buy on Amazon, it was an attitude I had to learn.

Kahneman suggests that we assume we know what happiness is but happiness is a by-product of our biases, beliefs, current environmental and emotional states. I didn't have a "happiness-radar" constantly bleeping as I was too busy peeling carrots or calling the garage back. I'd constructed an idea of what I thought I wanted out of assumptions of how others lived. This is why meditating is *training*. I was probably more happy than I knew before this experiment started. Meditating taught me to zone in and recognize happiness hot spots. Happiness, it seems, doesn't appear in one big baton-twirling moment, but in a series of minuscule vignettes.

I've had to learn to notice the tiny leaps of joy I now experience. It's a weird word – *joy*. I don't think I used it very much before. It's a sense of lightness. I want to smile (not all the time, that would be weird), but I often feel happy for no reason. And that's the winning ticket. *No bloody reason*. Finding this emotion is like happiness hide-and-seek. It's not always obvious, but is often blu-tacked to kindness. One time in the bakery where I often write, a young mother got her pram stuck by the till, causing a bottleneck. "Sorry," she repeated, reversing the pram back and forth. An older woman reached out and touched her arm. "No," she said firmly. "We've all been there."

This momentary act of kindness, so easily lost in amongst the hubbub of the bakery, was gold dust and choked me up. I felt a warmth. Okay, *Goddammit*, it was a feeling of *love*. I wallowed in that moment like a big love hippopotamus.

These feelings of gratitude arrive without warning, reminding me how much I love my family. It helps that feeling love is good for me. According to social psychologist, Barbara Fredrickson, these "micro-moments" of love "[fortify] the connection between your brain and your heart and make you healthier." Learning that everyone experiences the same ups and downs has been a necessary lesson.

Much of what I've learned relates to change. According to psychiatrist and author, Lori Gottlieb, "change involves the loss of the old and the anxiety of the new." Change *is* scary, simply because

I'm conditioned to prefer what I know. I couldn't change anyone else, so I had to start with myself. The *play* button had already been pressed – this was my life. Expecting change to come in the future was futile. I had to do this *now*.

There are well-documented stages of change and I reckon I hit them all. I had to meditate over and over before anything "happened". Issues were bubbling under the surface, but I didn't catch on straight away. I believed I was the first person *ever* to figure this stuff out. Researching later, I realized I was just standing in the line for Middle-Aged Woman Exploring Her Psyche. Erik Erikson, a developmental psychologist, even devised an eight-tiered system depicting these stages. *Dammit*; Erik stole my thunder.

My anxiety about the new segued into Erikson's life-stage shifts. He suggests that post-forty, we strive to make our mark in the world, contributing to society in positive ways. This transitioning required me to let go of the old script I'd been hanging onto and to write a new one. By putting so much emphasis on the health and psychological benefits of meditating, I'd overlooked a sense of Why I'm Here. I thought I wanted more of things – success, time, calmness, connection. In fact, I just needed to understand *why* I felt the way I did. It's a bit naff, but I needed to get out of the way of myself. Change involved a *new normal*. I may have been a bit late to the party, but at least I've figured out there's a party going on.

In My Right Mind

It's taken effort and time, but meditating doesn't have to be a strait jacket; ironically, it's been freeing. I've learned to be responsible for myself – what I think, feel and do is up to me. I'd thought I wanted to see which practice made me less shouty or bad tempered, but I hadn't considered what made me behave that way. I had to acknowledge the different versions of myself. The nice, patient self along with the grumpy, worried-about-my-kids self. Neither is better or worse. I know to be kinder now, to ignore

Cruella's sneers when she flicks her fur stole and criticizes me. This experiment has helped me do that.

People come to meditation for many reasons, but I didn't know what I was getting into. Meditation isn't what many people think it is. If you're already intentionally and consciously finding a few minutes a day for yourself, it wouldn't be a huge leap to meditate in the same time slot.

Meditation doesn't have an on-off switch. It's not as simple as doing it or *not* doing it. Sitting still is only part of it. What happens after that ten, twenty or thirty minutes is just as important. I feel that I learned as much about myself from talking about meditation, as from measuring it. It can be tough dealing with what a meditation practice kicks up, which is why the teacher and support network is as important as any method being taught. One spiritual path is not better than another, but one path is better than none.

As far as I'm concerned, meditating is the most sensible thing in the world. It's my personal prescription to a better, smoother-running life. I've discovered the cure to my dis-ease – and anyone else can do the same with the required commitment. For it to "work" – I had to put in the hours and accept how I felt. Ultimately, meditation *did* work – just not in the way I thought it would. The feeling of relief and "coming home" I experience the moment I sit down is incomparable to anything else in my life. My only wish is that I'd gained this awareness years ago.

Meditating is not a panacea. It won't stop bad things from happening. There will be more grief, more illness, more unexpected events. My phone is still glued to my hand – I haven't figured out how to do without it yet. Meditation hasn't made me levitate, wear saffron or got me likes on Instagram, but it has made my life feel fuller and more colourful. My emotions are streamlined and I don't feel suffocated by worry. Becoming emotionally sober has taken time. Sure, I have tools now, but still there are no failsafes.

I'd wanted to "find my right mind", but the truth is I already had it. This was an inner journey, so it's not surprising these changes are mostly "in" me. When I lost my sight, I had to remember how to see. Now I have to remember *to see*.

No data can persuade me to meditate – I already know why I need to do it.

Meditation is not a shelter or a hiding place, but it can be a sanctuary and a light source. For the record, many of us would probably benefit from meditating – though possibly not for the reasons we think. We are not so different. Rumi asks: "When will you begin that long journey into yourself?"

Mate, I'm on it.

ACKNOWLEDGEMENTS

Many have helped me during this weird, enlightening, but fun adventure. Barbara Jachs has been my sidekick throughout – nothing would have been possible without collaboration from her and Tristan Bekinschtein.

I am indebted to the teachers, leaders and advisors who have taught, led and advised me. In no order, I'd like to thank: Roy Sutherwood, Geshe Tashi Tsering and the Jamyang Buddhist Centre, Glen Svensson, Dr Dyan Haspel-Johnson, Jane Ellsbury, the Revd John Pritchard (and colleagues at St John's Church), Prakashjot Kaur, Garry Gelade and The Buddhist Society, Lisabetta Vilela at Harmonious-healing.com (sorry I didn't get to include Tai Chi), Colin Beckley (and the teachers at the Meditation Trust), Dhamma Dipa teachers and staff.

Thank you to my beta readers and fact checkers: Jane Mackelworth, Martha Oster, Glenys Wilson, Mary Hennock, Gail Emerson, Aileen Oh, Christian Darkin, Christopher Bowden, Juliette Galante, Karin Matko, Jim Green, Tony Mazurkiewicz and Angela Mariscal at the John Main Centre for Meditation and Inter-religious Dialogue at Georgetown University, The WCCM, Desmond Biddulph, Seth Butcher, Karta Singh of the Amrit Nam Sarovar Kundalini Yoga school, Enzo Tagliazucchi, Myles Katz, Sven Kimenai and the team at Synthesis Retreat, Chris Timmerman, Elif Clarke, Rupert Trusler, Simon Whitehead, Louise Renwick, Beth Parkin, Genet, Jackie and Jo. Thanks to the team at Dreem.com for providing the EEG headset.

Thanks go to my agent, Caroline Hardman, Jo Lal at Trigger Publishing, and editor Kate Latham. I'm grateful to all of my friends who are no doubt relieved that I have stopped talking about this experiment. If I have made a mistake or missed someone out, I'm sorry. I am human.

My family has been very patient. Thank you to Ed and the children for not laughing (too much) at me wearing my headset and for your unwavering support. Thanks Mum, for endless reading; and Dan, for throwing all those ideas around.

The kids still miss you, Aunty Felicity. And Dad – this book is for you.

FURTHER READING, LISTENING AND WATCHING

I've got to know myself through books on spirituality, psychology and neuroscience, and through articles, blogs, podcasts and cliched plaques on café walls. Consuming this content all comes under the heading of a "practice". I list them in what I hope are useful categories. This is by no means the whole list and you could lose years of your life surfing the net for spiritual and wellbeing resources. This is simply a starting place.

My TEDx talk. "The Art of Your Mind" by Vanessa Potter and information about The EEG Beach Exhibition can be found on my website vanessapotter.com. Connect with me at VanessaPotterWrites on Instagram.

Books

GENERAL

Brach, T, *Radical Self-acceptance: A Buddhist Guide to Freeing Yourself from Shame* [audiobook], Sounds True, USA, 2008

Brown, M, *The Presence Process: A Journey into Present Moment Awareness*, Namaste Publishing Inc., 2010

His Holiness the Dalai Lama, Cutler, H C, *The Art of Happiness: A Handbook for Living*, Simon & Schuster, 2000

Dennis, R, *And Breathe: The Complete Guide to Conscious Breathing – the Key to Health, Wellbeing and Happiness*, Orion Publishing Group Ltd., 2016

Fadiman, J, *The Psychedelic Explorer's Guide: Safe, Therapeutic, and Sacred Journeys*, Park Street Press, 2011

Goleman, D, *The Meditative Mind: The Varieties of Meditation Experience*, Jeremy P Tarcher/Penguin, USA, 2000

Green, J, *Giving Up Without Giving Up: Meditation and Depressions*, Bloomsbury Continuum, 2019

Harris, D, with Warren, J, and Adler, C, *Meditation for Fidgety Skeptics*, Penguin Random House, 2017

Kabat-Zinn, J, *Full Catastrophe Living: How to Cope with Stress, Pain and Illness Using Mindfulness Meditation*, Piatkus, 2013

Kornfield, J, *After the Ecstasy, the Laundry: How the Heart Grows Wise on the Spiritual Path*, Bantam Books, 2000

Kravitz, J, *Breathe Deep, Laugh Loudly: The Joy of Transformational Breathing*, Ini Freepress, 1999

Lynch, D, *Catching the Big Fish: Meditation, Consciousness, and Creativity*, Penguin Random House, 2016

Ricard, M, *Happiness: A Guide to Developing Life's Most Important Skill*, Little, Brown & Company, 2006

Roberts, A, *Albion Dreaming: A Popular History of LSD in Britain*, Marshall Cavendish Editions, 2012

Salzberg, S, *Real Love: The Art of Mindful Connection*, Flatiron Books, 2017

Shaw, M, *Passionate Enlightenment: Women in Tantric Buddhism [New Ed]*, Princeton University Press, 1995

Tolle, E, *The Power of Now: A Guide to Spiritual Enlightenment*, New World Library, 1999

Tsering, G T, *Buddhist Psychology: The Foundation of Buddhist Thought, Volume 1*, Wisdom Publications, U.S., 2006

Williams, R, *Being Christian: Baptism, Bible, Eucharist, Prayer*, SPCK Publishing, 2014

The Science of Meditation

Goleman, D and Davidson, R J, *Altered Traits: Science Reveals How Meditation Changes Your Mind, Brain, and Body*, Avery, 2017

Farias, Dr M, and Wikholm, C, *The Buddha Pill: Can Meditation Change You?* Watkins Publishing Limited, 2015

Kahneman, D, *Thinking, Fast and Slow*, Penguin, 2011

Peters, Prof S, *The Chimp Paradox: The Acclaimed Mind Management Programme to Help You Achieve Success, Confidence and Happiness*, Random House, 2012

Shapiro Jr, D H, and Walsh, R N, *Meditation: Classic and Contemporary Perspectives*, Aldine Transaction, 2008

Psychology and Wellbeing

Brown, B. *Daring Greatly: How the Courage to Be Vulnerable Transforms the Way We Live, Love, Parent, and Lead*, Penguin Life, 2015

Brown, B, *The Power of Vulnerability: Teachings of Authenticity, Connection, and Courage*, Sounds True [audiobook], 2012

Brown, B, *I Thought It Was Just Me (But It Isn't): Telling the Truth about Perfectionism, Inadequacy, and Power*, Audible Studios [audiobook], 2010

Cope, S, *Yoga and the Quest For The True Self*, Bantam USA, 2000

Daizen Victoria, B, *Zen at War*, Rowman & Littlefield Publishers, Inc., 2006

Erikson, E, *The Life Cycle Completed: A Review*, W W Norton & Company, 1998

Fredrickson, B L, *Love 2.0: Finding Happiness and Health in Moments of Connection*, Plume, 2014

Gottlieb, L, *Maybe You Should Talk to Someone*, Houghton Mifflin Harcourt, 2019

Huxley, A, *The Doors of Perception: And Heaven and Hell*, Vintage Classics [New Ed], 2004

Hofmann, A, *LSD: My Problem Child*, OUP, 2013

Hoffman, C, *Greetings from Utopia Park: Surviving a Transcendent Childhood*, Harper, 2016

Losada, I, *Sensation, Adventures in Sex, Love & Laughter*, Watkins Publishing, 2017

Mongan, M, *HypnoBirthing: The Mongan Method*, Souvenir Press Ltd., 2016

Neff, K, *Self Compassion: Stop Beating Yourself Up and Leave Insecurity Behind*, Hodder & Stoughton, 2011

Offit, P A, *Bad Advice: Or Why Celebrities, Politicians, and Activists Aren't Your Best Source of Health Information*, Columbia University Press, 2018

Pollan, M, *How to Change Your Mind: The New Science of Psychedelics*, Penguin, 2019

Purser, R E, *McMindfulness: How Mindfulness Became the New Capitalist Spirituality*, Repeater Books, 2019

Rubin, G, *The Happiness Project: Or, Why I Spent A Year Trying to Sing In The Morning, Clean My Closets, Fight Right, Read Aristotle And Generally Have More Fun*, Harper, 2011

Sarno, J E, *Healing Back Pain: The Mind-Body Connection*, Grand Central Publishing, 2001

Storr, W, *Selfie: How the West Became Self-Obsessed*, Picador, 2018

Washburn, M, *The Ego and the Dynamic Ground: A Transpersonal Theory of Human Development*, State University of New York Press, 1995

Podcasts and Online Meditations

There are numerous talks on meditation, science and wellness out there; just go search a little (Richard Davidson's are good). There are great TED talks by Andy Puddicombe on mindfulness, Rick Doblin on psychedelic assisted therapy, Brené Brown on empathy and Matthieu Ricard on happiness.

Matthieu Ricard, "The Habits of Happiness" [podcast]

The Greater Good Science Center at UC Berkeley has a huge research-backed resource in the form of a podcast series called "The

Science of Happiness". These 25-minute episodes (the time I can jog for) offer short practices on themes such as happiness, gratitude, patience, connection, mindfulness, laughter, love and combatting depression or anxiety.

I reckon I have listened to all of David McRaney's "You Are Not So Smart" podcasts during this experiment. These feature researchers, scientists and psychologists informally discussing "why we do the things we do". Definitely check out his work.

There are literally hundreds of online meditations available and a number of apps that are either free (in part), donations-based or have monthly subscriptions. Here are some I have used:

Loving-kindness meditation: https://thebuddhistcentre.com/text/loving-kindness-meditation

Free online meditations from Tara Brach, Kristin Neff and Sharon Salzberg

https://app.imagineclarity.com [app]

https://insighttimer.com [app]

https://journeymeditation.com [app]

Retreats, Meditation Centres, Teachers and Resources

MBCT AND MBSR

The following offer courses, mindfulness retreats and resources:

The Mindfulness Project, www.londonmindful.com

Oxford Mindfulness Centre, www.oxfordmindfulness.org/learn-mindfulness/resources/

TM

Teachers and courses can be found at:

Official Transcendental Meditation site, https://uk.tm.org

The Meditation Trust, www.meditationtrust.com

David Lynch Foundation UK, www.davidlynchfoundation.org.uk

TANTRIC MEDITATION

Details of the women's Tantric workshop I attended can be found at https://tarayogacentre.co.uk/courses/tantra/

Buddhist meditation centres and teachers that provided courses or workshops I have attended are at:

Tara, https://tarakmc.org/

Jamyang Buddhist Centre London, https://jamyang.co.uk

The Buddhist Society, www.thebuddhistsociety.org

Glen Svensson, www.glensvensson.org

CHRISTIAN MEDITATION AND CENTERING PRAYER

St John the Evangelist, Upper Norwood, www.sjun.org.uk

The John Main Center, https://johnmaincenter.org

The World Community For Christian Meditation, www.wccm.org

Contemplative Outreach, www.contemplativeoutreach.org

HYPNOTHERAPY RESOURCES:

I worked directly with Dr Dyan and Jane Ellsbury and have also used several of the self-hypnosis downloads.

Dr Dyan Haspel-Johnson, http://drdyan.com

Jane Ellsbury, https://janeellsbury.co.uk

Uncommon Knowledge, www.hypnosisdownloads.com

KUNDALINI YOGA

I was taught by Prakashjot Kaur, www.prakashjot.com

Amrit Nam Sarovar, www.amritnam.com

3HO, www.3ho.org

Yogi Bhajan, www.yogibhajan.org/main

VIPASSANA

Vipassana Meditation, www.dhamma.org/en/index

Vipassana in Europe: Mahasi Sayadaw, http://mahasi.eu

PSYCHEDELIC RETREATS

I attended the Synthesis retreat: www.synthesisretreat.com

Alalaho, www.alalaho.com

The Psychedelic Society, https://psychedelicsociety.org.uk

Imperial College London, Centre for Psychedelic Research, www.imperial.ac.uk/psychedelic-research-centre

Multidisciplinary Association For Psychedelic Studies, https://maps.org

SOUND BATH

Make It Sacred, www.makeitsacred.co.uk

BREATHWORK

The Big Breath Company, https://thebigbreathcompany.com

Elif Clarke, www.elifclarke.com

Stanislav Grof, www.stanislavgrof.com

The Wim Hof Method, www.wimhofmethod.com/practice-the-method

Sven Kimenai, https://svenkimenai.com

Rebirthing Breathwork International, www.rebirthingbreathwork.com/foundation

Transformational Breath Foundation, www.TransformationalBreath.com

PARENTING COURSE

Ed and I followed this course and found it helpful at home: www.positiveparentingsolutions.com

RESEARCH AND REFERENCES

IMAGE SOFTWARE

Allen M, Poggiali D, Whitaker K et al. Raincloud plots: a multi-platform tool for robust data visualization [version 1; peer review: 2 approved]. Wellcome Open Res 2019, 4:63. DOI: 10.12688/wellcomeopenres.15191.1

MBCT

Kabat-Zinn, J, "Mindfulness-Based Interventions in Context: Past, Present, and Future", Clinical Psychology Science and Practice, 10(2), 2003, 144-156

TM

American Heart Association, "Meditation May Reduce Death, Heart Attack And Stroke In Heart Patients", ScienceDaily, 2012. www.sciencedaily.com/releases/2012/11/121113161504.htm

Borland, C, and Landrith, G, "Improved Quality of City Life Through the Transcendental Meditation Program: Decreased Crime Rate", Department of Psychology, Maharishi International University, Fairfield, Iowa, US. Research completed July 1976

Hagelin, J S et al., "Effects of Group Practice of the Transcendental Meditation Program on Preventing Violent Crime in Washington, DC: Results of the National Demonstration Project, June–July 1993", 1998 https://pdfs.semanticscholar.org/

Hatchard, G D, et al., "The Maharishi Effect: A Model for Social Improvement. Time Series Analysis of a Phase Transition To Reduced Crime In Merseyside Metropolitan Area", Psychology, Crime & Law, 1996 2:3, 165-174, DOI: 10.1080/10683169608409775

International Yogic Flying Competition 2016, at MERU, Holland, YouTube: https://www.youtube.com/watch?v=UUnxnuUVEOs

Lazarus, A A, "Psychiatric Problems Precipitated by Transcendental Meditation", Psychological Reports, 1976, 39, 601-602. https://meditatinginsafety.org.uk/wp-content/uploads/2017/05/Lazarus-1976.pdf

Lindahl, J R, et al., "The Varieties of Contemplative Experience: A Mixed-methods Study of Meditation-related Challenges in Western Buddhists", PLoS ONE 12(5): e0176239. https://doi.org/10.1371/journal.pone.0176239

Orme-Johnson, D W, and Fergusson, L, "Global Impact of the Maharishi Effect from 1974 to 2017: Theory and Research", Journal of Maharishi Vedic Research Institute, 2018, 8, 13-79. www.patriziotressoldi.it/cmssimpled/uploads/images/MaharishiEffect_Review18.pdf

Sedlmeier, P, et al., "The Psychological Effects of Meditation: A Meta-analysis." Psychological Bulletin, 2012, 138(6), 1139–1171. https://doi.org/10.1037/a0028168

Sedlmeier, P, Loße, C, and Quasten, L C, "Psychological Effects of Meditation for Healthy Practitioners: An Update", Mindfulness 2018, 9, 371–387. https://doi.org/10.1007/s12671-017-0780-4

Vibhuti Pada: Yoga Sutras Book III (para 43/levitation) Hermes, July 1987 by Raghavan Iyer: www.theosophytrust.org/920-vibhuti-pada-yoga-sutras-book-iii-patanjali

Loving-Kindness

Aknin, L B, Hamlin, J K, and Dunn, E W, "Giving Leads to Happiness in Young Children", PLoS ONE, 2012, 7(6): e39211. https://doi.org/10.1371/journal.pone.0039211

Galante, M J, "Internet-based Randomised Controlled Trial of the Effect of Loving-Kindness Meditation on Wellbeing and Helping Behaviour, 2014", PhD Thesis, Cardiff University. https://ethos.bl.uk/OrderDetails.do?uin=uk.bl.ethos.620113

Klimecki, O M, et al., "Differential Pattern of Functional Brain Plasticity After Compassion and Empathy Training", Social Cognitive and Affective Neuroscience, 2014, 9(6), 873–9, https://doi.org/10.1093/scan/nst060

Shantideva, A Guide To the Bodhisattva Way Of Life, Chapter One, (28), "The Benefit of the Spirit of Awakening (The Benefit of the Bodhi Heart)". www.buddhism.org/Sutras/2/BodhisattvaWay.htm

Zen

Darley, J M, and Batson, C D, "From Jerusalem to Jericho: A study of Situational and Dispositional Variables in Helping Behavior", Journal of Personality and Social Psychology, 1973, 27, 100-108

Geher, G, "My Favourite Psychology Study: The Good Samaritan is In The Situation", Psychology Today, 2017. https://www.psychologytoday.com/gb/blog/darwins-subterranean-world/201703/my-favorite-psychology-study

Koller, J M, "Ox-Herding Stages of Zen Practice", Department of Cognitive Science, Rensselaer Polytechnic Institute

Christian Meditation

Bourgeault, C, "Centering Prayer – The Very Basics", The Contemplative Society. www.contemplative.org/contemplative-practice/centering-prayer/

Chopra, D, and Winfrey, O, "The Difference Between Meditation and Prayer" [video], 2012. www.oprah.com/own-super-soul-sunday/deepak-chopra-the-difference-between-meditation-and-prayer-video

Fisk, J, "Centering Prayer and Christian Meditation. What are the Differences Between These Two Forms of Contemplative Prayer?" https://johnfisk.wordpress.com/2011/07/18/centering-prayer-and-christian-meditation/

Sinha, P, "Conversation with NY Times Columnist Rob Walker at the Carlos Museum", Emory News Center, 2012. https://news.emory.edu/stories/2012/02/upress_conversation_with_ny_times_columnist_rob_walker/campus.html

Hypnosis Parts 1 & 2

Andreescu, B, interview. https://www.youtube.com/watch?v=1kRjvvUmjAY

Couto, M, "Canada's Bianca Andreescu Says Meditation, Visualization Formed Winning Mindset", The Canadian Press. https://globalnews.ca/news/5873474/bianca-andreescu-mindset

Halsband, U, et al., "Plasticity changes in the brain in hypnosis and meditation", Contemporary Hypnosis 2009 26(4) 194–215. https://doi.org/10.1002/ch.386

Kundalini Yoga

Kabat-Zinn, J, "Practical and Profound: Mindfulness in Healthcare" [video], Mindful Healthcare Summit, 2019. www.mindfulhealthcaresummit.com/speaker/jon-kabat-zinn

Keltner, D, "Hands On Research: The Science of Touch" [video], The Greater Good Science Center, https://greatergood. berkeley.edu/article/item/hands_on_research

Shannahoff-Khalsa, D S, "An Introduction to Kundalini Yoga Meditation Techniques That Are Specific for the Treatment of Psychiatric Disorders", The Journal of Alternative and Complementary Medicine, 10 (1) 2004, 91-101. https://www.liebertpub.com/doi/10.1089/107555304322849011

Vipassana

Dhar, P L, and Khurana, A, "Effect of Vipassana Meditation on Quality of Life, Subjective Well-being and Criminal Propensity Among Inmates of Tihar Jail, Delhi", 2003. http://buddhism. lib.ntu.edu.tw/BDLM/toModule.do?prefix=/search&page=/search_detail.jsp?seq=288120

Rumi, J, The Guest House [Translated by Coleman Barks], https://www.scottishpoetrylibrary.org.uk/poem/guest-house

Stern, M, "'Black Mirror' Creator on Exploring the Dark Side of Pop With Miley Cyrus and Mocking Twitter's Jack Dorsey", Daily Beast. www.thedailybeast.com/black-mirror-season-5-on-netflix-creator-charlie-brooker-on-exploring-miley-cyrus-and-twitters-jack-dorsey

Psychedelics

Carhart-Harris, R L, et al., "Psilocybin with Psychological Support for Treatment-resistant Depression: an Open-label Feasibility Study", The Lancet, Psychiatry, 3(7), 2016, 619-627. www. sciencedirect.com/science/article/pii/S2215036616300657

Dell'Erba, S, et al., "Synesthetic Hallucinations Induced by Psychedelic Drugs in a Congenitally Blind Man", Science Direct, 2017. https://doi.org/10.1016/j.concog.2018.02.008

"Drugs Misuse: Findings from the 2018/19 Crime Survey for England and Wales Statistical Bulletin: 19 September 2019", 2019. https://assets.publishing.service.gov.uk/government/uploads/system/uploads/attachment_data/file/832533/drug-misuse-2019-hosb2119.pdf

Griffiths, R R, et al., "Psilocybin Produces Substantial and Sustained Decreases in Depression and Anxiety in Patients with Life-threatening Cancer: A Randomized Double-blind Trial", Journal of Psychopharmacology, 2016, 30(12), 1181–1197. https://doi.org/10.1177/0269881116675513

Lee, H-M, and Roth, B L, "Hallucinogen Actions on Human Brain Revealed", Proceedings of the National Academy of Sciences, 2012, 109 (6) 1820-1821. https://doi.org/10.1073/pnas.1121358109

Nielson, E M, et al., "The Psychedelic Debriefing in Alcohol Dependence Treatment: Illustrating Key Change Phenomena Through Qualitative Content Analysis of Clinical Sessions", Front Pharmacol. 2018, 9:132. www.frontiersin.org/articles/10.3389/fphar.2018.00132/full

Psychedelic Research Group, Imperial College London, "Psychedelic Ceremonial Study", https://ceremonystudy.com

Smigielski, L, et al., "Characterization and Prediction of Acute and Sustained Response to Psychedelic Psilocybin in a Mindfulness Group Retreat", Scientific Reports, 2019, 9, 14914. https://doi.org/10.1038/s41598-019-50612-3

ABOUT THE AUTHOR

Before becoming a self-experimenting author Vanessa Potter spent 16 years as an award-winning producer, making ads for television. In October 2012 a catastrophic illness changed the course of her life, propelling her down a different, science-communication path. A number of unorthodox science-art collaborations with Cambridge neuroscientists led to an immersive exhibition, two books and a TEDx talk. She lives in South East London with her husband and two children.